Childhood Re-imagine

Childhood Re-imagined considers Carl Jung's psychological approach to childhood and argues that his symbolic view deserves a place between the more traditional scientific and social-constructionist views of development. Divided into four parts, this book covers:

- Jung on development
- theoretical and methodological discussions
- the Developmental School of analytical psychology
- towards a Jungian developmental psychology.

This book discusses how Jung's view of development in terms of individuation is relevant to child development, particularly the notion of regression and Jung's distinction between the child archetype and the actual child. It shows how Jung's understanding of the historically controversial notion of recapitulation differs from that of other psychologists of his time and aligns him with contemporary, post-modern critiques of development. The book goes on to investigate Fordham's notion of individuation in childhood, and the significance of this, together with Jung's approach, to Jungian developmental psychology and to wider interdisciplinary issues such as children's rights. Main also examines the plausibility and usefulness of both Jung's and Fordham's approaches as forms of qualitative psychology.

Through its detailed scholarly examination of Jungian texts and concepts *Childhood Re-imagined* clarifies the notion of development used within analytical psychology and stimulates discussion of further connections between analytical psychology and other contemporary discourses. It will be of particular interest to those involved in analytical psychology, Jungian studies and childhood studies.

Shiho Main is a fellow at the Centre for Psychoanalytic Studies, University of Essex, UK, and an associate lecturer with the Open University.

Childhood Re-imagined

Images and narratives of development in
analytical psychology

Shiho Main

Routledge
Taylor & Francis Group

LONDON AND NEW YORK

First published 2008
by Routledge
27 Church Road, Hove, East Sussex BN3 2FA

Simultaneously published in the USA and Canada
by Routledge
270 Madison Ave, New York, NY 10016

Routledge is an imprint of the Taylor & Francis Group, an Informa business

© 2008 Shiho Main

Typeset in Times by
RefineCatch Limited, Bungay, Suffolk
Printed and bound in Great Britain by
MPG Books Ltd, Bodmin, Cornwall
Paperback cover design by Lisa Dynan

All rights reserved. No part of this book may be reprinted or
reproduced or utilized in any form or by any electronic,
mechanical, or other means, now known or hereafter
invented, including photocopying and recording, or in any
information storage or retrieval system, without permission in
writing from the publishers.

This publication has been produced with paper manufactured to
strict environmental standards and with pulp derived from
sustainable forests.

British Library Cataloguing in Publication Data
A catalogue record for this book is available from the British Library

Library of Congress Cataloging-in-Publication Data
Main, Shiho, 1972–
   Childhood re-imagined : images and narratives of development in
analytical psychology / Shiho Main.
      p. cm.
   Includes bibliographical references and index.
   ISBN 978–0–415–38495–7 (hbk.) – ISBN 978–0–415–38496–4 (pbk.)
1. Child psychology.   2. Jungian psychology.   I. Title.
   BF722.M34 2008
   155–dc22   2008006908

ISBN: 978–0–415–38495–7 (hbk)
ISBN: 978–0–415–38496–4 (pbk)

For my parents

Contents

List of figures   xi
Acknowledgements   xiii

Introduction   1

PART I
Jung on development   9

1   **Psychological development**   11

   The individuation process 11
   Development as outgrowing 15
   Does the unconscious develop? 16
   Cultural development: nature and culture 21

2   **Regression**   30

   Regressive fantasies 31
   The regression of libido/psychic energy 35
   Beyond childhood: symbolic interpretations of regression 38
   Conclusion 42

3   **Symbolic child psychology**   44

   To what extent is child development relevant to
      psychological development? 44
   What is 'the child'? 45
   Is 'the child' related to the images of the actual child in
      Jung's view? 47

What is the relationship between the 'archetype of the child'
    and the 'archetype in childhood'? 50
What is the significance of the second half of life in relation to
    'the child'? 52
What is Jung's contribution to the discussions of psychological
    development? 56

PART II

Theoretical and methodological discussions
on development   59

4 'Recapitulation' and 'development' in analytical psychology   61

What is recapitulation theory? Its significance in the field of
    psychology 62
Jung's version of recapitulation theory: How is the notion
    of progress related to his view of recapitulation? 64
Questioning the notion of progress: What are the critiques
    of the idea of development? 70
Jungian and post-Jungian views on recapitulation: How is the
    notion of progress related to their views of recapitulation? 73
Dialogues between the theories of Jung and post-Jungians and
    contemporary critiques of the idea of development 77
Conclusion 78

5 Methodological issues in developmental psychology
and analytical psychology   81

Methodological shift in developmental psychology 82
Developmental practice in analytical psychology 92
Can analytic practice inform and contribute to discourses of
    developmental psychology? 95
Conclusion 100

PART III

The Developmental School of analytical psychology   101

6 Jung, Fordham, and the 'Developmental School'   103

When and how did the 'Developmental School' emerge? 103
What does the 'Developmental School' do? 106

*To what extent and in which aspects is the Developmental
    School 'developmental'? 109*
*What are the elements and rhetoric of development in
    analytical psychology? 112*
Conclusion 117

7   **The children's rights movement and Fordham's
    work with children**   **118**

What does Fordham mean by the individuality *of children in his
    theory of individuation in childhood? 119*
*In what way is the children's rights movement useful for the
    discussion of Fordham's work with children? 121*
*Discussion: Fordham's work with children in the light of the
    children's rights movement 123*
Can Jung's view of children and childhood be updated? 139
*Can the view on children and childhood in analytical psychology
    be updated? 142*
Conclusion 144

**PART IV
Towards a Jungian developmental psychology   147**

8   **Jung as a qualitative psychologist**   **149**

*Could Jung be introduced to developmental psychology as a
    qualitative psychologist? 150*
*Could Fordham be introduced to developmental psychology as a
    qualitative psychologist? 168*
Conclusion 170

9   **Conclusion**   **172**

Notes   177
Bibliography   186
Index   197

Figures

3.1 The actual and symbolic child-parent relationship   50
3.2 Three kinds of child-parent relationship   55
3.3 Multiple possibilities of the child-parent relationship   55

Acknowledgements

I am deeply indebted to many people who supported me in various ways over the years that I was working on this book.

First and foremost, I wish to thank Professor Renos Papadopoulos for his constant support, particularly for reading the entire work at an early stage and offering numerous helpful comments and suggestions on it. As the supervisor of my PhD, on which this book is based, he made generous and substantial contributions to this work, guiding the overall direction of my project and the ideas developed in my thesis and offering not only academic but also personal support throughout my studies at the University of Essex. Many thanks also to Professors Andrew Samuels, Joan Raphael-Leff, and Karl Figlio, who offered much valuable advice. Thanks, too, to the other members of staff and students of the Centre for Psychoanalytic Studies at the University of Essex for providing the inspiring and stimulating research environment in which most of the early work of this book was carried out. I wish to thank Dr Karen Evers, Dr Gottfried Heuer, Martha Stevns, and Barbara Wagnar, for their help in my understanding certain German words and expressions. I also wish to thank Deirdre Fottrell in the Department of Law at the University of Essex who kindly offered a meeting in which she clarified my questions about the children's rights movement. Many thanks also to Christopher Hauke for reading the manuscript and offering encouraging comments. I am grateful to Kate Hawes, Jane Harris, and others involved in the production of this book at Routledge for their patience and support. A special thank you goes to my husband Roderick for his continual encouragement and valuable comments on the manuscript and to my son Alasdair for providing inspiration. Finally, I am immensely grateful to my parents for their unfailing support.

Chapter 4 of this book is based on the article of the same title published in *Harvest: Journal for Jungian Studies*, 2000, vol. 46, no. 2, pp. 7–32.

Introduction

In this book, childhood is re-imagined from the perspective of analytical psychology. The book is concerned with what childhood means symbolically rather than with literal childhood. It takes a different approach from the two most widely recognised approaches to childhood today: the view of childhood as consisting of purely objective facts discoverable by scientific methods, and the view of childhood as consisting entirely of social constructions created and recreated by human subjectivity conditioned by specific times, places, societies, cultures, and so forth.[1] Unlike these approaches, the present study does not aim to determine causal relationships or correlations between the physical and psychological functioning and development of a child (brain and behaviour, for instance) or to identify the roots of particular images about childhood in society or culture (as the image of the innocent child might be traced to Romanticism, for instance). Instead, it explores the view of childhood as a symbol or a metaphor – a metaphor for a path towards self-realisation – inspired by the view of 'the child', that is, the child archetype as a symbol of the self, which was proposed by the Swiss psychologist, Carl Gustav Jung (1875–1961). The book looks at Jung's psychological approach to childhood, which claims to be scientific but not in the same way as mainstream psychology is considered to be scientific, and also explores what is beneath various images of childhood, but not in the same way as social constructionism explores what underpins particular images of childhood. The book also considers Jung's concept of 'the child' in relation to the long-standing psychoanalytic view of a child as dependent; Michael Fordham's (1905–95) views of the child as independent of its parents; and the dominant view of childhood as adults' past affecting their present, as found in both depth psychology in general and Fordham's view in particular.

The book explores whether this symbolic view of childhood can find a place alongside the scientific and social constructionist views and can contribute insights and perspectives distinct from those of the other views. Attending to the unconscious as well as conscious dimensions of the relationships between children and adults, the book raises the question whether the symbolic view of childhood could be useful for those involved in various work related to children and childhood – in research, charity, education, social work, law and social policy, arts, or entertainment. Issues related to childhood are often unconsciously bound up with issues related to the adults involved. And yet the unconscious dimension is rarely taken into consideration, even though it is often the main factor affecting the children themselves, the adults involved, and the relationships between them.

The theme of childhood is addressed in this book by examining various images and narratives of psychological development which co-exist within analytical psychology. The book aims to establish a dialogue between Jung's psychology and developmental psychology in the light of historical, social, personal, and interdisciplinary contexts, by looking at how the words 'development' and 'developmental' are used and what kind of assumptions underpin the use of these words. It examines the dominant discourses of natural, normal development as well as marginalised discourses about the development of what was and is usually thought of as primitive and therefore inferior. This examination involves connections between notions of development and other influential ideas: for example, relating to scientific, technological, and social development, cultural development, civilisation, ontogeny and phylogeny, body–mind parallels, the power of social discourses, the children's rights movement, images of children and childhood, and the relationship between the individual and society. The book also aims to enhance awareness in analytical psychology of the shift that has appeared in developmental psychology in terms of both theoretical understanding of the notion of development and methodological approaches to developmental issues, and to contribute to the discussion of development not only within analytical psychology but also within wider interdisciplinary areas where psychological development matters: sociology, law, social policies, education, health studies, cultural studies, economics, politics, and so on.

Previous works within analytical psychology relevant to issues of development are many (for example, Fordham, 1957, 1976, 1985b, 1994; Giegerich, 1975; Jacobi, 1965; Jung, 1928a, 1934a; Knox, 2003; Lambert, 1981; Marcus, 2007; Neumann, 1954; Urban, 1994; and von Franz, 1990). However, the various authors of these works tend to use the word 'development' in very different ways, without explicitly questioning and examining the Jungian notion of development itself. The notion of development is usually addressed implicitly, either in terms of Jung's theory of individuation or in terms of psychoanalytic approaches to child development.

Fordham's work stands out for its emphasis on both a Jungian perspective and a psychoanalytic orientation, that is to say, through his claim for individuation in childhood. Andrew Samuels' classification of Schools of post-Jungians (1985; see Chapter 6) has certainly contributed greatly to the image of Fordham as the founder of the 'Developmental School' of analytical psychology. However, how Fordham is 'developmental' seems to be understood in different ways in different contexts, and therefore clarification is needed as to what 'development' means and how 'developmental' issues are understood within analytical psychology.

In the area of modern infant research, Mario Jacoby (1999) presents a systematic examination of the issues regarding early child development. His work follows Daniel Stern's approach (1985) in the sense that psychoanalytic perspectives on early infancy are integrated with the results of modern infant research. However, in Jacoby's approach, this modern research has generally been drawn on without questioning its underpinning assumptions. Therefore, this book attempts more explicitly to consider critical approaches to modern infant research.

Knox's detailed works (2003, 2004) compare Jung's core concepts with common themes emerging among both recent developmental cognitive scientists and attachment theorists. In particular, she notes parallels between Jung's concept of the archetype and the concept of the image schema in cognitive developmental psychology, and between Jung's concept of the complex and the concept of the internal working model in attachment theory. She seems to suggest that analytical psychology should follow the successful path of attachment theory in combining psychoanalytic perspectives and cognitive scientific evidence and therefore should promote Fordham more strongly, since his work fits better into the models employed in both attachment theory and cognitive developmental psychology. Her work is concerned with the interaction between nature and nurture as it relates to models of development, and with finding links between the emergence of symbolic meaning in Jung's work and in cognitive science and attachment theory. The present book covers wider developmental issues than the nature/nurture debate, pays greater attention to the bipolarity of the archetypes, and focuses more on what Jung distinctively meant by symbols.

Within the developmental psychological camp, where depth psychology is not always sympathetically portrayed, Erica Burman describes psychoanalysis as 'the repressed other of psychology' (1994, p. 104) that could excavate 'what is passed over, or absent, within psychology' (ibid.). She presents a critical review of the history of developmental psychology, explicitly addressing issues that have emerged from modern developmental psychology in their historical and socio-political contexts, and thus sheds light on complex gender and cultural issues within and around this field. However, as is usually the case in histories of psychology and psychoanalysis, Jung and analytical psychology are absent from her discussions, where Freud, Klein, Winnicott, and Bowlby are introduced.

Some researchers have re-examined psychoanalytic texts from the perspective of marginalised discourses about development or alternative approaches to developmental issues. For example, Carol Gilligan looks at Freud's theory from a feminist point of view and charges that a 'problem in theory became cast as a problem in women's development' (1982, p. 7). She suggests that recognising the differences in women's experience and understanding might change understanding of women's development, adult development, which has predominantly been characterised in the masculine voice, and, consequently, human development. Michael Billig (1999) looks at Freud's case studies from the view point of conversation analysis and argues that analysis of the details of conversation could help to reconstruct the context of the cases more fully. His arguments shed light on various cultural contexts of development: for example, how the child is instructed in the use of language and in conversational morality, is implicitly taught how to remember (open up a conversation) and how to forget (dismiss topics rhetorically), and is influenced by the content of talk as well as by its rhetoric, both of which vary from culture to culture (ibid., pp. 136ff). Similar charges have been levelled against Jung's texts in relation to marginalised discourses about, for instance, gender (for example, Hopcke, 1989; Wehr, 1988) and race (for example, Adams, 1996; Dalal, 1988; Maidenbaum and Martin, 1991; Samuels, 1993). However, the primary focus of these approaches is not on development. There therefore remains scope for further study in these areas.

This book looks at analytical psychological understanding of psychological development and approaches to the issues of development in the light of the shifts that have emerged in developmental psychology. On the theoretical level, this means the shift from earlier to more recent understandings of the notion of development, the former predominantly supported by the notion of progress and the latter challenging this unquestioned assumption and its linearity and hierarchy. On the practical level, it means the shift from modernistic, positivistic, often quantitative research methods to postmodern, qualitative research methods. The original contribution of this book is to make explicit the ways in which analytical psychology could consider the historical implications of various developmental theories and research, the status of theories of 'development' as individual narratives and social discourses, and perspectives on certain public as well as private attitudes towards issues of psychological development.

There are various images and narratives of 'development' in analytical psychology. However, these images and narratives seem to exist independently of one another and have not benefited from an examination of their mutual implications. In this book, I use the word *images* to refer to clusters of meaning that are grouped within a particularly distinct form (not necessarily pictorial). These forms are embedded in the individuals' psychological world and have both conscious and unconscious, abstract and concrete dimensions. Without entering into a detailed definition, it may suffice to emphasise that these forms work at different levels of human functioning including the cognitive, emotional and ideational. The word *narratives* is used in this book to refer to stories either told by individuals or created collaboratively between a speaker (or writer) and an audience (or reader) through the processes of meaning-making in certain contexts. Narratives may address and reflect an individual's world-view, personal and emotional experiences, and conscious and unconscious motivations as well as obvious and less obvious historical, cultural, social, political, and other influences. Consideration of narratives in the clinical context has raised important issues and I shall touch upon some of these issues in this book, but here I shall use the word 'narratives' in a more general sense.[2] I distinguish between the words *images* and *narratives*, on the one hand, and the word *discourses*, on the other. Social discourses are widely exchanged and recognised in a particular society or community and their implications and meanings are interpreted with reference to that social context. Social discourses seem to have an influence on our thought processes and language use in a more collective sense than individual images and narratives. Burman explains the term 'discourses', in talking about the discourses which developmental psychology both constructs and informs, as referring to 'socially organised frameworks of meaning that define categories and specify domains of what can be said and done' (1994, p. 2). She is concerned with accounts that lie behind the language itself, and 'how, why and in what ways sets of ideas in developmental psychology have functioned outside as well as within its relatively restricted domain' (ibid.). However, discussions of development within analytical psychology do not seem to have been connected explicitly with social discourses about development outside of analytical psychology. I shall attempt to clarify the various partial images and narratives of development in analytical psychology and connect these images and narratives with more widely recognised discourses outside analytical psychology. I shall attempt to examine what kind of coherent discourses analytical psychology could offer and how these could contribute to other disciplines as well as to analytical psychology itself.

Another intention in using images and narratives as the sources for our investigation is to attempt to communicate analytical psychological understanding of development in a language closer to our everyday use of language, in this case, taking account of social and cultural contexts that have recently received a considerable appreciation of their importance. Images and narratives could be contrasted with symbols and myths, the latter pair of terms perhaps better explaining the characteristics of analytical psychology than the former. Symbols and myths have particular characteristics which images and narratives do not necessarily convey, such as, numinosity and autonomy, or perhaps what might be thought of as the 'irrational'. This book explores to what extent analytical psychological insight could be explained in terms of images and narratives and in what way introducing symbolic and mythic elements makes it difficult for us to make sense of what is communicated through language.

The book is divided into four parts: Part I Jung on development; Part II Theoretical and methodological discussions on development; Part III The Developmental School of analytical psychology; and Part IV Towards a Jungian developmental psychology. Part I discusses what Jung wrote about development. Here I examine Jung's view of development in terms of its process, in relation to regression, and in respect of child development. First of all, I examine what Jung has to say about psychological development, that is to say, the individuation process (Chapter 1). Second, I discuss how Jung considers regression in relation to progression as well as development (Chapter 2). Finally, I discuss to what extent and in what way his view of development is relevant to child development (Chapter 3). I explore how Jung's theory of individuation could be understood in various ways, and how the process could be described by different authors. Bearing in mind the complexity of the concept of psychological development, I shall construct my argument so as to present Jung's view of development in a coherent way and make sense of how he engaged with other psychological issues.

Part II examines developmental approaches in analytical psychology in relation to contemporary developmental psychology, both theoretically and methodologically. Chapter 4 discusses the notion of development in analytical psychology in relation to the historically controversial notion of recapitulation. I look at recapitulation theory, which originally arose in biology and embryology, later combined with particular historical ideas, and then was adopted in modified form in psychology. I discuss the historical and social implications of these two notions and point out their underpinning ideas in relation to the social and intellectual milieux of their origin. By locating Jung's view of development in this historical context, I hope to gain an overview of the significance of Jung's theory in the wider field of psychology. The important thing to note is that the notions of development and recapitulation are closely connected primarily in terms of their implications. The notion of development is usually understood in terms of progress, advancement, and betterment. Development is generally also understood in terms of change from lower to higher levels, and therefore in terms of a hierarchy. These images have their roots in the notion of recapitulation, which postulates development as a process of progressive change from lower to higher levels. However, I argue that Jung's understanding of recapitulation theory was different from that of other psychologists in his time, and therefore his understanding of development could be different from the common perception held in his time. My examination starts from the assumption that Jung's understanding of development could be very different from what has been generally accepted. In a general sense, my research shows that Jung's understanding of development is actually quite similar to contemporary critiques of the notion of development, which point out the unquestioned hierarchical and patriarchal structure and attitudes in Western society and draw attention to the dynamic interactions and processes of development rather than the determinants of it. Chapter 5 discusses what are considered to be 'developmental' methods within analytical psychology in the light of the methodological shift within developmental psychology. I look at how recent critiques of modern psychological practice have made explicit the conflict as well as complementarity between modern, positivistic, standardised, quantitative research and postmodern, diverse, qualitative research. I also look at debates on philosophical and political issues as well as debates on issues of psychological practice itself. I consider how analytical practice might contribute to psychological practice as a research tool.

Part III discusses how the Developmental School of analytical psychology could be located within and outside analytical psychology; that is to say, with its own narratives of development what kind of roles and functions does it perform within analytical psychology, and with analytical psychology's narratives of development how might it present itself to other disciplines and interdisciplinary fields of discussion? My approach is to examine the significance of the Developmental School of analytical psychology in terms of its historical background, theoretical and practical controversies and its political situation within analytical psychology, and contributions it might be able to offer to other fields of studies. First, in Chapter 6, I trace the history and background of the Developmental School in relation to Jung's and Fordham's work. I examine the wider socio-political context at the time in order to focus on the more specific service and training needs that were then emerging. This involves an examination of both the conscious intentions of its founders and the specific historical time in which the 'School' was founded, when certain concerns, narratives and images were dominant and others were subjugated and marginalised. Moreover, I explore the kinds of controversial issues that were created by the establishment of this particular institution. Second, in Chapter 7, focusing on Fordham's notions of individuation in childhood and of children's individuality, I locate Fordham's theory in wider social and historical contexts and examine the significance of his theory in relation to children's rights. My aim is to gain a kind of insight that might enable analytical psychology to have dialogues with contemporary issues. My assumption is that we will find many productive points of discussion in the children's rights movements, which are concerned not only with psychological issues but also with historical, social, cultural, educational, anthropological, ecological, political, economic, racial, religious, and gender issues. I also hope to shed light on the difficulties involved in this.

In the final part, Part IV, I discuss how postulating Jung as a qualitative psychologist might help us appreciate his distinctive understanding of and attitude towards both notions of development and psychological research on development (Chapter 8). Part IV explores to what extent Jung shows his qualitative stance in his work and in what way he does not entirely fit into the framework of qualitative psychology. I discuss how Jung's engagement with language, diversity, and subjectivity could be articulated from his work and applied to debates on emotion, personality, and sense of self and relationships. I also discuss Jung's perspectives on two kinds of subjectivity and objectivity and compare them with the views on subjectivity and objectivity held by qualitative psychologists and other psychologists. I compare Fordham's qualitative stance and potential contribution to contemporary

developmental psychology with those of Jung, and address controversies arising from these attempts to connect analytical psychology and contemporary
developmental psychology. Finally, I make some suggestions for future
research through which both analytical psychology and contemporary developmental psychology might enrich each other.

Part I

Jung on development

Chapter 1

Psychological development

The general idea of development is often associated with 'progress', 'advancement', and 'betterment'. However, it is arguable whether and to what extent these images apply to Jung's understanding of psychological development. This chapter first discusses Jung's idea of psychological development, which he theorises as the 'individuation process', particularly in relation to his concept of the 'self'. Next, it looks at the ways in which Jung describes development as outgrowing. Then it discusses whether he proposes other kinds of development specific to the unconscious. Finally, it considers Jung's understanding of development in relation to his view of culture and discusses how his notion of cultural development has different implications from those of more general images of development.

The individuation process

Individuation is a vast topic to discuss in a single chapter, since it is related to many other complex issues in analytical psychology. Nevertheless, I shall discuss various implications of its role specifically as a developmental process, identifying some of the confusions involved in it.

Jung's idea of development arises from his concern with the psychological meaning of life. Based on psychoanalytic and introspective observations of his own and others' psychological processes, he came to the view that the lives of neurotic people often lack meaning, even though they may have attained what they were seeking outwardly. He argues that their neurotic symptoms will disappear if they can 'develop into more spacious personalities' ([1963] 1995, p. 162). He states: 'For that reason the idea of development was always of the highest importance to me' (ibid.). The kind of development he has in mind is also described by him as 'to live the "symbolic life" ' (ibid., p. 163).

For readers not already familiar with Jung, his key concepts and where his perspectives come from might not seem straightforward. Jung's theory of psychological development is based on his concepts of archetypes[1] and, in particular, the self.[2] These two concepts remain particularly controversial in terms of their definitions and applications; especially with regard to how

Jung conceptualised them and how they could be understood in the light of theories and knowledge adopted from psychology and other academic disciplines. He proposes the concept of the collective unconscious (see, e.g., Jung 1936), a part of the psyche that is not personally or consciously acquired but inborn and universal. He distinguishes the collective unconscious from the personal unconscious, the latter of which largely consists of personal complexes that are related closely to the inferior functions of one's personality and relationships with others in everyday life. Jung believed that there is a deeper layer of the psyche than the personal unconscious. Among many ways of describing archetypes, Jung himself sometimes writes that archetypes are the contents of the collective unconscious. Irrepresentable themselves, they nevertheless have the potential to form representations but can only be consciously perceived as images or patterns.[3] Jung named some of these images: for instance, 'persona' for the superficial personality adapted to the external world or society; 'shadow' for the reflection of the negative aspects of oneself (usually represented as of one's own sex); 'anima' and 'animus' for representations of the unknown contrasexual aspects of oneself (and therefore also of one's inner world); the 'wise old man' for the existence of transcendent wisdom; and many others. Regarding the 'self', Jung states, among various explanations, that this is the final goal of the psyche. He says:

> During those years, between 1918 to 1920, I began to understand that the goal of psychic development is the self. There is no linear evolution; there is only a circumambulation of the self. Uniform development exists, at most, only at the beginning; later, everything points towards the centre . . . I knew that in finding the mandala as an expression of the self I had attained what was for me the ultimate.
>
> ([1963] 1995, p. 222)

Jung says that in 1927 a dream brought confirmation of his ideas about the centre and the self (ibid.). He speaks of this dream and concludes with his understanding of the psychological meaning of life:

> This dream brought with it a sense of finality. I saw that there the goal had been revealed. One could not go beyond the centre. The centre is the goal, and everything is directed towards the centre. Through this dream I understood that the self is the principle and archetype of orientation and meaning. Therein lies its healing function. For me, this insight signified an approach to the centre and therefore to the goal. Out of it emerged a first inkling of my personal myth.
>
> (ibid., p. 224)

Jung reports that after this dream he gave up drawing or painting mandalas, as it enabled him to take an 'objective view' of the things that filled his being (ibid.). He attached great importance to his experience of pursuing his inner images. He writes:

> It has taken me virtually forty-five years to distil within the vessel of my scientific work the things I experienced and wrote down at that time . . . The years when I was pursuing my inner images were the most important in my life – in them everything essential was decided. It all began then; the later details are only supplements and clarifications of the material that burst forth from the unconscious, and at first swamped me. It was the *prima materia* for a lifetime's work.
>
> (ibid., p. 225)

In one way, Jung's theory of psychological development could be seen as largely the story of his own psychological experience of life and his search for his own development. However, implications of and insights which could be gained from his theory seem too rich to dismiss it as a mere reflection of his personal struggle with the psychological meaning of life.

Even though we do not go in detail or depth into Jung's psychology as a whole but focus only on development, it is hard to avoid the complexities of his theorisation. His concept of 'individuation' is about 'psychological development'. However, he speaks of 'psychological development' as 'psychic development' on the one hand (e.g., 1928a) and 'development of personality' on the other (e.g., 1934a). In one way, it could be understood that the former is concerned with the structure of the psyche and the latter with the functions of the psyche. The same confusion occurs regarding his concept of the self. On the one hand, the self is the totality of the psyche, including the conscious and the unconscious, and on the other hand, it is the wholeness of the personality (e.g., 1928c). Another confusion surrounds the concept of the self as the goal of individuation, for the self is presented both as the whole psyche which organises the archetypes and as one – albeit the ultimate – archetype which is organised in the whole psyche. However, as Colman suggests, this confusion may be solved by considering the self as the 'process of the psyche' and not as a structure, functions or contents of the psyche (2000, pp. 14–18). This understanding of Jung's term 'the self', as a psychological process, may actually represent his understanding of psychological 'development'. This reflects a general shift towards the view that the psyche cannot simply be divided into a structure and its functions. It leads us to consider the dynamics of the psyche as a whole.

Jung's theory of the 'individuation process' can be understood in terms of a variety of dynamics. First, it may be understood as the process concerned with *differentiation, recognition*, and *integration* (e.g., Jung, 1945). In this process, one is to withdraw one's projections so that one can recognise reality in the outside world, and then one has to integrate the projected archetypal images which emerged from the unconscious into consciousness. Put another way, one is to realise that the negative aspects of others which one sees are in fact the shadow of one's own unconscious psyche: one is to accept this alien part of one's psyche and to become aware of one's own shadow side. This may also be described in terms of becoming an individual separated from the collective, or of differentiating consciousness from the unconscious. Second, the individuation process may be understood in terms of the *compensation* of opposites, maintaining the balance of the conscious and the unconscious, maintaining the balance of outer and inner adaptation, transformation of libido (progression/regression), or balancing superior/inferior functions (e.g., Jung, 1938/54, paras 187–98). Third, the individuation process may be understood in terms of *birth* or initiation; or as *rebirth*, creation of a third element, the transcendent function, or symbol formation (e.g., Jung 1940, paras 281–4). By this, two elements create a third element, which does not belong to the original two but is something new, like producing gold in an alchemical process. It may also be described as *symbolisation* or *spiritualisation*. Fourth, the individuation process may be understood as working towards achieving the totality of the psyche, achieving wholeness of personality, or as the process towards the centre (e.g., Jung, 1942/48, paras 286–95). This is often symbolised by a quarternity image, a circular figure, or a spiral, each of which represents either a container or a solution of the conflicts in the dynamics of the psyche.

Regarding the theoretical understanding of the 'individuation process', a question arises as to what kinds of psychological development are actually aimed at in Jungian analysis. It seems that various kinds of development overlap with the various aims of analysis. Jolande Jacobi sums up the different points of view on the individuation process, which refers, in her view, to 'both the "natural" as well as the "methodically" or "analytically assisted" course of development' (1965, p. 79). She distinguishes:

1   (a) the 'natural' process which is the ordinary course of human life;
    (b) the 'methodically' or 'analytically assisted' process worked out by Jung.
2   (a) a process experienced and worked out as an 'individual way';
    (b) an initiation resulting from participation in a collective event.
3   (a) a gradual development consisting of many little transformations;
    (b) a sudden transformation brought about by a shattering experience.
4   (a) a continuous development extending over the whole life-span;
    (b) a cyclic process constantly recurring in unchanged form.
5   (a) a process in which only the first phase is accomplished;
    (b) a process in which both phases follow in sequence.
6   (a) a process prematurely interrupted by outer or inner circumstances;
    (b) an undeveloped process remaining in atrophied form;
    (c) a 'sick' or 'defective' process.

(ibid.)

Overall, there would be no problem in calling the above process 'development' instead of 'individuation'. The only difficult category would be group 6, which concerns what may be called regressiveness. I shall discuss regression more fully in the following chapter. Here it can just be noted that regressiveness too can be regarded teleologically as a chance for development in a new direction. In this respect, both the threat that regression pauses to development and the need for regression as part of the process of development are important for individuation. Different manifestations of the 'individuation process' are aimed at and observed in analysis, and, therefore, being synonymous with the 'individuation process', the 'developmental process' would vary in both Jungian theory and practice.

As we have seen above, the process of development does not have only one definition but can be viewed from different perspectives. It apparently does not simply consist of advancement within a hierarchy. Jung reached the conclusion that the goal of psychological development, the individuation process, is the self, and that this goal involves movement towards a centre. Nevertheless, within that developmental process so many dynamics are intermingled before reaching the goal, all of them integral parts of the developmental process, that they need to be incorporated in various ways into an overall understanding of development. From one point of view, Jung's entire psychology can be presented, more precisely, as his developmental psychology.

Development as outgrowing

Jung also talks about development in terms of a person outgrowing himself or herself in the course of analysis. Jung writes: 'Now and then it happened in my practice that a patient grew beyond himself because of unknown potentialities, and this became an experience of prime importance to me' (1929a, para. 18). He further writes:

> I therefore asked myself whether this outgrowing, this possibility of further psychic development, was not the normal thing, and whether getting stuck in a conflict was pathological. Everyone must possess that higher level, at least in embryonic form, and must under favourable circumstances be able to develop this potentiality. When I examined the course of development in patients who quietly, and as if unconsciously, outgrew themselves, I saw that their fates had something in common. The new thing came to them from obscure possibilities either outside or inside themselves; they accepted it and grew with its help. It seemed to me typical that some took the new thing from outside themselves, other from inside; or rather, that it grew into some persons from without, and into others from within. But the new thing never came exclusively either from within or from without. If it came from outside, it became a profound

inner experience; if it came from inside, it became an outer happening. In no case was it conjured into existence intentionally or by conscious willing, but rather seemed to be borne along on the stream of time.

(ibid.)

The above account of development as outgrowing could seem too metaphorical and some may find it not very helpful in concrete terms. However, the account seems to encompass many of the key themes which represent the distinctiveness of Jung's view of development. For instance, we can observe such characteristics as symbolic, paradoxical, cyclical, spontaneous, and numinous aspects of the psyche involved in development. Connected with 'the child' as a symbol of the self, which we shall discuss in Chapter 3, this could be seen, metaphorically speaking, as the child growing out of childhood. Paradoxically, though, the child may be entering yet another childhood by means of rebirth, and so the process of outgrowing continues. Connected with the objective psyche in which individual psyches participate, the emergence of the new from within and without in this process could be linked with characteristics of active and passive objectivity of the objective psyche and passive and active subjectivity of an individual's psyche, which we shall discuss in Chapter 8. Jung's idea of development as outgrowing described above clearly indicates a bigger picture than what goes on within oneself or between one and one's social environment. It certainly requires a perspective that accepts the depth of the unconscious as an essential part of psychological development.

Does the unconscious develop?

When it comes to psychological development, what is usually considered is something at least observable if not measurable, such as personality, behaviour, or some aspects of consciousness. To raise the question of whether the unconscious develops may not be practical. However, the purpose of exploring this question is to clarify what is often meant by development at the conscious level and to probe the limitations of applying that meaning to the whole psyche in Jung's model.

Another dominant image of development is change, which also has a strong connection with the image of development as 'progress', 'advancement', and 'improvement'. John Morss argues that developmental psychologists have confidently assumed that 'change with time is fundamentally progressive' (1990, p. 228). Since change is usually visible, this image of 'development' seems to concern conscious development but not unconscious development, if there is such a thing. For Jung, however, the whole psyche encompasses both the conscious and the unconscious, and therefore for Jung possibilities of unconscious development as well as conscious development need to be considered. Some people may argue that we cannot know whether or not or how the unconscious develops, as the unconscious is fundamentally unknown to us. Nevertheless, Jung attempts to conceptualise the unconscious, so we should be able to conceptualise the possibility of unconscious development. In fact, Jung argues:

> The great question now is: in what do these unconscious processes consist? And how are they constituted? Naturally, so long as they are unconscious, nothing can be said about them. But sometimes they manifest themselves, partly through symptoms, partly through actions, opinions, affects, fantasies, and dreams. Aided by such observational material we can draw indirect conclusions as to the momentary state and constitution of the unconscious processes and their development.
>
> (1928c, para. 272)

Therefore, at least at a theoretical level, it seems possible to postulate various connections between development and the unconscious. Consideration of the possibility of unconscious development is then indispensable, in order to fully address Jung's account of psychological development.

I am not attempting here to arrive at any conclusion as to whether or not the unconscious does develop, but am simply trying to explore further the meaning of the word 'develop' in relation to the unconscious. This theoretical explanation involves focusing more on the unconscious as distinct from the conscious mind and yet as a part of the whole psyche. It aims at identifying some possibilities of unconscious development but without definitely concluding that this development exists. The unconscious may seem not to develop, so long as we are possessed by the dominant images of development which apply only to the conscious level. For the same principles may not easily apply to the unconscious. However, there are at least two ways of addressing the question of how, in Jung's view, the unconscious might develop. One way is to challenge one of the general images of development and widen its meaning to include what is normally not regarded as development but is so regarded in Jung's view. The other way is to accept the general images of development but consider another possibility of interpreting the meaning of development. Specifically, this includes questioning whether the word 'development' should be understood only as an intransitive verb (v.i. to develop) or also as a transitive verb (v.t. to develop something/somebody) and as a reflexive verb (v.refl. to develop oneself). That means we can consider whether the unconscious develops (v.i.), the unconscious develops something (v.t.), and the unconscious develops itself (v.refl.). I shall pose questions as to how the unconscious might develop, what the unconscious might develop, and how the unconscious might develop itself and what would be the implications of these. In that way, we can explore whether the existing notion of development only applies to the conscious or might also apply to the unconscious or the whole psyche. Accordingly, additional characteristics of development may have to be suggested.

The first question is whether development should be understood exclusively in terms of constant, linear and progressive change, in a way that excludes stability. In his paper 'The tyranny of change' (1996b), Jungian analyst Renos Papadopoulos observes that change in general is usually associated with positive development. He argues that change tends to be closely connected with 'hope and the aspiration for something better', and, especially in the context of therapy, it is connected with patients' expectations of positive and constructive transformations in their lives (ibid., p. 1). However, Papadopoulos claims that development always involves stability as well as change. He states: 'Every human organism, every group, every organisation, every system must have both – change and stability. Growth takes place when change is coupled with stability' (ibid., p. 7). He also states: 'Too much stability creates stagnation and stifles development, whereas too much change without a measure of stability may contribute to disintegration and chaos' (ibid., p. 1). Accordingly, change is a 'multidimensional image' and could be perceived as involving not only the expectation of renewal and recovery but also the threat of instability (ibid.). It would be one-sided to connect development only with change, without taking sufficient account of stability. Nor could stability alone explain the whole dynamics of development.

How, then, do the ideas of change and stability apply to Jung's understanding of development? On the one hand, Jung seems to claim that change is a characteristic of the development of the archetypes. He states: 'Every archetype is capable of endless development and differentiation. It is therefore possible for it to be more developed or less' (1944a, para. 563). On the other hand, Jung seems to claim that stability, too, is a characteristic of the development of the archetypes. He states: 'what is more, it remains in its original form – unchanged, for nothing changes in the unconscious' (ibid.). Speaking of the unconscious psyche, Jung often refers to primitive identity, what Lévy-Bruhl calls *participation mystique*,[4] whose characteristics are, in short, non-differentiation between conscious and unconscious, between subject and object, between 'I' and other. It seems paradoxical that the unconscious is characterised by change and differentiation and, at the same time, by non-differentiation and stability. It could be argued that the archetypes concern different kinds of development on the conscious and the unconscious levels. In this respect, Coleman's view of the self, which I discussed earlier, could also be applied to other archetypes: the archetypes could be regarded as the 'process of the psyche', in which something unknown is connected to visions, thoughts, and language. The stability of the archetypes would be their continuous existence in the unconscious and their potentiality to emerge into consciousness as archetypal images. The change of the archetypes would then be the various manifestations of archetypal images which are perceived consciously. Thus, the archetypes in the collective unconscious, seen as the process of the psyche, involve both change and stability. If we consider that development means only differentiation and change, the unconscious would appear not to develop. However, if we consider that development also means continuity and stability (as part of self-regulation), the unconscious would appear to develop – or at least to be integrally involved in the development of the psyche as a whole.

Nevertheless, since stability is not often associated with development, it might still be hard to comprehend that stability is also a part of the process of development. Jung writes that 'the unconscious is seen as the collective pre-disposition to extreme conservatism, a guarantee, almost, that nothing new will ever happen' (1930b, para. 61). He explains this stability by means of what he calls 'archetypal conditions', i.e., 'inherited instincts, functions, and forms that are peculiar to the ancestral psyche' and imply the 'probability that a man will behave much as his ancestor behaved' (ibid.). Thus, for Jung, this stable ground of the unconscious is the foundation of human psychology. In order to examine psychological development, which includes the process of the unconscious, we need to consider both the stable condition of the unconscious and the potentiality for change in its manifestation.

The need for thinking in terms of both change and stability can be exemplified by considering the concept of homeostasis. Homeostasis is a concept originally applied to the physiological mechanism which maintains the constancy of organic conditions, but it is often used as a metaphor for self-regulating systems in wider contexts including human psychology. Steven Rose employs the term *homeodynamics*, for the tendency of a biological sys-tem towards self-regulation, instead of *homeostasis*. He argues that the set point at which the internal variables are maintained is not fixed but that 'there is a super-rhythm imposed upon homeostatic oscillations' (1998, p. 155). He shifts the focus from gene-centred determinism to interaction within organisms, and demonstrates that 'the moment-to-moment stability of the organisms is maintained not statically but dynamically' (ibid., p. 157). Rose's concept of homeodynamics could be applied to psychological mechanisms and when thinking about psychological development, it leads us to pay more attention to dynamic interactions in the psyche rather than static determin-ants of the psyche. Whether it is called homeostasis or homeodynamics, a psychological system which contains both change and stability, both dynamic and static states, may be called psychological self-regulation. Rose also maintains: 'Lifelines are not purely homeostatic: they have a beginning at conception, and an end at death.' However, if this principle does not apply to the unconscious, which, in Jung's view, has no beginning and no end, we may have to admit the limit of the application of the physiological mechanism to the psychological one.

The second question is whether the unconscious itself develops or whether the unconscious develops something, for instance, one's psyche in the way one relates to one's unconscious. Jung's concept of the collective unconscious offers us a picture of something beyond the personal, beyond human know-ledge, beyond conscious awareness or perception. The unconscious may be considered to develop when this overwhelming non-personal realm of the psyche makes a strong effect on the conscious mind.

Taken as a transitive verb (to develop something), it could be seen that the unconscious develops one's psyche: one's conscious perception (of the unconscious), one's personality, one's thoughts, ideas, questions, interests, curiosity, and relationships, including the relationship with the unconscious within oneself as well as in the minds of other people. It is hard to deny that the unconscious has at least some influence on one's psychological processes. One of the characteristics of the collective unconscious is described as the aforementioned *participation mystique*, the state of non-differentiation. It has the characteristic of continuity without end. It could be that consciousness cannot share its continuity and stability with the unconscious and therefore attempts to change in order to maintain its separateness from the unconscious. Jung argues that ' "beginning" and "end" are primarily necessities of conscious cognition' (1934b, para. 812) and doubts whether the same applies to the continuity of the psychic process as a whole. He writes:

> Beginning and end are unavoidable aspects of all processes. Yet . . . it is extremely difficult to see where one process ends and another begins, since events and processes, beginnings and endings, merge into each other and form, strictly speaking, an indivisible continuum.
>
> (ibid.)

In this continuum, the unconscious could develop or deepen certain images which grow into our conscious mind. We say that we develop our interests, ideas, questions, and thoughts. We also say that we develop relationships. This kind of development has no limit and no goal though it has a beginning. Our ideas and relationships can be deepened continuously and endlessly. There are aspects of development that deepen and cultivate something. What we develop over the years, or as we age, has predominantly been discussed in terms of nature and nurture, i.e., innate capacity/mechanisms and environmental/social influences, whether focus is given to one or the other, or the interaction between them, depending on different assumptions about causes of development (I shall discuss this further later in the chapter). Nevertheless, adding yet another dimension and thinking in terms of the unconscious seems to make the nature/nurture debate rather irrelevant or even inappropriate. For Jung, there is non-differentiation in the collective unconscious, and the collective unconscious influences one's mind from both within (as a part of one's psyche) and from without (as the source of universal phenomena manifesting in specific forms in the individual mind).

Taken as a reflexive verb (to develop oneself), it could be considered that the unconscious develops the unconscious itself. The unconscious may become 'better' (whatever this may mean), or become bigger by means of overwhelming or possessing the conscious mind, or become mature by means of developing the capacities of the conscious mind. However, the unconscious may also take care of itself, pay attention to itself, and nurture, nourish, cultivate, and deepen itself (even in the process of becoming better). There may be aspects of development that are self-nurturing and self-cultivating. Nevertheless, nurturing does not necessarily refer to the mother–infant relationship or the relationship between a child and its caretaker. For the subject can be the object by developing itself.

To consider the word 'develop' as a transitive verb or as a reflexive verb creates a different pattern of development from linear development. The deepening, nourishing, and cultivating aspects of development imply a more complex picture of development than a linear model of chronological development.

In this section, I have raised the question of the various possible connections between development and the unconscious. However, I should also accept the limits of exploring this question. Jung states: 'We should not, however, labour under the illusion that we have now discovered the real nature of the unconscious processes. We never succeed in getting further than the hypothetical "as if" ' (1928c, para. 272). I do not presume to suggest any 'right' answer to this question but remain open to this crucial issue in order to reconsider the dominant images of development.

Cultural development: nature and culture

With regard to the dominant images of development, it is generally agreed that developmental psychology is primarily concerned with the issue of nature and/or nurture, which is normally taken as the conflict and/or inter-action between biological factors and socio-cultural or environmental factors. Similarly, Jung is concerned with the relationship between nature and culture. However, due to his particular understanding of culture, Jung's concern with nature and culture seems to be different from the nature/nurture debate in developmental psychology.

Jung seems to regard nature as the biological, organic, and physical factors of development, as it is in the nature/nurture debate. However, when discussed in relation to nature, Jung's understanding of culture does not equate with the environmental, social, political, economic, and other factors that are normally regarded as constituting culture today. Rather, culture for Jung consists of the 'unnatural' or spiritual aspect of the human being. Jung writes:

> The psyche as such cannot be explained in terms of physiological chemistry, if only because, together with 'life' itself, it is the only 'natural factor' capable of converting statistical organizations which are subject to natural law into 'higher' or 'unnatural' states, in opposition to the rule of entropy that runs throughout the inorganic realm. How life produces

complex organic systems from the inorganic we do not know, though we have direct experience of how the psyche does it. Life therefore has a specific law of its own which cannot be deduced from the known physical laws of nature.

(1947/1954, para. 375)

Jung seems consistently to use the words nature and culture for the physical and spiritual aspects of a human being, though he describes the conflict between nature and culture in different, sometimes even contradictory ways. Sometimes, he views nature and culture as a co-existing pair, arguing that

Our psychology takes account of the cultural as well as the natural man, and accordingly its explanations must keep both points of view in mind, the spiritual and the biological. As a medical psychology, it cannot do otherwise than pay attention to the whole man.

(1927/1931, para. 160)

He also argues: 'The endless dilemma of culture and nature is always a question of too much or too little, never of either or' (1917/1926/1943, para. 41). Other times, he suggests that, in human development, a change takes place from nature to culture, asking: 'Could by any chance culture be the meaning and purpose of the second half of life?' (1930–31, para. 787) He claims that the transition leading from the first half of life to the second is 'a transformation of nature into culture, of instinct into spirit' (1925, para. 335). Other times again, he makes a distinction between nature and culture, paralleling the conflict between nature and culture with the conflict between 'individual consciousness and collective feeling'[5] (1913, para. 486). He also finds a parallel with the 'dilemma of five and four' (1950, para. 680). He observes that in mandalas painted by one of his patients the presence of four elements symbolises the ' "ideal" man' while the presence of five elements symbolises the 'material and bodily man' (ibid.). He explains:

Five is the number assigned to the 'natural' man, in so far as he consists of a trunk with five appendages. Four, on the other hand, signifies a *conscious* totality. It describes the ideal, 'spiritual' man and formulates him as a totality in contrast to the pentad, which describes the corporeal man.

(ibid.)

It is now clear that Jung is concerned not with nature and nurture, that is, the inner and outer conditions of development, but with nature and culture, which for him means the physical and spiritual aspects of a human being. Accordingly, in Jung's account, cultural development could be considered to be spiritual development. Nevertheless, it is still unclear how 'culture' and 'spirit' can be connected. Locating Jung's perspective on culture in historical context and comparing his ideas with the common belief in his time might help us understand what Jung meant by nature and culture.

There are significant correspondences between Jung's account of nature and culture and what is observed in the alchemical process. Jung was seriously concerned with alchemy from the late 1920s onwards (e.g., Marlan, 2006, pp. 267–72). Alchemy concerns the attempt through laboratory work to produce gold by means of the lapis or 'stone'. However, Jung considers alchemy not only as a chemical procedure for producing gold but also as the process of symbolisation that occurs in the alchemists' state of mind during their work. Jung observes:

> For many alchemists the allegorical aspect undoubtedly occupied the foreground to such an extent that they were firmly convinced that their sole concern was with chemical substances. But there were always a few for whom laboratory work was primarily a matter of symbols and their psychic effect. . . . Although their labours over the retort were a serious effort to elicit the secrets of chemical transformation, it was at the same time – and often in overwhelming degree – the reflection of a parallel psychic process which could be projected all the more easily into the unknown chemistry of matter since that process is an unconscious phenomenon of nature, just like the mysterious alteration of substances.
>
> (1944b, para. 40)

What we can observe here are the two different levels involved in both an alchemical process and Jung's view of psychological development: that is to say, an obvious, physical or material process, on the one hand, and a transformative and symbolic, deeply and inexplicably psychological and unconscious process, on the other. Moreover, Jung argues that 'the alchemist's hope of conjuring out of matter the philosophical gold, or the panacea, or the wonderful stone, was only in part an illusion, an effect of projection' (1944a, para. 564). What alchemists projected upon the unknown chemical substance, Jung argues, was 'the impersonal, collective archetypes' (ibid., para. 557) and what was projected into the phenomena of chemical change was 'the process of individuation' (ibid., para. 564). As we discussed earlier, the process and the goal of the individuation process could be interpreted in various ways. Nevertheless, in respect of the parallel processes between material and psychic, or physical and spiritual, it could be suggested that there is transformation between the two via an unconscious pathway. Jung explains that the process of individuation is 'the experience of the self' and 'a vital happening which brings about a fundamental transformation of personality' (1945, para. 219). He also explains that the 'self' in this context is 'a new centre of personality' created by means of a process of centring (ibid.), 'the centralizing processes in the unconscious that go to form the personality' (1944a, para. 564). The symbolism of alchemy plays an important role here because it expresses the individuation process (1944b, para. 40; 1945, para. 219). Just as Jung suggests that alchemy can help us understand the symbols of the individuation process (1945, para. 219), so alchemy can help us understand Jung's notion of psychological development.

Jung's concept of the self fits perfectly within the alchemical model. He states:

> Alchemy describes what I call the 'self' as *incorruptibile*, that is, an indissoluble substance, a One and Indivisible that can not be reduced to anything else and is at the same time a Universal, to which a sixteenth-century alchemist even gave the name of *filius macrocosmi*.
>
> (ibid., para. 220)

In Jung's view, alchemy involves what he regards as 'psychic' reality, which for him includes both physical and spiritual dimensions, hence nature and culture. He writes:

> The breath-body is not something 'spiritual' in our sense of the word. It is characteristic of Western man that he has split apart the physical and the spiritual for epistemological purposes. But these opposites exist together in the psyche and psychology must recognize this fact. 'Psychic' means physical *and* spiritual. The ideas in our [alchemical] text all deal with this 'intermediate' world which seems unclear and confused because the concept of psychic reality is not yet current among us, although it expresses life as it actually is.
>
> (1929a, para. 76, n. 2)

Jung's notion of psychological development is the search for the 'whole man', one who is both physical and spiritual. Accordingly, Jung's notion of the self would be represented by this whole man. Jung states:

> 'Ars totum requirit hominem!' exclaims an old alchemist. It is just this *homo totus* whom we seek. The labours of the doctor as well as the quest of the patient are directed towards that hidden and as yet unmanifest 'whole' man, who is at once the greater and the future man.
>
> (1944b, para. 6)

Here we need to consider how Jung's understanding of alchemy is related to the medieval understanding of alchemy. For Jung states:

> In dealing with alchemy we must always consider what an important part this philosophy played in the Middle Ages, what a vast literature it

left behind, and what a far-reaching effect it had on the spiritual life of the time.

(1944a, para. 556)

Close links between Jung's theory and alchemical texts have been discussed by scholars and practitioners of analytical psychology (e.g., Marlan, 2006). Also from outside of the Jungian camp, Åsa Boholm, a social anthropologist, acknowledges that Jungian psychology has played a pioneering role in understanding the symbolism of alchemy (1992, p. 119). Discussing the cultural context of the society of the Middle Ages, Boholm refers to the idea of 'cosmic identity',[6] according to which 'all things in the universe are organically interrelated' (1992, p. 121; see Montgomery, 1973, p. 243). Noting the contradictoriness of this idea for a modern reader, he explains:

> Since the organic cosmos was understood to be at the same time both spiritual and physical, it was quite logical that physical changes brought about new spiritual states and that the alchemist as practitioner would be affected spiritually by his experiments, with the corollary that his state of mind directly influenced the experimental process. The project of alchemy is therefore both physical *and* spiritual.
>
> (Boholm, 1992, p. 121)

What Jung calls 'psychic reality' seems to echo this idea of 'cosmic identity' in the Middle Ages. According to Boholm, the medieval world-view was utterly different from contemporary perspectives fostered by modern Western natural science. Nature[7] was considered not to be a static 'thing' but to be 'in a state of perpetual flux' (ibid., p. 115), and it was understood not only as 'a physical world of causes and effects *sui juris*' but also as 'spiritual and animated' (ibid., p. 116). Animals and plants were ascribed magical and supernatural properties (ibid., p. 117), and the universe was depicted as a 'unitary organic system' (ibid., p. 118). Owing to this particular perspective in the Middle Ages, 'No separation was felt to exist between natural science and theology, and questions about Divinity, planets, animals, and the causes and mechanisms which operated in the world, were closely intertwined' (ibid., p. 120). Boholm refers to Thorndike's survey of the history of magic and experimental science in the Middle Ages, which establishes that alchemy was closely related to other subjects, such as medicine, astronomy, astrology, zoology, and botany, and was a legitimate subject of natural philosophy and 'experimentation' in the Middle Ages (1992, p. 120; see Thorndike, 1927, II, p. 521).

Clearly, Jung's perspective on nature and culture bears a significant similarity to the alchemists' belief in the nature of the universe, as both physical and spiritual. We have seen that the alchemists' world-view was not particular to themselves but was common among other scholars in the Middle Ages.

Therefore, Jung's perspective on nature and culture is not totally different from the general understanding of the universe in the Middle Ages, even though it seems very different from the predominant understanding of the natural and cultural worlds in modern times in terms of biological and social contexts.

Here another question arises: does Jung neglect the outer, environmental, social conditions when considering psychological development? If not, how does he deal with them? It might be unfair to represent Jung's view of culture solely in terms of the spiritual aspect of the human psyche, as he is also concerned with culture in terms of civilisation. Spiritual development and civilisation: these two dimensions seem to be rather contradictory. Civilisation should be more concerned with socio-cultural contexts in the modern sense of this word, and in this respect Jung does not totally exclude the social aspect. Indeed, he explicitly acknowledges it, when he states that 'society is one of the necessary conditions of his [man's] existence' (1945, para. 224). However, he does not regard it as an important element when considering psychological development. For Jung, more important is psychic reality, how individuals experience the world and what the world means to individuals, rather than what is generally seen as the external and social world. In fact, Jung states that society is 'nothing more than a term, a concept for the symbiosis of a group of human beings. A concept is not a carrier of life' (ibid.). He explains:

> The sole and natural carrier of life is the individual, and that is so throughout nature. 'Society' or 'State' is an agglomeration of life-carriers and at the same time, as an organized form of these, an important condition of life. It is therefore not quite true to say that the individual can exist only as a particle in society.
>
> (ibid.)

For Jung, society appears to be a threat not only to individual but also to cultural development. In Jung's account, 'society' understood as 'a political collective called the "State" ' is 'in every respect detrimental to culture' (ibid., para. 222). For, it is 'a political directorate which ministers to the power struggles of special groups and promises economic benefits to the masses' (ibid.). For Jung, cultural or spiritual development contradicts society, the state, and the mass. Therefore, the latter are not just meaningless but can be even harmful for psychological development. In Jung's view, concern with social conditions could overwhelm the important human aspect which Jung regards as culture.

When Jung speaks of the individual and society, what he is actually concerned with is the conflict between the individual and the collective and between consciousness and unconsciousness. He describes these conflicts: 'Society is the greatest temptation to unconsciousness, for the mass infallibly swallows up the individual – who has no security in himself – and reduces him to a helpless particle' (ibid., para. 225). When a political aim predominates, 'Consciousness, instead of being widened by the withdrawal of projections, is narrowed, because society, a mere condition of human existence, is set up as a goal' (ibid.). Jungian analyst Christopher Hauke describes this crisis as 'the loss of self', which arises from 'identity with the mass' as well as from 'identity with archaic imagery arising from the unconscious' (2000, p. 172).

Here the difference between 'individualism' and 'individuation' needs to be clarified, in order to avoid misunderstanding of the individual in relation to the collective. Jung explains that 'individuation' is 'the better and more complete fulfilment of the collective qualities of the human being', while 'individualism' is 'deliberately stressing and giving prominence to some supposed peculiarity rather than to collective considerations and obligations' (Jung, 1928c, para. 267). Therefore, individuation does not imply a selfish, anti-social attitude which leads to isolation (see Hauke, 2000, pp. 168–74). Psychological development is a form of individual development which does not contradict collective development. In line with this, Hauke (using the term culture in much the same way as Jung) writes that Jung's 'concept of individuation is clearly as much a cultural project as it is a psychological project' (2000, p. 172). Thus, individuation allows one to connect with collectiveness in other forms than society, while individualism stands in isolation within a limited understanding of collectiveness, that is, society which consists of the power of the masses.

The issue of the individual versus society, the political collective, and the mass is clearly shown in the conflict between culture and civilisation. Jung extensively cites a Swiss educationist, Pestalozzi (1927) regarding the distinction in value between culture and civilisation. Jung quotes Pestalozzi: 'Culture has the power to unite men as individuals, in independence and freedom, through law and art. But a cultureless civilisation unites them as masses, without regard to independence, freedom, law or art, through the power of coercion' (1945, para. 227, n. 10). The translators of *The Collected Works of C. G. Jung* note the Germanic distinction between *Kultur* and *Zivilisation*: the former means 'culture, deriving ultimately from tillage and worship (*cultus*)' as 'a natural organic growth', while the latter means 'civilization' as 'an affair of the city (*civis*) and thus something artificial' (ibid.). They observe that Pestalozzi subscribes to this Germanic distinction and employs the word 'Zivilisation' in a pejorative sense. It is apparent from Jung's further citations of Pestalozzi that he agrees with this distinction between culture and civilisation. Jung quotes Pestalozzi's statement that 'The collective existence of our race can only produce civilization, not culture' (ibid., para. 225, n. 9). What is more, for Pestalozzi, human culture would not be advanced by any form of education established for the masses; our race develops only by means of humane education for the individual, not for the masses or for civilisation (ibid., para. 224, n. 8). Jung apparently distinguishes cultural development from civilisation. For Jung, civilisation is merely a product of the political-collective domination of individuals, or the non-humane mass, which can only produce the illusion that civilisation equates with human progress. He seems to have an unfavourable attitude to the word 'civilisation', pointing out the particular human attitude that prioritises the mass under the name of society.

Jung's attitude can be observed in his use of the word 'progression' as opposed to 'development' in at least one context. Jung states: *'progression should not be confused with development'* (1928b, para. 70). In the original German *Gesammelte Werke*, Jung distinguishes the German words 'Progression' and 'Fortschritt', translated into English as 'progression' and 'progress'.[8] However, Jung seems here to use the German word 'Progression' with a different implication. Gottfried Heuer drew my attention to the German word 'Fortschrittsgläubigkeit'. In this word, 'Fortschritt' (progress) and 'Gläubigkeit' (trustfulness) are combined, but the meaning of the word is quite different from 'progress'. 'Fortschrittsgläubigkeit' means blind belief; for example, that 'a technical progress is the same as a betterment of humanity' (Heuer, personal communication, 2000). Jung might have had in mind this kind of excessive belief which should be distinguished from the idea of development: it is merely an illusion or an effect of projections to believe that humanity is progressing.

Jung's statements about culture are not straightforward, because of his own conflicts about the idea of cultural development. This is represented by the conflict between the individual, on the one hand, and the collective, the mass, society, and civilisation, on the other. Jung's writings on Christianity and alchemy would also be relevant to a discussion of cultural development as spiritual development. We shall not explore this extensive topic here, though a later chapter (Chapter 3) will consider the God-image in relation to the child archetype, as one of the representations of the self.

In summary, Jung's distinction between nature and culture shows that his view of culture is very similar to the medieval world-view, and therefore different from the modern perspective. His distinction between culture and civilisation also shows that his view of culture corresponds not only with the world-view of medieval times but also with some critiques of modern belief systems, inasmuch as he challenges the positivistic attitude towards socio-cultural development. Therefore, Jung's perspective on culture paradoxically resembles both the medieval world-view and certain contemporary perspectives such as postmodernism.

This chapter has critically examined from Jung's perspective some of the dominant images of development, which are often associated with progress, advancement, and betterment; change; and nature and nurture. I have looked at an alternative Jungian perspective on psychological development, which is concerned with continuous processes that do not necessarily entail linear progress but can be interpreted in various ways; integration of projections, compensation of opposites, creation of the third, and symbolisation which could all be called individuation; outgrowing, with its spontaneous, cyclical, paradoxical, and symbolic aspects; change and stability, which together form a system of self-regulation that has a self-nurturing or self-cultivating characteristic; and nature and culture, which represent not the inner and outer conditions but the psychical and the spiritual aspects of a human being. This may indicate how distinctive or idiosyncratic Jung's ideas are rather than how similar they are to some of the ideas of other psychologists or thinkers. Because of Jung's strong resistance to social conformity, his theories might suggest a particular perspective on human psychology, relatively free from political and social trends or the fashionable views of his time, and which might also be applicable today.

Chapter 2

Regression

This chapter will discuss psychological development from the viewpoint of regression. It will illustrate different perspectives on regression, in terms of fantasies, psychic energy, and symbols, in which Jung's notion of development is addressed. By means of these perspectives, it will challenge the dominant images of what is usually regarded as contrary to development, that is to say: (1) going back to an 'undeveloped' stage; and (2) hindering or stopping the process of development. One of the crucial questions is whether the 'earlier' stages should be regarded as 'undeveloped', in other words, whether development is to be understood in terms of chronological sequence. Another important question is what adaptation means for Jung; rather, what role adaptation plays in his model of psychological development.

In general, regression is often understood as contrary to progression. Regression is sometimes understood as contrary to development as well, when progression is equated with development. However, though Jung views progression and regression as opposites, he does not seem to equate progression with development. How, then, in Jung's account, are the notions of regression, progression, and development related?

In depth psychology, regression often plays an important role in the development of individuals. Jung's is not the only theory to view regression as necessary for one's psychological well-being. However, while it is common among various approaches in depth psychology to connect regression with particular experiences in early childhood, Jung, unlike other theorists, considers regression as a phenomenon beyond the personal. In his view, regression does not simply lead to one's getting in touch with personal issues from early childhood (within oneself and with significant other or others) but releases the energy of archetypes. This chapter aims at clarifying in what way Jung's view of regression is distinctive by examining what he means by regressive fantasies, the regression of psychic energy (or libido), and symbolic interpretations of regression.

Regressive fantasies

Jung's view of regression is first connected with his understanding of the nature and function of fantasies. He regards regression as a natural phenomenon, which does not prevent psychological development. In his 'Two kinds of Thinking' (1911–12/1952), he first notes two types of regression: one is 'reactivation of original perceptions' (ibid., para. 25) and the other is 'regression to infantile memories' or 'an "historical" regression' (ibid.).

With regard to the first type of regression, Jung writes that dream-thinking 'regresses back to the raw material of memory' (ibid., para. 25), referring to Freud's statement about the dream-thoughts and his notions of progression and regression in his *The Interpretation of Dreams* (1900).[1] Jung seems to have no objection to the idea that regressive phenomena are observed in dreams. According to Jung, progression for Freud is the hallmark of waking thought: 'the advance of the thought stimulus from the systems of inner or outer perception through the endopsychic work of association to its motor end, i.e., innervation' (Jung, 1911–12/1952, para. 25). Regression is the reverse found in dreams: 'regression of the thought stimulus from the preconscious or unconscious sphere to the perceptual system, which gives the dream its peculiar atmosphere of sensuous clarity, rising at times to almost hallucinatory vividness' (ibid.). This could be identified as topographical regression in Freud's account.[2] Thus, regression here is considered as the process from thoughts to perceptions, from the conscious to the pre-conscious or unconscious.

With regard to the other type of regression, Jung argues that dreams 'elaborate' memories of early childhood, referring to Freud's view (Jung, 1911–12/1952, para. 25). However, Jung further argues that this regression goes beyond the childhood memories to what Jung calls *archaic thinking* (also called dream-thinking, fantasy-thinking, subjective thinking, non-directed thinking). By archaic thinking, Jung means that there is a kind of thinking in dreams, fantasies, and myths, which is subjective, can be inferred only indirectly, and is not directed outwards. This is contrasted to the other kind of thinking, which Jung calls *directed thinking* (also called adapted thinking, logical thinking, reality-thinking, or thinking in words). He presents the difference between archaic thinking and directed thinking in relation to the different characteristics between the unconscious and the conscious. In terms of the psychic functions, archaic thinking is 'effortless, working as it were spontaneously, with the contents ready to hand, and guided by unconscious motives' (ibid., para. 20) and directed thinking 'operates with speech elements for the purpose of communication, and is difficult and exhausting' (ibid.). Directed thinking is also described as the 'ideal language' (ibid., para. 14) in the sense that it 'in its origin and essence, is simply a system of signs or symbols that denote real occurrences or their echo in the human soul' (ibid., para. 13). In terms of psychic structure, much of archaic thinking 'belongs to the conscious sphere, but at least as much goes on in the half-shadow, or entirely in the unconscious, and can therefore be inferred only indirectly' (ibid., para. 39), and directed thinking is 'an altogether conscious phenomenon' (ibid.). The distinction between archaic thinking and directed thinking is clear in terms of both psychic functions and psychic structure. Nevertheless, these two kinds of thinking are also related. Jung explains that through archaic thinking, directed thinking 'is brought into contact with the oldest layers of the human mind, long buried beneath the threshold of consciousness' (ibid., para. 39). Accordingly, the unconscious bases of dreams and fantasies are 'not in themselves infantile' (ibid., para. 38), just as myths, which are based on unconscious fantasy-processes are 'far from being infantile' (ibid.). Jung sees the archaic basis of the mind as a matter of plain objective fact rather than as being dependent on individual experience or personal choice (ibid.). Therefore, for Jung, this type of regression does not concern mere recollection of childhood memories but the fantasies which are based on the archaic thinking in the unconscious.

This archaic thinking, which activates fantasies, is found not only in dreams but also in children and in myths; and because of that, confusion occurs between regressive fantasies and the infantile psyche or its memories. Jung states: 'Any introversion occurring in later life regresses back to infantile reminiscences which, though derived from the individual's past, generally have a slight archaic tinge' (ibid., para. 40). As opposed to Abraham[3] who regards myths as 'the infantile psychic life of the race', Jung describes myths as 'the most mature product of that young humanity' (ibid., para. 29). When Jung observes that there is 'a parallel between the mythological thinking of ancient man and the similar thinking found in children, primitives, and in dreams' (ibid., para. 26), his main concern is neither with children nor with so-called primitives. What he is really concerned with is mythological or fantasy-thinking, which is projected from the unconscious.[4] In other words, Jung is concerned not with how children or so-called primitives develop but with how this fantasy-thinking plays a role in the process of psychological development. Jung questions how fantasies are made, what their nature is (ibid., para. 33), where the fantasies get their material (ibid., para. 34), and 'where the mind's aptitude for symbolical expression comes from' (ibid., para. 37). Accordingly, his notion of the other type of regression, which he calls 'historical' regression, led him to question the nature of fantasies in the unconscious.

In relation to this 'historical' regression or 'regression to infantile memories', we shall now look at regression in a case of neurosis. As we have seen, Jung regards regression as a natural phenomenon and therefore disagrees with the view of regression and regressive fantasies (that is, infantile memories and fantasies), in terms of the aetiology of neurosis.

How Jung understands regression to infantile memories will be clearer if we look at his objections to Freud's concept of regression, in relation to the idea of development. Freud holds a view of regression which goes back to fixated stages in one's childhood, where the precursor of a current symptom originates. For Freud, development means resolving infantile sexuality, specifically the Oedipus complex. However, Jung disagrees with the view that sexualises an adult's fantasies about childhood (infantile fantasies manifested in the adult) and pathologises such fantasies as a cause of present neurosis. Likewise, he disagrees with the view that sexualises fantasies in childhood (infantile fantasies manifested in the child) and pathologises such fantasies as a precursor of later neurosis. Jung's objection to Freud's concept of regression and his objection to Freud's concept of childhood are closely connected. Jung considers that what Freud calls 'perverse' and what is called 'amnesia of childhood' are misnamed. Jung argues that it is incorrect to call them pathological and that both infantile sexual manifestations and the 'anterograde amnesia of children' are normal (1913, paras 368–9). Moreover, Jung doubts that regressive fantasies are always sexually oriented and cause neurosis. He writes: 'I do not even seek the reason for regression in primary incestuous or any other sexual desires' and that 'a purely sexual aetiology of neurosis seems to me much too narrow' (1916, para. 565). For Jung, childhood itself cannot be pathological and therefore cannot be the direct determinant of neurosis.

For Jung, what distinguishes normal from neurotic is not regressive fantasies, which can be observed in both normal and neurotic cases, but the presence of actual conflict. In 'The Theory of Psychoanalysis', he argues that neurosis stems from actual conflicts in the present rather than from childhood experience (1913, para. 373). Making a distinction between normal and neurotic cases, Jung sees neurosis as a reaction to the actual conflict, which is solved without much difficulty among normal people but causes the neurotic to get stuck (ibid., para. 408). This view and what Jung found in his word association tests are linked, in terms of actual conflicts. The association experiment made visible the actual conflicts, which Jung called 'complexes', and led him to think of the complexes as constellating[5] the subject's reaction (1906a, paras 733–4). He writes that 'the results of the association experiment argue strongly in favour of the regression theory' (1913, para. 408).

Identifying the problem in neurosis with the complex, Jung explicitly distinguishes fixation and a particular kind of complex, namely, the incest complex, which are used as pathological terms in Freud's account, from the cause of neurosis. Jung asserts that the infantile fantasies themselves are natural but what is peculiar to neurotics is their exaggeration of the importance of the infantile past (1916, para. 564). He argues that, 'if the fixation were indeed real, we should expect to find its influence constant; in other words, a neurosis lasting throughout life' (ibid.). Again, for Jung, the problem in neurosis is not the infantile fantasies themselves but the overemphasis on such fantasies recalled as the infantile past. Likewise, Jung also disagrees that the incest complex is the cause of neurosis. He observes that the fact that a traumatic experience in childhood was partly or wholly unreal has led psychoanalytic

theory to claim the incest complex as a highly important element in pathological fantasy. However, he believes that 'the incest complex was not a special
complex of neurotic people; it proved to be a component of the normal
infantile psyche' (1913, para. 353). Accordingly, Jung's impression of Freud's
use of the word 'regression' was that it is a concept associated with 'infantile
sexuality' and 'incest' (ibid., para. 373) and came to refer to the phenomenon
of reactivation or secondary exaggeration of infantile reminiscences (1916,
para. 565). For Jung, however, the incest complex can be observed in any
infantile psyche, and therefore itself cannot be the cause of neurosis.

Thus, for Jung, Freud's concept of regression as a symptom of unsolved
infantile sexuality is highly questionable: regressive fantasies should not be
reduced to the infantile past or labelled with pathological terms, such as
'perverse', 'fixation', 'amnesia', etc. Regressive fantasies are not fixated fantasies stemming from the repressed unconscious. For Jung, what might be
repressed is the complex, but the fantasies are not something repressed in the
unconscious. Jung distinguishes fantasies of an impersonal nature from those
of a personal nature, the former of which correspond to the collective
unconscious (e.g., 1940: paras 289–91). This leads us to Jung's distinction
between the personal unconscious, from which the complex arises, and the
collective unconscious, from which fantasies of an impersonal nature arise.

It could be that Jung's two kinds of thinking and Freud's two principles
(both of which were formulated more or less in the same year, 1911, after
their participation in the conference at Clark University in the USA)
signalled a great difference between the two psychologists for their later
theorisation on development. From the perspectives of their concepts of two
kinds of thinking,[6] the differences between Jung's and Freud's notions of
infantilism become apparent. One could even say that the differences in their
understanding of regression are in fact differences in their understanding of
infantilism. In Jung's view of two kinds of thinking, both archaic thinking
and directed thinking exist naturally and have an equal significance in the
human psyche. However, Jung later charges that Freud's concept of the
'pleasure principle', which Jung regards as the foundation of Freud's
theories, shows 'fanatical one-sidedness on sexuality, concupiscence' (1934c,
para. 340). Jung further comments that 'Repression, sublimation, regression,
narcissism, wish-fulfilment and the rest are all concepts that relate to the
grand drama of the pleasure principle' (ibid.). He suggests that a neurosis can
be seen not necessarily as an excess of infantilism but as an excess of adaptation, which should not be taken as a mere repression of infantilism or a
'substitute formation' (ibid., para. 343). (We will address adaptation later in
this chapter.) Jung's notion of infantilism is based on one of his two kinds of
thinking, that is, archaic thinking, as mentioned earlier, which is also called
early, infantile, fantasy, or dream-thinking. As this archaic thinking itself is
natural and normal for Jung, the early infantile state, infantile memory,
infantile thought and fantasies are also natural and normal. Thus, Jung's two

kinds of thinking, which are fundamentally different from Freud's two basic principles, lead to an utterly different interpretation of regressive phenomena from Freud's.

Jung not only de-pathologises and de-sexualises regressive fantasies but also attributes a teleological significance to them (1913, para. 404). In the case of neurotics, regression can be a chance for a new life. What Jung means by a new life is a new direction of adaptation. He suggests that when outward adaptation is too demanding, it is time to direct the libido inwards for the purpose of inner adaptation. Jung suggests that the fantasies of a neurotic can be 'the first beginnings of spiritualization, the first grouping attempts to find new ways of adapting' and that the neurotic's 'retreat to the infantile level does not mean only regression and stagnation, but also the possibility of discovering a new life-plan' (ibid.). This seems in a way similar to some other depth psychological views of regression, e.g., Kris' notion of 'regression in the service of the ego' (Kris, 1952), Balint's notion of benign regression (Balint, 1968), Winnicott's idea of therapeutic regression (Winnicott, 1954) or 'regression to dependence' (Winnicott, 1959–64, p. 128), in the sense that regression becomes a key to further psychological development. Nevertheless, Jung's approach to symbolic interpretation takes him beyond the view of regression as personal experience, as will be discussed later in this chapter.

From Jung's point of view, regressive fantasies are not infantile in the Freudian sense of being primarily pathological and personal, but infantile in the sense of being archaic, which is natural and normal. Accordingly, for Jung, it is neither a particular childhood experience nor an unresolved childhood trauma or complex that activates regressive fantasies but the archaic basis of the mind in the unconscious.

The regression of libido/psychic energy

Jung's *energic viewpoint* explains what goes on in the psyche when it becomes regressive: instead of seeing it as fixated or stuck, he presents the psyche as a ceaseless movement of libido, that is, psychic energy. Just as he objects to the view of regressive fantasies as sexually repressed or fixated, so he objects to the view of psychic energy as sexually oriented. An *energic viewpoint* of neurosis was presented in 'Psychoanalysis and Neurosis' (1916) as an alternative to the purely sexual standpoint that underpins psychoanalytic theory (ibid., para. 566). Jung considers that psychological phenomena are manifestations of psychic energy, which he calls libido, and that the libido is 'by no means only sexual' (ibid., para. 567). In 'On Psychic Energy' (1928b), he presents the progression and regression of libido as one of the most important energic phenomena of psychic life (ibid., para. 60). According to Jung, progression means outer adaptation, 'a continuous process of adaptation to the environmental conditions' (ibid., para. 74), and regression means inner adaptation, 'an adaptation to the conditions of the inner world' (ibid., para. 75). On one level, progression is 'a forwards movement of life in the same sense that time moves forwards' (ibid., para. 77), and regression is 'the backward movement of libido' (ibid., para. 62). On another level, however, 'Libido moves not only forwards and backwards, but also outwards and inwards' (ibid., para. 77) when the movement of libido corresponds to the two opposite types of attitude. Progression, as adaptation to outer conditions, is analogous to extraversion, and regression, as adaptation to inner conditions, is analogous to introversion (ibid., para. 77).[7] In the process of progression the pairs of opposites are united and reach a state of regular interaction and mutual influence (ibid., para. 61), and in the process of regression the value of the conscious opposites decreases and the value of unconscious factors increases (ibid., paras 62–3).

Seen from the energic point of view, the therapeutic relationship between regressive fantasies and adaptation could be understood as follows. According to Jung, fantasies are theoretically inexhaustible in analysis, so when the production of fantasies ceases after a time (1913, paras 422–3), it means that 'no more libido is regressing' (ibid., para. 423). He writes: 'The end of the regressive movement is reached when the libido seizes hold of the actualities of life and is used for the solution of necessary tasks' (ibid.). He also describes these tasks as 'certain necessary obligations to life' (ibid.), 'the incomparably more important duties to themselves' (ibid., para. 424), the 'task of adaptation the patient had to fulfil' (ibid.), and 'their life-tasks' (ibid., para. 425), in contrast to 'the general duties of life' and 'the precepts of current morality' (ibid., para. 424). It is apparent that when Jung talks about the regression of libido (or psychic energy), he is more focused on one's new life task, the new adaptation, the new direction in which the psychic energy should go, which calls for recognition, than on the cause of regression. Moreover, Jung writes: 'It is usually *the moment when a new psychological adjustment, that is, a new adaptation, is demanded*' (1916, para. 563) that neurosis breaks out, and it usually happens when a situation is at its most critical rather than by a mere chance. Jung warns of a danger in cases 'where the patient continues to produce endless fantasies, whether for his own pleasure or because of the mistaken expectations of the analyst' (1913, para. 423). In these cases, Jung claims, 'The consequence was that the libido always sank back again, as it was given no opportunity for further activity' (ibid., para. 424). From these cases, it is also apparent that Jung takes account of the very point at which the psyche requires a change in its balance through a new direction of its energy.

Jung's notion of progression and regression involves a dialectical relationship between them rather than the usual association with progression as its positive aspect and with regression as its negative aspect. With regard to the energic psychic process, progression and regression are regarded as 'transitional stages in the flow of energy' (1928b, para. 76). Jung uses the word 'canalization of libido' (ibid., paras 79–87), which means 'a transfer of psychic intensities or values from one content to another' (ibid., para. 79). In his writings, the following statement appears (1917/1926/1943, para. 182, 1928d, para. 281): 'The unconscious progressiveness and the conscious regressiveness together form a pair of opposites which, as it were, keeps the scales balanced.' Such dialectical relationship as Jung's progression and regression (or progressive and regressive transformations of energies) can be seen in other psychological theories, for instance, Jean Piaget's assimilation and accommodation,[8] Michael Fordham's deintegration and reintegration,[9] Melanie Klein's paranoid-schizoid position and depressive position,[10] and Margaret Mahler's separation and individuation.[11] These theories also suggest the dialectical relationships involved in development are not between positive and negative factors but between two equivalently indispensable factors. Jung explains that in the dialectical relationship between progression and regression 'energetics is concerned only with quantity and makes no attempt to explain quality' (1928b, para. 73). Moreover, he even explicitly denies the negative connotation of regression: 'regression is not necessarily a retrograde step in the sense of a backwards development or degeneration, but rather represents a necessary phase of development' (ibid., para. 69).[12] In this respect, development could therefore be understood not as a linear progression but as an interaction between movements backwards and forwards. Chronology here does not apply to the movement of progression and regression. Regression, seen as inner adaptation or the inward movement of psychic energy in Jung's account, does not in any sense mean being 'fixated' or 'stuck', and therefore does not stop or hinder development.

Looking at development from the energic viewpoint, both dynamic and static characteristics can be observed, which were discussed in Chapter 1 as one of the alternative perspectives to the general images of development. It was discussed there how development concerns not just 'change' but both 'change and stability'. Change is signalled when Jung distinguishes progression from development, saying that 'the continuous flow or current of life is not necessarily development and differentiation' (1928b, para. 70). Emphasising continuous movements of psychic energy, Jung uses the word development here as a synonym of change or differentiation. He writes: 'the psychic life of man can be progressive without evolution and regressive without involution' and that evolution and involution have no immediate connection with progression and regression (ibid.). He further explains that this is because progression and regression actually have a static character, although they are life-movements with their own directions (ibid.). What Jung seems to convey is the distinction between an action of psychic energy and its effects. Ceaseless movements of energy are able to maintain stable psychic conditions without necessarily changing either its outer conditions or itself. As we have seen earlier (in Chapter 1), Jung elsewhere understood development also as a continuous process and not just in terms of changes. In order to maintain such stability, psychic conditions need the dynamics of psychic energy. He writes that it is the contents of the collective unconscious that are liable to 'retard the pace of development' and to force it into regression until the store of energy which activated the unconscious has been used up (1917/1926/1943, para. 159). For no progress can be made, so long as the collective unconscious and the individual psyche are coupled together without being differentiated (ibid.). Here development would not simply mean change and differentiation but would be a self-regulating process which has both variable and invariable characteristics. It is confusing that Jung sometimes seems to use the word development in its general sense (as merely change for the better, a sense to which he usually objects), and other times uses it in the sense of his particular understanding of it (as change and stability). However, in either case, he resolves the problem of regression, seen as hindered development or 'fixation', through maintaining that progressive and regressive movements of psychic energy do not produce a hierarchical development of human psychology based on chronology. Even static moments can play a part in development, and therefore being 'stuck' and 'static' should be distinguished. While static moments of regression can engender fantasies, stuck moments of regression imply involution or degeneration and do not engender anything. Progression and regression together imply another dialectical relationship, i.e., change and stability in the process of development.

In sum, the energic view explains the process of development by means of the combination and compensation of progression and regression. From an *energic viewpoint*, Jung takes account of inner adaptation as well as outer adaptation, while generally adaptation is used only in terms of outer adaptation and inner adaptation is neglected. He holds the view that regression and progression are equally significant for development. Regression and progression of libido mean inner and outer adaptation, which are related to the balance of conscious opposites and unconscious factors, on the one hand, and to introversion and extraversion of psychological types, on the other. Progression for Jung does not mean progress in a hierarchical or judgemental sense and the progression–regression pair is not of the same kind as the pairs of evolution–involution, success–failure, or normal–pathological. For these reasons, in Jung's account, 'progression' cannot be equated entirely with 'development'.

According to Jung, what governs the progression and regression of libido is symbols. He writes: 'The psychological mechanism that transforms energy is the symbol', by which he means 'a real symbol and not a sign' (1928b, para. 88). In the next section I shall examine the symbolic meaning of regression.

Beyond childhood: symbolic interpretations of regression

Jung's concept of symbols well illustrates his attempt to present his perspective on what he regards as distinctively psychological development (the spiritual or cultural dimension), which does not rely on biological or social dimensions of development (nature or nurture), albeit they are interrelated to a certain extent.

Jung explains that a symbol 'represents the libido, or psychic energy in its creative aspect' and has 'a large number of analogous variants, and the more of these variants it has at its disposal, the more complete and clear-cut will be the image it projects of its object' (1911–12/1952, para. 180). He makes a distinction between signs and symbols. While the sign always has a fixed meaning, being a conventional abbreviation for or a commonly accepted indication of something known, the symbol is 'an indefinite expression with many meanings, pointing to something not easily defined and therefore not fully known' (ibid.). While signs can be understood semiotically as representing definite things, symbols should not be taken literally (ibid.). Likewise, Jung explains the symbol as, more specifically, a 'libido symbol':

> The *tertium comparationis* for all these symbols is the libido, and the unity of meaning lies in the fact that they are all analogies of the same thing. In this realm the fixed meaning of things comes to an end. The sole reality is the libido, whose nature we can only experience through its effect on us.
>
> (ibid., para. 329)

Connected with an energic view, Jung's notion of the libido symbols points to a dimension of the human psyche which operates with meaning in different ways from the usual ways in which other dimensions of the psyche discover, understand, or create and recreate meaning in certain objects.

Jung postulates the phase to which the psyche regresses as prior to the emergence of sexuality, and even as prior to one's childhood. For instance, against the sexual aetiology of neurosis, Jung first presents 'the presexual stage' as an earlier stage of development than the sexual stage, to which regression will go (ibid., para. 206). He argues that the presexual stage is the nutritional phase in the first years of life, which has no characteristics of sexuality (ibid., 1913, paras 263–9).[13] Indeed, it is because there is no sexual libido in that stage that he advocates looking at the concept of libido not in terms of sexuality but from the energic point of view (1913, paras 267–70). Nevertheless, the concept of the presexual stage does not appear in Jung's later theorisation. Discontinuing the idea of the 'presexual stage', Jung instead speaks of the 'pre-infantile period', to which regression goes. Regression to the pre-infantile period calls forth 'the wordless occurrences', which cannot be translated directly into the world of consciousness, due to their opposition to the conscious mind (1917/1926/1943, para. 120). The connection is made clear between where regression goes and the archaic, subjective, non-directed thinking that we have looked at earlier in this chapter.

The same idea is depicted as 'before childhood'. He writes: 'the regression continues right back into childhood' and 'ends up in the time before child-hood' (ibid., para. 117). In another place, he writes that the regressive ten-dency is one's seeking for 'the universal feeling of childhood innocence, the sense of security, of protection, of reciprocated love, of trust, of faith – a thing that has many names' (1930b, para. 55). This could be understood as the psychological need to get in touch with symbols. Moreover, Jung writes that 'the psychic development of the individual produces something that looks very like the archaic world of fable, and that the individual path looks like a regression to man's prehistory' (1935a, para. 18). Accord-ingly, in the theory of the archetypes, regression crosses over any parti-cular stages and goes beyond them. This is because the archetypal images are representations of something beyond the presexual stage, and even beyond the pre-infantile phase, that is to say, they lie in the world of symbols. The archetypes are crystallised out in the collective unconscious. For Jung, the collective unconscious is 'an image of the world which has taken aeons to form' (1917/1926/1943, para. 151). In line with his theory of archetypes, Jung thus consistently appreciates regression in terms of access to the symbolic world.

The energic viewpoint is explicitly linked to a symbolic interpretation of regression (Jung, 1928b, paras 42–7). The energic and symbolic views of regression together alter the causal view. Jung writes:

> The symbolic interpretation of causes by means of the energic stand-point is necessary for the differentiation of the psyche, since unless the facts are symbolically interpreted, the causes remain immutable sub-stances which go on operating continuously, as in the case of Freud's old trauma theory.
>
> (ibid., para. 46)

Concerning the theory of development, Jung believes that the final or teleo-logical point of view is necessary, since the causal view on its own is one-sided. For the final view leads us to look at symbols, while the causal view leads us to look at facts. Jung writes: 'Cause alone does not make develop-ment possible. For the psyche the *reductio ad causam* is the very reverse of development; it binds the libido to the elementary facts' (ibid.). For Jung, regression does not mean contrary to development but reducing the causes of development to the facts does mean contrary to development.

When we compare a symbolic interpretation of regression with a causal one, it is apparent how differently the process of regression can be interpreted. From the causal standpoint, regression is determined by a 'mother fixation', but from the final standpoint the libido is considered to regress to 'the *imago* of the mother' for the purpose of finding there 'the memory associations by means of which further development can take place' (Jung, 1928b, para. 43). Jung asserts that 'Psychic development cannot be accomplished by intention and will alone; it needs the attraction of the symbol, whose value quantum exceeds that of the cause' (ibid., para. 47).

Likewise, symbolically, regression seeks rebirth and not incestuous cohabitation (1911–12/1952, para. 332). For the basis of the 'incestuous' desire is not cohabitation but 'the strange idea of becoming a child again, of returning to the parental shelter, and of entering into the mother in order to be reborn through her' (ibid.). Jung states: 'The road of regression leads back to childhood and finally, in a manner of speaking, into the mother's body' (ibid., para. 506).

Jung explains that the majority of symbols are more or less close analogies of sexuality because the symbol derives its motive power from the instinctual process and sexuality is one of the strongest instincts (1911–12/1952, para. 338). Symbols of parents are also not always images of real parents but may be God-images beyond the concretism and sensuousness of memory (1921, para. 201). Regression to the parents is instantly transformed into progression if it is taken symbolically, but regression remains if the symbols are interpreted merely as signs (ibid.). Accordingly, it appears that there are close analogies between the biological and spiritual dimensions in Jung's account, as there are close analogies between sexuality and most symbols. However, it also appears that there are distinctive characteristics of the spiritual dimension when symbols are seen as transformers.

Jung argues: 'The symbols act as *transformers*, their function being to convert libido from a "lower" into a "higher" form' (1911–12/1952, para. 344).[14] This could be seen as transformation from the biological to the spiritual dimension. He also states: 'The exclusive importance of the cause, i.e., its energic value, thus disappears and emerges again in the symbol, whose power of attraction represents the equivalent quantum of libido' (1928b, para. 46).

If Jung sees the biological dimension of human beings as 'lower' and the spiritual dimension as 'higher' when he speaks of libido converted from a 'lower' into a 'higher' form, does it mean that in regression libido is in a 'higher' form? In order to understand what Jung means by 'lower' and 'higher', we need to consider how symbolic interpretation stands in relation to the complementary function. We saw in the previous section that progression and regression contribute equally to the process of development and that their transformation takes place in a complementary way which maintains the balance of the opposites. However, a 'higher' form of libido seems to be involved in something more than a mere dialectical dynamic.

Jung calls progressive development towards a new attitude the *transcendent function* (1917/1926/1943, para. 159). He also describes the beginning of the transcendent function as the collaboration of conscious and unconscious data ([1916]/1957, para. 167). He explains that the transcendent function is equivalent to a renewal of life and that 'In the regenerated attitude the libido that was formerly sunk in the unconscious emerges in the form of some positive achievement' (1921, para. 427). When we consider opposites such as lower and higher, it is easy to associate them with dialectical relationships, in this case perhaps with a judgemental relationship, for instance, between inferior and superior. However, Jung's focus might not be on the opposites themselves – what is higher and what is lower – but on the distance or gap between them, which is the same for both.

'Birth' and 'rebirth' have particularly important symbolic meanings. Jung explains them in terms of the transcendent function:

> The confrontation of the two positions generates a tension charged with energy and creates a living, third thing – not a logical stillbirth in accordance with the principle *tertium non datur* but a movement out of the suspension between opposites, a living birth that leads to a new level of being, a new situation. The transcendent function manifests itself as a quality of conjoined opposites. So long as these are kept apart – naturally for the purpose of avoiding conflict – they do not function and remain inert.
>
> ([1916]/1957, para. 189)

In the transcendent function there is something more than compensation; there is a third element which is beyond the original opposites. In that sense, what Jung calls the 'higher' form can be viewed as the birth of the third element. Following on from this, it becomes necessary also to examine the concept of the quaternity, which Jung finds represented in mandalas and other symbols of the self. This will be addressed in the next chapter.

Conclusion

In this chapter, I have discussed Jung's idea of development in terms of his concept of regression. I have illustrated that Jung's theory of regression can be understood in terms of a theory of fantasies, libido, and symbols. Jung de-pathologises, de-sexualises, and impersonalises regressive fantasies, suggesting a teleological view, an energic view, and symbolic interpretations of these fantasies. It becomes clear that, for Jung, regression is not contrary to development but reductionism to facts is. He frees fantasies from the past and gives an account of their dynamics in the present, including their meanings for the future. Instead of looking merely at dichotomies – pathological and normal, symptomatic and meaningful, sexual and non-sexual (or energic), causal and teleological, personal and collective, literal and metaphorical (or symbolic) – I have illustrated that each of these notions needs to be viewed not just in relation to its opposite but in relation to the potential emergence of the third element, that is, the symbolic meanings and effects which it might bring about.

From Jung's perspective, fantasies can be seen as providing a path to new adaptation as well as a channel to the collective psyche, from where symbols stem. Fantasies grow, until the time when 'no more libido is regressing' (Jung, 1913, para. 423) and the regressive movement ends, whereupon the libido is used for new adaptation. Libido regression or the regression of psychic energy (towards inner adaptation, in other words, introversion) means the development of fantasies. Likewise, libido progression or the progression of psychic energy (towards outer adaptation, in other words, extraversion) means the end of fantasies. In that sense, Jung does not present a linear model of development. For it is not true that the more one adapts outwardly, the more one develops. Too much outer adaptation can result in neurotic problems. There is no endless development in that sense. One cannot go forwards and outwards endlessly, as one has to come backwards and inwards at some point in order to maintain the balance of one's psychic energy and personality.

I have distinguished Jung's notion of 'development' from that of 'progression' or 'adaptation to environmental conditions', which is a form of one-sidedness, due to its one-directedness: forwards or outwards. For regression takes the counter-position to compensate the one-sidedness, going in the other direction: backwards or inwards. Then I have considered Jung's notion of development in relation to that of 'transformation' of libido/psychic energy; its function of balancing the opposites. I have also discussed Jung's notion of development in relation to that of the 'transcendent function', the emergence of the third element.

However, a question remains as to whether regression in an adult and regression in a child are different in a symbolic sense. We also need to discuss how the symbolic explanation of 'development' can be applied to early states of mind and how it influences Jung's images of 'the child' and actual children. The next chapter will discuss various issues regarding the child and the adult as well as 'the child' and the actual child.

Chapter 3

Symbolic child psychology

This chapter first examines how and to what extent child development is relevant to psychological development in general and to Jung's psychology in particular. It next examines how Jung viewed the child and how his conception of the child is related to his understanding of psychological development. Finally, it discusses the confusion in understanding Jung's concept of the child as well as his contribution to discussions of psychological development.

To what extent is child development relevant to psychological development?

Developmental psychology used to be seen as almost equivalent to child psychology. Psychologists took the development of the child as representative of human development, so that their theories about child development were seen as theories about development *per se*. The child is sometimes seen positively as a 'developing child' who is the carrier of human progress and other times negatively as an 'undeveloped child' who is primitive and inferior compared to grown-ups. A specific image of the child underpins each developmental theory.

As many critiques point out, any particular image of the child that is used to support developmental theories is biased with a particular historical, social, and cultural background and excludes other possibilities of child development. Erica Burman argues that discourses of childhood are part of cultural narratives (1994, p. 48). She maintains that any portrayal of development as natural and inevitable is in fact conditioned not only by differing conceptions of the age range within which developmental phases are supposed to take place but also by cultural and class variation in life expectancy and other factors such as political majority, legal responsibility, sex, child-rearing strategies, and differences in moral code (ibid., pp. 48–50). More precisely, Sheila Greene argues that the 'normal' development promoted by child psychologists has a specific kind of bias: a 'middle-class, Western and male-centred view of the universe' (1997, p. 43). Consequently, 'children from the culture, class or gender that is excluded from the definition of what is developmentally the norm are fated to be categorized as deviant, and therefore problematic' (ibid.). Thus, developmental theories based on specific images of the child limit themselves to their applications to particular groups of children.

Despite Jung's obvious concern with psychological development, his theories have not been recognised as comprising a developmental theory. Why is Jung's psychology not considered a form of developmental psychology? Probably, it is not because he did not have a theory of development but, at least in part, because he did not have a theory of *child* development. His theory of development was not rooted in child-centred psychology in the same way as the theories of many other contemporary and later psychologists.

Jung's psychology is generally thought to be about adult psychology and not about child psychology, as he was mainly concerned with adult patients and had few consultations with children.[1] However, he was very much concerned with 'the child' as an archetype or a symbol of the self. In this respect, Jung closely observed 'the child in the adult' (1934a, para. 286). Jung's psychology may also be largely concerned with child psychology, but in the form of psychology of 'the child'.

What is 'the child'?

For Jung, 'the child' predominantly means the archetype of the child. Therefore, the question to be asked should not be *who* the child is but *what* 'the child' is in Jung's view. The child archetype, which usually appears as the child motif in myths and fairy tales as well as in dreams and fantasy, is not a human child but a symbol (Jung, 1940, para. 260, n. 21). As an archetype, it cannot be described in itself, although there are numerous specific manifestations of the child motif. It exhibits duality and integrates opposites, such as beginning and end, initial and terminal, the pre-conscious and the post-conscious essence of humans, that is, the 'unconscious state of earliest childhood' and an 'anticipation by analogy of life after death' (ibid., para. 299), and many other paired elements. In particular, the child motif emerges as the archetype of the 'child god' or as the 'Christ child' (ibid., para. 268), in dreams and myths as the 'divine child' (Jung, 1952, para. 713), the motif of the child-hero or the squaring of the circle (ibid., para. 738), in alchemy as the stone, which may change into gold (ibid.), and as many other figures. The 'child of chaos' is considered as Saturn in Gnosticism and Mercurius in Alchemy (Jung, 1943/1948, para. 275). Child motifs for Jung also include roundness, the circle, the sphere, the quaternity, and other forms of wholeness. Jung argues that 'the child is a symbol of the self and the quaternity is a symbolical expression of this' (1946, para. 378). Furthermore, the archetype of the child appears, according to Jung, as the 'eternal child' in man, which is abandoned and exposed but, at the same time, divinely powerful (Jung, 1952, para. 755).

As an archetype, 'the child' contains many contradictions. For example, Jung refers to the child archetype in terms of the 'divine child' or an 'eternal child', or as a symbol of the self. The 'divine child' is characterised by eternity or immortality. In this sense, we could characterise 'the child' as a *non-developing child* (as an eternal child). As a symbol of the self, 'the child' could also be described as *the most developed child* (as wholeness, as the goal of individuation). Marie-Louise von Franz considers what in particular the mythological motif of the child means when it functions as a symbol of the self, i.e., 'one of the many images which illustrates the mystical, divine core of the human being' (1990, p. 19). She notes its duality: on the one hand it has the capacity of the self and on the other it has an infantile shadow. The element of youthfulness, the spirit of truthfulness, absolute spontaneity and genuineness of the personality are characteristics of the child that can be understood in both positive and negative ways. James Hillman discusses these contradictions in terms of the archetype of senex and puer (1967). We might expect that straightforwardly the image of the senex is the wise old man and the puer aeternus is the eternal child. However, he argues that *'the senex is there at the beginning'* (ibid., p. 311; emphasis in original), that 'the senex is there in the child' (ibid., p. 323) and that the archetype cannot so simply be divided into youth and age (ibid., p. 309). He views 'the archetype of senex-puer' as a single archetype which has two faces. It is described as 'a two-headed archetype, or a *Janus-Gestalt*' (ibid., p. 314), the 'union of sames' (ibid., p. 334), and 'the *senex-et-puer* unity, which holds the polar extremes of the spirit' (ibid., p. 338). However, when senex and puer split within the same archetype, each split half is one-sided. Puer and senex each have both positive and negative aspects (ibid., p. 314). According to Hillman, *'the difference between the negative and positive senex qualities reflects the split or connection within the senex-puer archetype'* (ibid., p. 325; emphasis in original) and *'there is no basic difference between the negative puer and negative senex'* (ibid., p. 330; emphasis in original). Therefore, the 'positive puer' or eternal child would refer merely to a transformed continuation of the senex. Hillman explains this connection as a 'secret identity of both faces that are actually one face' (ibid., p. 334) and that 'The bi-polar spirit would be ambivalent, logically incoherent but symbolically cohesive, as we find in the paradoxes of mysticism' (ibid., p. 340). If we consider that the child is one of the two faces of the same archetype, the child archetype could be seen as itself a meaningful paradox. Accordingly, 'the child' who never develops (remaining as *puer*) and 'the child' who has already developed (being *senex*) are paradoxically the same, not logically but symbolically.

Chronological development does not apply to 'the child', which, as a symbol, partakes of and emerges from the timeless realm of the collective unconscious. Jung's psychology does not take the same standpoint as so-called child-centred psychology, in as much as the child means the symbol and not the actual child. Nevertheless, it may be called symbolic child psychology or symbol-centred child psychology, in which the child archetype plays an important role.

The child as an archetype may seem remote from any real child. However, in one way, the archetype of the child represents various child-images together, experienced by or imagined as actual children as much as projected upon them. Jung does not commit himself to a particular archetypal image of the child. He remains open about what childhood exactly is, by emphasising the potentiality of the archetype to manifest or be represented in any forms or images in a given situation. The symbolic meaning of the child archetype is prioritised for its autonomy and spontaneity. In this way, Jung's concept of the child archetype does not support a recognisable theory of child development.

Is 'the child' related to the images of the actual child in Jung's view?

I have discussed how the child archetype is a symbol of the self and does not necessarily equate with the actual child. Having said that, Jung's distinction between 'the child' and the actual child is sometimes unclear. His statements about children are confusing: whether he speaks of 'the child' as the archetype or as an actual child or as a metaphor for something else is not always obvious. Samuels observes that a metaphor cannot be separated from its original content regardless of the extent to which the word is understood literally.[2]

Speaking of children and childhood, Jung makes various remarks. He notes the difference between the adult's past (actual childhood) and the adult's memories/narratives/fantasies of the past (images of childhood). He talks about one's own son or daughter from the parents' point of view (as a part of the parents' psyche) as well as from the child's point of view (as the filial psyche whose experience of the parents is both actual and archetypal). He parallels the child's psyche with the early state of mind, the regressed state of mind, the primitive psyche, and archaic, irrational, dream or fantasy thinking. Nevertheless, the complexities of these narratives of children and childhood stem from the fact that they are all interrelated, while some of them are also strongly connected with 'the child'. When the unconscious is involved, psychic experiences in transference, countertransference, dreams and fantasies could easily be invaded by the archetypal images of 'the child' as well as other archetypal images.

When Jung describes the child's psyche from his experiences of child analyses and observations, it is unclear whether in his account the actual child has any connection to the archetype of 'the child'. He seems to hold that: (1) there is no centre in the child's psyche (1928a, para. 103); and (2) most of the child's psyche is related to its parents' mind (1910/1946, 1926/1946, 1927/1931a, 1928a, 1934a). From these, Jung might seem to accept (3) no subjectivity and individuality in childhood. When he describes the actual child as part

of its parents, it is contrasted with the symbolic child, representing wholeness: the symbolic child is both dependent on and independent from the
parents but the actual child is only dependent on the parents. If that is the
case, his images of the actual child could in fact be one-sided or partial
images of 'the child'.

However, there is some evidence against the case that Jung views the actual
child exclusively in relation to its parents. Jung does show an awareness of
children's individuality, by looking beyond parental influence. Talking about
a case of a girl of 13 years old, where Jung believes that the mother in fact
needs treatment, he states:

> Nothing is more stunting than the efforts of a mother to embody herself
> in her child, without ever considering that a child is not a mere append-
> age, but a new and individual creature, often furnished with a character
> which is not in the least like that of the parents and sometimes seems to
> be quite frighteningly alien. The reason for this is that children are only
> nominally descended from their parents, but are actually born from the
> ancestral stock. Occasionally you have to go back several hundred years
> to see the family likeness.
>
> (1926/1946, para. 222)

This echoes his idea expressed in the introduction to Wickes's 'Analyses der
Kinderseele' (1927/1931a, paras 86–92). Having noted psychic causality, that
is, the causal significance of parental problems for the psyche of the child,
Jung writes:

> But what he [the child] is as an individuality distinct from his parents can
> hardly be explained by the causal relationship to the parents ... It is a
> combination of collective factors which are only potentially present in
> the parental psyche, and are sometimes wholly invisible. Not only the
> child's body, but his soul, too, proceeds from his ancestry, in so far as it is
> individually distinct from the collective psyche of mankind.
>
> (ibid., para. 93)

Jung further comments:

> Because of its universal distribution the collective psyche, which is still so
> close to the small child, perceives not only the background of the parents,
> but, ranging further afield, the depths of good and evil in the human
> soul. The unconscious psyche of the child is truly limitless in extent and
> of incalculable age.
>
> (ibid., para. 95)

Thus, looking at the depth of the actual child's psyche, what Jung seems to suggest lies there is the collective unconscious, where the child archetype is located. That is how the confusion arises between the actual child and the child archetype in the collective unconscious.

When his focus was on the collective unconscious, it may seem that Jung was rather blinded to the actual child by his strong attachment to 'the child'. He claims: 'The collective unconscious is a natural and universal datum and its manifestation always causes an unconscious identity, a state of *participation mystique*' (1946, para. 504). As Jung himself admits, in the collective unconscious his concept of 'the child' may have involved an unconscious identity with his view of the actual child. In fact, his view of the child psyche seems to come from his view of the primitive psyche. Lévy-Bruhl's expression, '*participation mystique*'[3] originally referred to the unconscious identity of primitive man with the universe, without differentiation between subject and object. What Jung claims is that this state of identity in mutual unconsciousness would also occur between children and parents, as a feeling of oneness with the parents. As a result, the child's psyche is considered, in Jung's view, to be closely related to the parents' psyche, especially the mother's, and to involve no differentiation between conscious and unconscious, subject and object. Accordingly, when a child exhibits pathology, Jung recommends looking at its parents' psychology. Jung's concept of 'the child' so dominates his thinking that it allows him to see actual children only collectively, rather than as individuals, just as when he speaks about primitives, they are always a collective group and their individual life is not considered. This means either that each personality among the actual children or primitives is neglected and the differences among them are not discussed, or that Jung may not be concerned either with children or with primitives on the individual/personal level but only with the collective psyche.

Jung did not systematically write about his perspectives on children and childhood, distinguished from his perspective on 'the child'. Consequently, though sometimes his statements about the child seem provocative as though referring to the immaturity of the actual child's psyche (for instance, 1927, para. 272; 1928a, para. 109), at other times, when speaking of a symbol, they seem to refer exclusively to the adult's psyche. Jung writes:

> We talk about the child, but we should mean the child in the adult. For in every adult there lurks a child – an eternal child, something that is always becoming, is never completed, and calls for unceasing care, attention, and education.
>
> (1934a, para. 286)[4]

In symbolic childhood, development can begin at any moment in life, for there is no differentiation of beginning and end. However, a question remains as to whether the same kind of non-linear development can apply to actual childhood, during which, Jung believes, the child's psyche is mostly unconscious and largely constituted by its relationship to its parents. He has a well-articulated theory of 'the child', which could have been tested against the development of the actual child. But strangely he never pursued this seemingly straightforward connection.

What is the relationship between the 'archetype of the child' and the 'archetype in childhood'?

We have seen how Jung not only makes a distinction but also creates a certain amount of confusion between his concept of 'the child' and his perception of the actual child. In this section we examine more fully what might cause this confusion.

The confusion seems to stem largely from the various, complex connections between parents and both (1) the actual child and (2) 'the child' on the conscious as well as unconscious levels. As with the actual child and the child archetype, so we have to consider the actual parent and the parental imago.[5] Both the actual child and 'the child' are related to both the actual parent and the parental imago. This seems rather complicated, but it is in the complexities of these relationships that the confusion on this issue is located. The relationships are illustrated in Figure 3.1.[6]

In Figure 3.1, 'a parent' means the actual parent, and 'a child' means the actual child. These two represent the child–parent relationship on the conscious level. 'The parental imago' and 'the child' are the archetypes, and these two represent the child–parent relationship on the unconscious level. The conscious and unconscious relationships are interrelated.

Jung describes the parental imago as the 'archetype in childhood' and distinguishes it from 'the archetype of the child' in terms of their manifestations and functions. I have discussed above how, with regard to 'the archetype of the child', Jung maintains that: (1) 'the child' is not a real child but a symbolic motif, which has archaic characteristics and appears in dreams and fantasies as well as in fairy tales and myths; (2) the archaic characteristics of 'the child' are inherent, timeless, and universally seen in human beings, as with any other archetype; and (3) 'the child' is a symbol of the self: 'The self is . . . the whole man, whose symbols are the divine child and its synonyms' (1952, para. 755). In contrast, where 'the archetype in childhood' is concerned, Jung claims that: (1) the most immediate archetype in childhood is

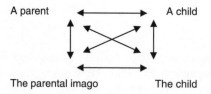

Figure 3.1 The actual and symbolic child–parent relationship.

the primordial image of the mother (1927/1931b, para. 75); (2) regression leads one back to one's childhood when the parental imago was active and may now be reactivated (1916, para. 569); and (3) the parental imago appears in the form of projections, as with any other archetype, and these need to be withdrawn (1945, para. 212). Therefore, when Jung speaks of the archetype in childhood, it seems to refer predominantly to parental imagos. Again, childhood could be understood symbolically rather than literally in terms of the deeper layer of the psyche to which symbols belong, that is to say, the collective unconscious. In this sense, the archetype in childhood, i.e., the archetype in the collective unconscious could mean any archetype.

The archetype in childhood and the archetype of the child are different on one level: the former is predominantly the parental imago and the latter is a symbol of the self. However, since both are archetypes in the collective unconscious where there is no differentiation, they cannot be entirely differentiated, for they are intermingled on another level. The mother imago is the first archetype manifested in childhood. This and the father imago are interrelated with the actual parents. The parental imago also manifests in adulthood either being transferred onto human objects (as projection through transference not only in analytic sessions but also in everyday life) (1946, para. 420) or appearing in a fantasy (1929b, paras 142, 212, 215). Accordingly, as far as concerns the manifestation of the parental imago, there should be no difference between actual childhood and psychologically revisiting childhood in adulthood.

Understood not literally but symbolically, childhood does not mean the early phase of life or the adult's past but signifies the world of symbols where all archetypes meet one another, that is, the collective unconscious. The child archetype could exhibit its symbolic themes connected with the parental imago anytime in life. Jung argues that it represents 'the self as such', that is, it is 'timeless and existed before any birth' (1946, para. 531). Regression connects these archetypes, activating them within the symbolic childhood. The 'archetype in childhood' (the parental imago) and the 'archetype of the child' (a symbol of the self) play a role in both outer and inner adaptation. Involved in *interaction* with other people and *intra-action* within oneself, the 'archetype in childhood' and the 'archetype of the child' contribute to both external relationships with others and to subjective or internal integration.

However, Jung did not mention the manifestation of 'the child' in actual childhood, while he observed the parental imago appearing at anytime in life, i.e., in symbolic childhood as well as in actual childhood. Jung's concept of the parental imago is always viewed from a filial standpoint (as personifications of father and mother) and not from a parental standpoint (in the relationship with daughter or son), and therefore the subject of development is always the child who experiences the parents rather than the parents in relation to their children. Consequently, the person in the position of 'a child' (not necessarily an actual child, for the person can be an adult and of any age) can be viewed in relation more to the parental imago than to the child archetype. It would be problematic to focus too much on the actual child–parent relationship, although any relationships between two people can be seen in terms of this relationship. When we are preoccupied with parents, the connection between 'a child' and 'the child' will be lost.

It is contradictory that 'the child' should, on the one hand, be timeless and potentially active at any time in life, since it belongs to symbolic childhood, yet, on the other hand, be, for Jung, invisible in actual childhood. Whereas the parental imago is connected with both actual childhood and symbolic childhood, 'the child' is connected not explicitly with actual childhood but only with the second half of life. In other words, whereas the parental imago is likely to be identified with the actual parent at any time in life, symbols of the self are less likely to be identified with oneself at any time in life in this perspective. Unless the second half of life means something other than an actual chronological period, 'the child' will be excluded from the actual childhood.

What is the significance of the second half of life in relation to 'the child'?

Jung emphasises the significance of the second half of life for the individuation process, but, curiously, he also emphasises the importance of 'the child' in the second half of life. It seems contradictory for Jung to claim that the second half of life is an important developmental period and yet that the eternal child, who does not belong to any period of life, is a significant motif in that period. This is another confusion arising between a child and 'the child': i.e., between our expectation of what, in actuality, unfolds chronologically in life and what, as a symbol, remains the same.

Jung points to lack of experience, one-sidedness, and dependency as the characteristics of the first half of life. However, it is unclear whether Jung connects these images of the first half of life with his perception of actual youth or of the eternal youth of 'the child'. If he connects such images with 'the child', the first half of life should again be understood metaphorically.

As we have seen earlier with regard to the archetype of senex–puer, Hillman disagrees with the division of life into first and second halves, since this involves splitting the archetype of the senex–puer (1967). He argues that 'we cannot fit psychological life into the historical conditions or the narrowly biological frames of a "first-half/second-half" ' (ibid., p. 310) and that 'The "second-half" is with us from the beginning' (ibid., p. 311). He particularly objects to the split between youth and age in terms of inferior and superior halves, with the puer representing only negative aspects and the senex representing only positive aspects of the personality. He suggests reversing the value when superiority/inferiority concerns the senex–puer archetype. He identifies the negative aspect of the puer as the same as the negative aspect of the senex. For instance, irrationality is usually regarded as characteristic of the first half of life, and accordingly, the puer represents the irrationality of man. However, irrationality is not only the negative aspect of the puer but also the shadow side of the senex. According to Hillman:

> Irrationality would not have to be banned to the crazy fringe and treated as peripheral; irrationality belongs to the nature of the old wise man. Before we can gain consciousness of the wisdom of nature, which is how Jung . . . describes the old wise man, we would first have to be in touch with the unconscious aspect of the wisdom that is ape.
>
> (ibid., p. 354)

What Hillman describes as the secret identity between the negative aspect of the puer and that of the senex is not usually recognised because of our immediate association of the puer with the first half of life. However, the first half of life could be explained equally well in terms of the senex, as could the second half of life in terms of the puer. Accordingly, in Hillman's view, development is seen as a non-linear form, in which the midpoint is *kairos*, i.e., 'the right moment' (ibid., p. 302, Hillman cites Jung, 1956, *Gegenwart und Zukunft*) and 'discovering a connection between past and future' (1967, p. 303). He writes:

> We work to overcome the puer in ourselves and behold before us images of the wise old man to be. . . . The critical time in this process that is represented by the midpoint of biological life is as well the mid-point of any attitude or psychological function that ages but does not change.
>
> (ibid., p. 330)

The notion of the first and second halves of life could be seen as a metaphor for the archetype of puer and senex. Like the puer–senex archetype, Jung's notion of the first and second halves of life could be seen not as polar opposites but as lying on the same side from the crucial turning point of psychological life, i.e., the centre of the psyche.

Jung's emphasis on the importance of the second half of life could be understood not in terms of maturity (based on chronological development) but in terms of reconnection to the unconscious (based on his notion of spiritual development). For a person to enter the second half of life would mean that his or her relationship with the collective unconscious changes, or rather that the archetypes suddenly start to affect them in a different, perhaps in the opposite, way.

However, if the midpoint of life is seen only on the conscious level reflecting one's chronological life, the division of life into first and second halves will create a kind of elimination of actual childhood and old age. It would encourage the view that it is too soon for young children to reflect on their lives and too late for old people to think about their future, and therefore these kinds of psychological development are irrelevant to them. But the midpoint or turning point in life, i.e., the point at which the conflict between psychological opposites becomes particularly acute (something Jung considered to happen mostly in middle age), may in fact emerge at any time regardless of the chronological phase of life. Jung's understanding of psychological development therefore does not exclude youth and old age.

There could be postulated more than one kind of relationship between the first half of life and the second half of life. One is chronological, and another is circular. Yet another is a combination of compensatory cycles. Once a person is born, he will already be in the cycle of the first half and second half of psychological life, in the process of going forwards, or doing something new, and going backwards, or resolving things that have been left behind, while searching for another dimension of life. One will encounter many opportunities for psychological rebirth. A turning point may come within the same cycle of life or become a point of transformation into another cycle of life. It could be a transformation that helps the person escape from one pattern of life, leads him or her into another channel, and helps him or her relate to his life in a different way. Transformation leads the individual to a new dimension of life, which is again cyclical but related to the original cycle of life in a compensatory way: a combination of compensatory cycles. Within these cycles, going forwards and backwards, progression and regression, are not a matter of chronological or linear development. In this cyclical form of life, every single moment could become a crucial point in the continuation of life.

Like Hillman's concept of the 'senex–puer' and Jung's metaphor of the 'first half–second half' of life, it could be considered that the *child–parent archetype* is a metaphor for an inseparable pair. From this viewpoint, a person could potentially be involved in three child–parent relationships (not only two): (1) the person as an actual child relates to his or her own parent; (2) the person as an actual parent relates to his or her own son or daughter; and (3) these two relationships create another child–parent relationship, i.e., between the child and parent within oneself (Figure 3.2). These relationships are obvious on the conscious level. On the unconscious level, the child archetype and parental imago are involved and make these three relationships even more complicated (Figure 3.3).

In these unconscious relationships, the question as to which comes first, child or parent, is circular. Therefore, the unconscious child–parent relationship is not linear or chronological but is represented as a circular or spiral form. Symbolically, being a parent could also include acting out the child–parent relationship in the role of parent, not necessarily having an actual child but having an alternative child in the form of another person or object with whom one is in close relationship. It does not matter whether or not one

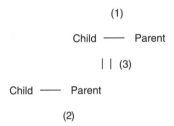

(1)

Child —— Parent

| | (3)

Child —— Parent

(2)

Figure 3.2 Three kinds of child–parent relationship.

Note: (3) shows the relationship within the same person.

is an actual parent, since one has both child and parent aspects in oneself on the archetypal level. Jung was interested in 'the child in the adult' (that is, in one way, or metaphorically, the child archetype, and in another way, literally being a daughter or a son). Likewise, he was interested in the adult, especially the parent in the child (that is, metaphorically the parental imago, and literally the father and mother), with whom he thought the child's mind is largely connected on the unconscious level. The relationship between the first half and second half of life leads us to the paradoxical relationship between the parent in the child and the child in the adult. The implication of this circular form of relationships could be that the child–parent relationship can be seen as either a child–child or parent–parent relationship, in the sense either that both the child and the parent equally have access to the child archetype and the parental imagos or that continuation of generations involves two roles: child and parent. Again, the actual and symbolic child–parent relationships cannot be completely separated from each other and yet they have very different implications: the actual child–parent relationship could be looked at in terms of overt behavioural patterns, or culturally and morally imposed social roles of parents, or various socially constructed images of children, whereas the symbolic child–parent relationship needs another dimension, i.e., the complexities of one's psyche in which there underlies the unconscious personalities, roles, and communications which could be alien to the conscious ones.

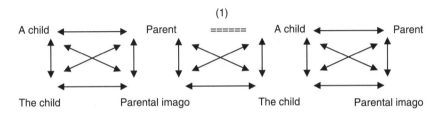

Figure 3.3 Multiple possibilities of the child–parent relationship.

Note: (1) shows the relationship within the same person.

What is Jung's contribution to the discussions of psychological development?

The keynote of Jung's understanding of psychological development, if it is explained in relation to the child, would be the paradoxical relationship between the parent in the child (the archetype in childhood, i.e., predominantly the parental imago) and the child in the adult (the archetype of the child, i.e., a symbol of the self). If Jung had focused more on the parents in the child rather than on the child in the adult, his theory could have been more easily related to discussions in developmental psychology, for it could more readily have been understood literally. However, when the child–parent relationship is taken symbolically, child development, for Jung, could be understood as the process of working on various symbolic images of 'the child' and other associated symbolic images, particularly related to the parental imago, throughout one's life.

Jung's symbol-centred child psychology may not be easy to understand, since the symbolic dimension does not rely on anything visible and concrete. However, unless we locate Jung's understanding of development in the realm of symbols, i.e., the collective unconscious, we will lose sight of what is distinctive about Jung's perspective. One thing that makes it difficult to grasp Jung's understanding of development is his use of analogies between psychology and myth. Arguably, Jung's psychology has been excluded from developmental psychology not because of the methodology of his studies but because of the particular use of language within them, which was not familiar to other psychologists.

Other psychologists also use analogies and metaphors, but more effectively, perhaps in a more intelligible way, than Jung did. For instance, the body–mind parallel has often been used for the explanation of psychology: when the relationship between what is considered physically proven and what is inferred from the physical (i.e., the psychological processes) is understood, it is often accepted as though the latter also concerns objective facts. In this way, analogies with the more readily observed physical processes are used to assist our conceptualisation and consequently inferences about the reality of psychic processes. However, for Jung, analogies themselves, rather than logical parallels, are referred to or heavily relied on as the means for our imagination to understand symbols, which are inexplicable themselves.

Steven Rose uses the word 'physics envy' (1997, p. 9) to describe a sense of inferiority among biologists whose questions about the world 'are not easily answerable in the reduced, mathematicizing language of physics' (ibid.). He argues:

> Science is assumed to be about both explaining and predicting. There is commonly supposed to be a hierarchy of the sciences, from physics

through chemistry, biology and the human sciences. In this scheme physics is seen as the most fundamental of the sciences.

(ibid., p. 7)

As a biochemist himself, Rose protests:

But we should not be afraid to cut ourselves loose from the reductionist claims that there is only one epistemology, one way to study and under-stand the world, one science, whose name is physics. Not everything is capable of being captured in a mathematical formula. Some properties of living systems are not quantifiable, and attempts to put numbers on them produce only mystification (as, for instance, with attempts to score intelligence or aggression, or calculate how many bits of information – memories – the brain can store). Biology needs to be able to declare its independence from spurious attempts to mathematicize it.

(ibid., p. 9)

The same principle would apply to psychology. Human psychology is expected to be explained by means of the 'laws' of, for example, biology or physiology. More loosely, attempts are also made to explain psychology by means of analogies with and metaphors from the softer science of sociology. In any case, psychologists' questions tend to be answered in language borrowed from other disciplines within the hierarchy.

However, Jung's psychology clearly differentiates itself from other discip-lines such as physics, biology, or sociology. Jung offers a distinctively psycho-logical explanation of development, introducing the symbolic meaning of psychic reality. It is questionable how the symbolic dimension which Jung brought into psychology can be fitted into the above hierarchy of sciences. Rose maintains: 'There is nothing inevitable about such a hierarchical view. It is a historically determined convention which reflects the particular traditions of the ways in which Western science has developed from its origins in the seventeenth century' (ibid., p. 8).

Jung's vocabulary could be seen as more psychological than that of other psychologists who largely rely on vocabularies borrowed from physical reductionism, biological determinism, and social constructionism[7] and social narratives. The fact that what Jung claims cannot be found in the structure or functions of the brain or in human behaviour does not disprove that there is a realm of the psyche which cannot be directly measured or observed or tested and yet has great impact on the conscious and unconsciousness: this should not prevent us from exploring further the unknown or, in Jung's term, the collective unconscious.

In this chapter, I have discussed how Jung's psychology can be seen as a strong form of child psychology, but predominantly in a symbolic sense. I have argued that unlike other developmental psychologists in his time and

after, Jung saw the child not as 'developing' or 'undeveloped' but, paradoxically, as both 'non-developing' (the eternal child) and 'most developed' (an
image of wholeness, the goal of individuation). I have also argued that his
symbolic child psychology illuminates the dynamics of psychological processes, both intra-action within and interaction between people, represented
by the archetype of the child (symbol of the self) and by the archetype in
childhood (parental imago). Like the puer–senex pair, the inseparable pair
of child–parent can be seen as an archetype, which implies wholeness and
is relevant to any moment of life, not only to early childhood, as has been
the case for many psychologists. Jung's psychology seems to suggest a non-
chronological model of development, which can be illogical and paradoxical.
In the next part, we will look at how Jung's distinctive notion of development
might be linked with his notion of recapitulation and how it might involve a
different kind of methodology from what has traditionally been used in child
psychology or developmental psychology.

Part II

Theoretical and methodological discussions on development

'Recapitulation' and 'development' in analytical psychology

Considering Jung's lifetime work on psychological development, what he meant by 'development' does not seem straightforward, and the terms 'development' and 'developmental' have been used in analytical psychology in various ways. Despite Jung's interests in various kinds of development,[1] his theory is not referred to in literature on developmental psychology as significantly as those of other psychologists and psychoanalysts, for instance, G. Stanley Hall and Sigmund Freud, who formulated stage models of development. In this chapter, we shall look at Jung's view on 'development' in comparison with the shifting understandings of development in the history of developmental psychology. By examining the close relationship between the notions of 'recapitulation' and 'development', particular foci will be placed on the notion of progress and stage models of development.

The aim of this chapter is to bring Jung's view on 'development' to light, by means of examining his view on 'recapitulation'. Recapitulation theory is generally known as the belief that ontogeny (the course of individual development) recapitulates phylogeny (the process of human evolution). In Jung's time, the notion of development often reflected the notion of recapitulation. But as Jung had a different understanding of recapitulation from other psychologists in his time, his understanding of development also appears to differ from theirs.

In nineteenth-century psychology, the idea of 'recapitulation' was linked to that of 'development' by means of the notion of progress. The notions of Western civilisation and science, which were thought to lead us onwards and upwards, reinforced the view of development as a progressive process (Greene, 1997, p. 36). Developmental psychologists connected evolutionary change with individual development by means of the notion of progress. This view contributed to their formulation of progressive stage models of development, in which the child goes higher up the hierarchy. However, Jung did not formulate a stage model of development, and as a result his theory was largely excluded from twentieth-century discussions of development.

However, within psychology, critiques of the idea of development have challenged the notion of progress that underpins stage models of development.

What develops, what are 'development' and 'developmental', and how the changes over time are to be described, have been questioned rather than taken for granted. Re-examining Jung's theory in terms of the revised understanding of development, in which the notion of progress is less important, we may find that Jung now has more to contribute to the debate.

In this chapter, I shall first examine the basic assumptions underpinning recapitulation theory as it is adopted in psychology. Second, I shall examine more closely Jung's distinctive use of recapitulation theory and his notion of development. Third, I shall discuss some critiques of earlier understandings of development which have emerged within developmental psychology. Fourth, I shall discuss some Jungian views of recapitulation theory and development. Finally, I shall highlight some issues in more recent approaches to development and discuss whether and on what ground there might be scope for dialogue between these critiques of the idea of development and the views of Jung and Jungians.

What is recapitulation theory? Its significance in the field of psychology

Recapitulation theory, as it is generally understood, is the belief that ontogeny recapitulates phylogeny.[2] However, there are various versions of recapitulation theory adopted in other fields of studies, and their central themes are remote from purely biological refutation. The use of recapitulation theory in the field of psychology was influenced not only by biology but also by other intellectual disciplines.

Evolutionary thinking

Let us first look at the biological influence on developmental psychology. Gould argues that it was primarily the concept of natural selection that was responsible for the wide influence of recapitulation theory as an import from evolutionary theory[3] into other fields during the nineteenth century (Gould, 1977, p. 115). However, developmental psychology is sometimes seen as having been constructed out of criticisms of Darwinism, namely non-Darwinism. John Morss claims that it was not Darwin's natural selection that developmental psychologists identified as the mechanism for evolutionary change and individual development. Rather, it was the single, universal track of development that they applied – extrapolating from bodily functioning to mental functioning. While Darwin's theory of natural selection was first announced in his *On the Origin of Species by Means of Natural Selection* in 1859, his original points were developed beyond his own formulations by 'Darwinism', which claimed the 'primacy of *natural selection* as the mechanism for evolutionary change' (Morss, 1990, p. 3). Opposing Darwinism, proponents of 'non-Darwinism' believed that it is 'high-level "laws" ' rather than natural selection that govern evolutionary change (ibid.). Among the non-Darwinians was Lamarck who argued for the doctrine of 'use-inheritance' (ibid.) or 'inheritance of characters acquired in an ancestor's lifetime' – a doctrine further cultivated by 'Lamarckism' (ibid., p. 31). Lamarck's account of hereditary mechanism explains the hierarchical model of mental functioning, maintaining that what are replayed in the early mental state of childhood, which is unconscious, are the experiences and feelings of ancestors. Ernst Haeckel is regarded as a follower of both Darwin and Lamarck: he followed Darwin in his application of embryological evidence to reconstruct the evolutionary sequence, and he followed Lamarck in his employment of the mechanism of modifications for evolutionary change (ibid., p. 18). Haeckel's biogenetic law clarifies the causal, dialectic relation-ships between evolutionary process and the course of individual develop-ment. According to Haeckel's 'Biogenetic Law', 'ontogeny is the short and rapid recapitulation of phylogeny. . . . the ancestry drives the individual development: Phylogeny is the *cause* of ontogeny' (ibid.). Hence, Haeckel's claim for a causal relationship between ontogeny and phylogeny supports the linear model of development for mental functioning as well as physical func-tioning. The biological assumption of evolutionary progress thus provides the basis for the psychological model of developmental progress.

Philosophical thoughts

A number of ideas in European intellectual history, besides biological ones, also had an influence upon developmental psychology, and were largely con-structed through critiques of Darwinian theory. One such idea was 'sensa-tionism', which emphasised processes of learning, and was closely related to the epistemological tradition of 'sensationalism',[4] which stressed the role of sensory experience in human acquisition of knowledge. It is important to note that this philosophical stance is thought to have influenced the devel-opment of evolutionary theories, including Darwin's work.

As further background to the emergence of evolutionist thinking and empirical developmental psychology, intellectual traditions from the late eighteenth to late nineteenth century are also considered to be relevant (Morss, 1990, p. 5). The notion of *progress* in human affairs was explored in the French Enlightenment of the eighteenth century and also in 'Romanticism'[5] of the early nineteenth century. Moreover, 'Nature-Philosophy' in German-speaking Europe was centrally concerned with developmental change, which was thought to be progressive and systematic, and conceived development as a general process in Nature (ibid.). In contrast, the materialism of the mid-nineteenth century challenged romantic idealism through its appeal to progress in the physical sciences rather than to the humanities (ibid., p. 6). At the same time, there were positivist formulations in the social sciences and philosophy and systematic formulations in associationist philosophy.[6] This associationism was the continuation of the sensationalist tradition of the seventeenth century, sharing its emphasis on the sensory origins of experience – sensation providing the irreducible mental elements for combinations, i.e., association of ideas. Associationism was also the basis for the prosperity of empirical psychology within this empiricist and materialist environment. The father of experimental psychology, Wilhelm Wundt, who established the first experimental psychology laboratory in Leipzig in the 1870s, considered psychology to be the study of conscious experience, and he borrowed the laws of association from the British empiricists and associationists in order to unite the analysed elements of consciousness in experience.

Thus, the notion of progress persists in non-biological intellectual disciplines; whether it is the romantic idealisation of progressive development in nature or the materialistic conviction of progress in science. Nineteenth-century associationism, which has its roots in sensationalism in the seventeenth century, emphasises the sensory origins of experience as the elements of associated ideas, and therefore it emphasises the process of learning, which became the basis for empirical psychology.

The notion of progress

The most central assumption in developmental psychology is that 'change with time is fundamentally progressive' (Morss, 1990, p. 228). Consequently, the notion of progress promoted stage models of development. The stage models of development provide a hierarchical picture of mental functioning, in which the earlier state is considered to be primitive, undeveloped, and inferior. This hierarchical picture of human development in line with the use of recapitulation theory sustains the view of the child as savage. It is a view implied by Hall and Freud (addressed later in this chapter) who could be seen as influential figures for Jung's early work, but the employment of recapitulation theory in psychology was not original to Hall[7] and Freud. The presumption of hierarchical models for human development based on the notion of progress was a metaphor in widespread use around that time.

Jung's version of recapitulation theory: How is the notion of progress related to his view of recapitulation?

Jung's first statement on recapitulation appears in 'Two Kinds of Thinking' in 1911,[8] which was later published as *Transformations and Symbols of Libido* in 1912.[9] Jung published this work just after his visit to the Clark Conference in 1909.[10] By the time he invited both Jung and Freud to Clark University in Massachusetts in 1909, Hall had formed his idea of child-centred education and established his 'genetic psychology', both of which were based on his understanding of recapitulation theory. At the conference,

Freud presented the case of little Hans.[11] He argued that the cause of the little boy's neurosis was 'repressed complexes' and that the neurotic symptoms were effects of repression. He described the instinctual and pressing character of sexual libido as the innate instinctual component of infantile repression (Freud, 1909). Jung gave his first two lectures on his association studies (Jung, [1963] 1995, pp. 141, 179); then he gave a further lecture on problems in the mental life of a 4-year-old girl, his case of Anna (Rosenzweig, 1992, p. 135).[12] In their lectures, Freud and Jung seem to share the views that, on the one hand, there is an innate predisposition in the child's psyche and, on the other hand, there are relationships both between the child's thought and the parent's or caretaker's mind and between the child's thought and earlier stages of human evolution. Unlike Hall's genetic psychology or Freud's model of psychosexual development, however, Jung's employment of recapitulation theory does not assert a stage-model of development but emphasises the characteristics of archaic thinking, through paralleling the child's thought with what he called primitive thought.

Narratives of the collective psyche: global parallelism

There is a debate as to whether Jung's use of the word 'primitive' is racist. In his texts, Jung indeed proposed parallels among the following: (1) the unconscious; (2) prehistoric humans; (3) psychotic and other states of mind where there is a direct or raw expression of unconscious impulses, unprocessed and unmediated by any conscious functions; (4) children; (5) people from what are sometimes called 'primitive' cultures and 'primitive' regions in the world today (referring particularly to blacks and other non-European people); and (6) the shadow and other repressed and undesirable material. Jung's ideas about the 'primitive' create a whole package of parallel processes.

This kind of parallelism among all of these states has been criticised. In particular, Farhad Dalal has highlighted the political, and more specifically, racist implications of this parallelism. Dalal claims that Jung's parallelisms between the modern black and the prehistoric human, between the modern black's consciousness and the white's unconscious, and between the modern black adult and the white child are racist (Dalal, 1988). He asserts that 'his [Jung's] use of "we" consistently denotes the European. The Other is always "they". It is difficult to locate a use of "we" that implies all of the human race' (ibid., p. 265). He maintains that Jung situates European man at a higher level of a racial hierarchy, regarding blacks as not just different but inferior (ibid., p. 278). Dalal claims that for Jung, '*Individuation is a process reserved for the white, the European*' (ibid., p. 275; emphasis in original).

Michael Vannoy Adams supports Dalal, questioning whether Jungian theory and practice are intrinsically and ineluctably racist (1996, p. 131) and whether contemporary Jungians are racist or multiculturalist (ibid., pp. xxi, 131). Adams writes that the expression 'going black' is originally a British expression equivalent to 'going primitive' or 'going native' and means 'going back': to revert in the colonialist, imperialist context, and to regress to an earlier and lower state in psychoanalytic terms (ibid., p. 51). He claims that the associations black–primitive–instinctive and white–civilised–rational are not only oppositional but also judgemental in the sense of inferiority–superiority (ibid., p. 53). He writes: 'The supposition is that the European psyche is higher and the non-European psyche lower on an evolutionary and developmental scale' (ibid.).

However, in his reply to Dalal's paper, Samuels points out that Jung's investigation of so-called primitives highlights symbolic and valuable aspects of Western, European man, rather than repressed or alienated ones (Samuels, 1988, p. 280). He also points out the significance of Jung's pioneering role in the re-estimation of Eastern culture and religion (ibid.). Moreover, in his reply to the same paper, Charles Rycroft indicates that Jung's ethnocentric arrogant attitude towards 'savages' and 'primitives' was almost universal among European intellectuals of his generation (Rycroft, 1988, p. 281).

It appears that this kind of parallelism is not Jung's original idea. It was typical of the scientific thought of the late nineteenth century to compare the child with the 'savage' (Morss, 1990, pp. 23–4). Morss calls the closing years of the nineteenth century the heyday of 'global parallelism' in terms of the conceptualisation of childhood (ibid., p. 24). He writes: 'Evidence from a vast range of sources – primates, "primitives," prehistory – was amalgamated into an encyclopaedic account of the thought processes of the child, unified by the principles of evolutionism' (ibid.). Hall[13] brought an anthropologist, Alexander Chamberlain, to Clark University, and Chamberlain published his studies (e.g., 1990) on the thought processes of the child in terms of a parallelism with what is thought to be 'savage' (Gould, 1977, pp. 117–18; Morss, 1990, p. 24). Also relevant were studies of dreams, which were paralleled with studies of what Morss calls 'aliens', such as prehistoric man, primitive tribes, or the criminal (Morss, 1990, p. 24). Freud also made comparisons between child thought, the thought of the mad, and the dream state (ibid.).[14]

Jung indeed did use these parallelisms (1911–12/1952, 1913, 1927/1931b, 1930/1950, 1943),[15] and when taken literally some of his statements could appear to be provocative (for instance, 1928/1931, para. 726). However, if we focus on the distinctiveness of his theoretical arguments, the meaning he attributed to them could be seen to be less judgemental or discriminative than Dalal claims. In other places what Jung refers to as 'primitive' on the psychological level is something always present in the human psyche. These parallelisms, on the one hand, demonstrate the continuity of the collective psyche, and, on the other, convey the differentiation of consciousness from the collective psyche.

Using these parallels, Jung presents the collective psyche as 'the universal possibility of a uniform mental functioning' (Jung, 1916/1966, para. 455–6; 1928c, para. 235).[16] His model of the collective psyche emphasises that there is a common core to human psychology, regardless of the period in human history. He distinguishes the 'universal' collective psyche from the collective psyche underneath it, the former being limited to a group of people (race, tribe, and family), in which differentiation is also observed (1916/1966, para. 456; 1928c, para. 235). Without the 'universal' collective psyche, there would be no differentiation and therefore no cultural differences among people. Jung writes:

> In accordance with phylogenetic law, we still recapitulate in childhood reminiscences of the prehistory of the race and of mankind in general. Phylogenetically as well as ontogenetically we have grown up out of the dark confines of the earth; hence the factors that affected us most closely became archetypes, and it is these primordial images which influence us most directly, and therefore seem to be the most powerful.
>
> (1927/1931b, para. 55)

As I addressed earlier in Chapter 2, when Jung refers to so-called primitives, his main concern seems to be with their mythical motifs rather than their development. When he uses words such as 'parallels', 'correspondences', 'similar mutations', and 'analogies' to refer to the relationship between ontogenesis and phylogenesis, he does so in terms of the universality and continuity of the collective psyche which manifests in different people in different times. According to Jung's use of 'recapitulation' as a metaphor for these analogies, it is not primitive psychology that child psychology recapitulates, but it is the collective psyche that both child psychology and primitive psychology reactivate.

When Jung speaks of primitive psychology, his emphasis is on the collective unconscious, in contrast to individual consciousness, the latter of which is characterised by separation and opposition (1933/1934, para. 290). When primitive psychology is contrasted with modern consciousness, however, it may provoke misunderstanding in sensitive readers who have in mind literal images of so-called primitives. Jung writes:

> Our understanding of these deeper layers of the psyche ['the universal basis of the individually varied psyche'] is helped not only by a knowledge of primitive psychology and mythology, but to an even greater extent by some familiarity with the history of our modern consciousness and the stages immediately preceding it.
>
> (1944b, para. 40)

Whether the issue of superiority/inferiority matters to the relationships between the collective psyche and individual consciousness is arguable. On the one hand, the manifestations and representations of the collective psyche in ancestry, in primitive people, in child's thought, in dreams, and in the delusions of madness are depicted by Jung as though they were inferior to the consciousness of a present, civilised, adult, normal person. On the other hand, the collective psyche can be seen as superior to individual consciousness, inasmuch as it is more powerful and never allows consciousness to eliminate it. Therefore, the superiority–inferiority of the conscious–unconscious may not be something on which we are able to make a definitive judgement.

Limits of hierarchical models: psycho-physical parallelism

Another factor which promoted stage models of development is the hierarchical model of mental functioning. Jung seems to use a parallelism between body and mind and apply biological recapitulation theory to human psychology.[17] He might have been influenced to some extent by Friedrich Zschokke, his biology professor who believed in biological recapitulation,[18] when he was at the medical school at Basel University (1895) (Hayman, 1999, pp. 30–1; Portman, 1976). However, when we look more closely at the hierarchical model borrowed from physical functioning and applied to mental functioning, the unconscious stands out as something particular to the latter. One of Freud's teachers in Vienna, Theodore Meynert, a brain anatomist and psychiatrist, adopted the hierarchical model of the nervous system. In this system, 'lower' levels were seen as becoming overlaid, and inhibited, by 'higher' levels.[19] The hierarchical model of evolutionary change and individual development allowed regression 'to lower levels even when higher states had been achieved' (Morss, 1990, p. 25). Likewise, in his theory of psychoanalysis in general and of neurosis in particular, Freud noted the difference between physical recapitulation and mental recapitulation (Gould, 1977, p. 157). In physical recapitulation, transient stages are remoulded or replaced by subsequent forms in order to create the later stages, but in mental recapitulation, an ancient stage does not vanish to make way for a later stage in ontogeny. In short, the stages of mind can co-exist (ibid.). The Haeckelian physical recapitulation of ancestral morphologies cannot simply be applied to mental recapitulation of ideas and behaviours (ibid.). Therefore, not only in Jung's work but also in Freud's, we can see the idea that the early stages of mental functioning remain throughout the courses of both ontogeny and phylogeny.

Nevertheless, there is a remarkable difference between Jung and Freud. For Freud, the earlier stages do not disappear, but are repressed in the healthy adult: 'The repressed, primitive core continues to "reside" in the adult brain' (ibid.). In contrast, for Jung, it is not merely the 'repressed' that remains in the adult psyche, but the entire 'collective psyche' exists in human mental functioning throughout the processes of individual development as well as human evolution. In both Freud and Jung, mental recapitulation seems to be paralleled to a certain extent and yet distinguished from physical recapitulation, but what is recapitulated in the mind and the forms in which a recapitulated ancient or earlier stage remains in the psyche are seen very differently by them. Again, what Jung calls archaic thinking seems to encapsulate the distinctiveness of his view of recapitulation.

Against the notion of progress: education, culture, and history

Like Hall,[20] Jung sees education from the viewpoint of recapitulation. Jung holds that education reinforces differentiation and integration of consciousness and the unconscious. However, unlike Hall, he does not believe that the process of education relives the state of the past. For Jung, the child does not recapitulate the ancestors and unfold from lower to higher stages in a hierarchical picture of development. He explicitly disagrees with the idea of progress, when it is concerned with culture, history, and education (1943, para. 250). He states: 'Culture means continuity, not a tearing up of roots through "progress" ' (ibid.) He questions a purely technical and practical education which disregards a state of the past in favour of the notion of progress. He suggests that education should not take less account of the continuity of history, which is the innermost law of culture.

For Jung, consciousness and the unconscious are equally important, in terms of psychological differentiation and continuity. He recommends the integration of both, not just the promotion of conscious functions, and implies the danger of excessive projections as a result of disregarding the collective. He writes:

> What we understand by the concept 'individual' is a relatively recent acquisition in the history of the human mind and human culture. It is no wonder, therefore, that the earlier all-powerful collective attitude prevented almost completely an objective psychological evaluation of individual differences.
>
> (1921, para. 12)

Jung's idea of the continuity of the collective psyche and differentiation from it throughout human history could both be seen as non-recapitulatory forms of human mental functioning in terms of progressive processes in time. In so far as the collective psyche is concerned, such time scales as ontogenetic, and phylogenetic history should not mean anything, because the collective psyche is eternal and chronological time does not apply. Jung's view of development can be explained as a relationship in which the individual's consciousness continuously attempts to differentiate from the collective unconscious, which is beyond time and space. Similarly, the collective unconscious continuously exists at the root of individual consciousness.

Thus, the notion of progress, which underpins the view of the child as 'savage' and the hierarchical model of mental functioning with its stage models of development, may have influenced Jung's psychology to a certain extent. However, Jung appears not to have used recapitulation theory in the same way as other psychologists, who, supported by the notion of progress in the nineteenth century, made use of recapitulation theory as a basis for stage models of development. The reason for this could be summarised as follows: Jung's particular use of recapitulation theory demonstrates his concern with a process in which the notion of progress is irrelevant, i.e., the continuity of the collective psyche and differentiation from it. His notion of differentiation does not necessarily require a hierarchical picture of development. For Jung, the past is an earlier stage of humanity, which includes pre-historical time or even signifies metaphorically beyond time, but is not necessarily a lower level. What is considered to be of a lower level in a hierarchical model of development is to be distinguished from Jung's notions of 'the deeper layers of the psyche', 'primitive psychology', 'the earlier all-powerful collective attitude', and 'a state of the past', which could, again, also be called archaic thinking. Therefore, Jung's use of this parallelism is irrelevant to linear models of development, due to the continuous existence of the collective psyche in present, civilised, adult humans.

Questioning the notion of progress: What are the critiques of the idea of development?

Within the field of developmental psychology, several critiques challenge evolutionary-based stage models and question the concept of development as a process that progresses with ageing. They question the notion of uni-directional and natural progression, which for most of the twentieth century lurked at the heart of the word 'development' and at the heart of developmental psychology. 'Developmentalism' is criticised, due to its 'imposition of an unwarranted uniformity of structure and directionality on to the changes associated with the ageing process' (Greene, 1997, p. 37).

Non-progressive development

Concerning the functions of development, there are claims not only for step or stage-like functions but also for other kinds: for example, continuous, inverted U-shaped, and upright U-shaped functions (Muir, 1999, pp. 6–9) which show particular features of human capacity that persist continuously throughout life, reach their zenith in midlife, and show high achievement in either early or old age, respectively. Some of these functions are related to particular views of development. More generally, there are various views of development, and each of them has a different view of the child (for instance, Das Gupta, 1994; Ford, 2004; Karmiloff-Smith, 1996; Muir, 1999, Oates and Grayson, 2004). According to the organismic world-view or Piagetianism, there are stages of development. Proponents of this view focus on the innate structure, which changes in successive stages as a result of the interaction between the organism and the environment, and the stages are not reducible. The social constructivist perspective promoted by Vygotsky follows this constructivist perspective but more fully emphasises the socio-cultural and ecological contexts. According to the mechanistic world-view or Behaviourism, there is continuous development. Proponents of this view focus on principles of learning, the input from environmental factors on the particular response of the organism. According to Nativism, the child is pre-programmed at birth; therefore, though there are variations within, a strict Nativist theory is considered to be non-developmental in form, denying learning and the maturation process. Connectionism denies both pre-specified blueprints and single, general-purpose learning mechanisms, but argues for interactions between architectural, computational, temporal, and representational biases or constraints. The Life-span perspective considers interactions between biological and environmental factors for the explanation of behavioural and biological change across the life-span. Therefore, there are claims for the construction of inner structure, biological predisposition, input by learning, socio-cultural factors, and interactions between organismic and environmental factors as the determinants of development, and there are non-progressive, even 'non-developmental' functions, views, and models of development.

Development: earlier meaning and more recent approaches

Greene challenges the old meaning of development as 'steady, progressive, development through predictable stages', which is supported by the nineteenth- and early twentieth-century Western conviction that science and civilisation bring us progress and universal truth (1997, p. 36). Rejecting extreme environmentalism and extreme hereditarian views, developmental psychologists nevertheless end up emphasising one direction or the other of the old dichotomy between genetic determinants and environmental/social determinants (ibid., p. 40). As one example of this basic dichotomy, Greene mentions the views of the child as 'passively responding to the forces operating upon him or her' on the one hand, and as 'an active agent in his or her own development on the other' (ibid., p. 43). In contrast, the new concepts of human psychological change across time encompass 'niche-picking, active, passive and evocative genotype-environment effects and proximal processes', highlighting the question of how the various mechanisms are involved in the interplay between genes and environment (ibid.). Developmental psychologists have begun to take a more self-critical stance towards the history of their discipline, and are now more willing to 'unpick the previous self-congratulatory discourse, to deconstruct and reinterpret' (ibid., p. 37). Consequently, the more recent histories of developmental psychology have rediscovered psychologists whose work 'was relatively neglected in its own time and certainly did not become part of the received history of the discipline', but has now been 'given its quality and undoubted resonance for psychologists of our time' (ibid.).[21] Jung could be a candidate for becoming one of these 'rediscovered writers'.

Likewise, Burman points out that we talk of development in terms of 'progressing', 'advancing' from one stage to the next, but that 'the norms by which we evaluate that development may be far from universal' (1994, p. 182). Burman reports the shift of psychological perspectives on the infant in the mid to late nineteenth century, first, 'as a biological organism abstracted from its familial and material environment', second, as an 'innocent [bearer] of wisdom', and third, as 'savage' or 'undeveloped' or 'primitive' (ibid., p. 10). Underpinning these perspectives, she notes, was the theory of 'cultural recapitulation' whereby 'the individual in her or his lifetime reproduces the patterns and stages of development exhibited by the development of the species – "ontogeny recapitulates phylogeny" ' (ibid.). The ontogeny/phylogeny debate in developmental psychology, as she points out, seems to be closely connected with images of the child framed in a certain hierarchy, whether biological, ideological, or cultural. Similarly, deconstruction of what Jung as well as other analytical psychologists meant by 'recapitulation' and 'development' could illuminate their underpinning assumptions in comparison with the history of these notions in developmental psychology.

Without being aware of the dominant discourses on development, we could remain caught up in the assumption that psychological development is a progressive process. In the book *Causes of Development* (Butterworth and Bryant, 1990), various scholars demonstrate different types of causal explanation for human development from the perspectives of cognitive developmental psychology, developmental biology, ethology, embryology, social psychology, and computer science. Each causal explanation identifies different crucial issues and employs sophisticated arguments. The editors of this book comment that 'any one type of explanation, particularly when applied to human development, is *necessarily* incomplete' (ibid., p. ix). It could be further argued that these claims are not even compatible. Because their definitions of development vary, their causal explanations of development naturally differ. As Carey asserts, 'we cannot explain developmental change until we know its nature' (1990, p. 135), so it is questionable whether it is appropriate to seek its causes, without first defining what development means.

Furthermore, Richardson sees development as a dynamic system in which each component functions as a sub-system, and he questions the value of discussing dichotomies such as nature/nurture, organism/environment, biological/socio-cultural factors, inner/outer conditions, mind/body, and the like. The dynamic interaction of the multiple components of the system are due to self-organisation, and not to an order either from outside or pre-formed

(2000, p. 35). In other words, the *relation* of the dynamic structure of the organisation of the external environment to the internal dynamic structure determines developmental and behavioural outcomes (ibid., p. 42). The earlier view of development would argue that both genetic factors and environmental factors are 'supposedly isolated causal agents' in development, but they are always simply part of a causal complex of interactions of factors of both 'genetic' and 'environmental' origin (ibid., p. 25). He presents the dynamic systems theories and ecological thinking as helpful ways of looking at development as self-organisation.

Reflecting these recent critiques within the discipline of developmental psychology, such issues within studies of children have been emphasised as the need to consider ecological validity, cultural variation, wider relationships than the mother–infant dyad, and most importantly, the autonomy of and active role played by the child. For instance, in studies of cognitive development, increasing emphasis has been given to the flexibility and self-organising aspects of the brain and cognitive functions inferred from them (e.g., Mareschal *et al.*, 2004). In studies of social and emotional development (e.g., Barnes, 1995) as well as cognitive development (e.g., Perret-Claremont *et al.*, 2004), wider social contexts in which the child lives and the interactions and transactions between the child and his or her social contexts have been taken more into account in the interpretations of research evidence and theorisation.

Jungian and post-Jungian views on recapitulation: How is the notion of progress related to their views of recapitulation?

Anthony Stevens applied evolutionary thinking to psychology and psychiatry and thereby introduced evolutionary psychology to the Jungian world. He is the main person who has seriously advocated an evolutionary perspective on Jung's theory of archetypes. His use of recapitulation seems to be a direct continuation of Darwinism, identifying natural selection as the mechanism of evolution and dialectic relationships between ontogeny and phylogeny. He holds that archetypes are biological entities and that '*archetypes evolved through natural selection*' (Stevens, 1982, p. 17; emphasis in original). He also considers that archetypes function as dynamic units of the phylogenetic psyche and maintains that Jung's term 'collective unconscious' is misleading (Stevens and Price, 1996, p. 6). For Stevens, 'Archetypes are conceived as neuropsychic units which evolved through natural selection and which are responsible for determining the behavioural characteristics as well as the affective and cognitive experiences typical of human beings' (ibid.).

However, among Jungians and post-Jungians, recapitulation theory seems to have been most widely discussed according to not Stevens' version (by means of natural selection) but Neumann's understanding (by means of the notion of progress), which was akin to the nineteenth-century developmental psychologists' version.

Different views of development in different schools of analytical psychology

What is 'development' and 'developmental' is a controversial issue also in analytical psychology. Samuels named the London School of analytical psychology the 'Developmental School' (1985).[22] Fordham himself objected to this, stating that Jung's psychology is all about development (Casement, 1995, pp. 329–30). Nevertheless, Fordham and the members of the Society of Analytical Psychology (SAP) still carry the image of being specifically concerned with development. One of the main reasons for this image could be their work with children. The issues regarding the Developmental School will be discussed further in Part III of this book. But at this point we shall discuss the strong connection between images of development and images of the child.

Neumann, whose position is within the 'Classical School' of analytical psychology, presented a stage model of conscious development in his *Origins and History of Consciousness*[23] (1954), based on his understanding of recapitulation theory. It is apparent that he has in mind a progressive, hierarchical, and linear model of individual and collective development. According to Neumann, 'The evolution of consciousness by stages is as much a collective phenomenon as a particular individual phenomenon. Ontogenetic development may therefore be regarded as a modified recapitulation of phylogenetic development' (ibid., p. xx). His attempt is to outline the archetypal stages in the development of consciousness. For Neumann, the determinants of the course of conscious development are internal, psychic, and archetypal factors rather than external environmental factors, because for him symbolism is evidence of humans' collective nature as it appears in the individual. Neumann's notion of individual 'development' seems to be a process of psychic differentiation between mother and infant, and between consciousness and the unconscious, which involves ego development and increasing adaptation to collective society (ibid., pp. 398–9). Neumann asserts: 'An important goal of childhood development and education is the utilization of the individual in the sense of making him a useful member of the community' (ibid., p. 399). Therefore, Neumann's stance is likely to be more developmental than Jung's, in terms of the earlier meaning of 'developmental', due to his notion of progress.

However, Giegerich, whose position is within the 'Archetypal School' of analytical psychology, disputes Neumann's theory of development of archetypes and his stage model of ego-development. Giegerich takes issue with Neumann, arguing that his work *Origins and History of Consciousness* is not about consciousness but myth, that is to say, it is a purely symbolic archetypal fantasy. Giegerich claims that one cannot assert the development of consciousness without empirical evidence, stating: 'There are changes in history, but there is not evolution' (1975, p. 141). Neumann's mythological concretism seems to Giegerich non-psychological, as it eliminates what should be imaginal (Samuels, 1985, pp. 74–5).[24] In favour of Hillman's circular approach to development,[25] Giegerich believes that myth is working continuously and contemporaneously in a constant state of interaction (ibid., p. 72). Consequently, archetypes always have the same characteristics. Giegerich's claim for the constancy of the archetypes does not seem to share the views of development and recapitulation as processes of progress and may have affinity with more recent discourses about the interactions of dynamic change over time.

Fordham, whose position is within the 'Developmental School' of analytical psychology, denies Neumann's views of recapitulation and development. Fordham argues that 'Ontogeny does not recapitulate phylogeny' (1957, p. 115, n. 25), disputing Neumann's notions both of progress and of the causal, dialectic relationship between evolution and individual growth. Fordham states:

> There is no recapitulation in the sense postulated by the biogenetic law or its reverse, rather there is the same basic pattern of the archetypal entity expressing itself in a different sphere and adapted to a different purpose in consequence of a different orientation of the ego.
>
> (ibid., p. 33)

Referring also to Neumann's *The Child* (ibid., p. 103), Fordham challenges Neumann's disregard of child analysis as a major methodological weakness of his thesis. Fordham objects to the application to child analysis of insights stemming from the study of myths, for myth is 'a product of a developed mind and has social as well as individual meaning' (ibid., p. 106). He claims: 'the environment is more significant than genetic influence' (ibid., p. 109). He also argues that 'stages do not exist' and that 'The idea of continuous growth would seem far more appropriate and nearer to reality' (ibid., p. 110). His objection to stage models and his belief in 'the same basic pattern of the archetypal entity' manifested and adapted according to needs throughout life could be seen to render the notion of progress irrelevant. His stance is not developmental in its earlier meaning, and in this sense, his view of development could be seen as closer to Jung's.

Unlike Neumann (the Classical School), Fordham (the Developmental School) and Giegerich (the Archetypal School) do not agree with stage models of development. Samuels observes that 'the two wings of the post-Jungian world join forces to attack the centre, the Classical School' (1985, p. 141), indicating the similar view of development within the Archetypal and Developmental Schools, which both perceive development as being largely generated as *'something already there in the child'* (ibid., p. 141; emphasis in original). For both Giegerich and Fordham, archetypes in principle do not develop (ibid., pp. 72, 74). However, it does not seem to be the pure nativist view (which emphasises a predetermined, innate capacity for development) that both Giegerich and Fordham take. They prefer a view focusing more on what goes on in interactions and dynamics. For Neumann, origins and stages, which are found in myths, seem to be the prime concern. However, origins do not matter for Giegerich, because archetypes do not change but remain constant throughout their interactions; therefore the linear model does not seem important to him, because there is no predictable periodicity for archetypes. In contrast, Fordham takes more account of interactions of the primary self than of the origins of this archetype, and he abandons stages in favour of the dynamics of deintegration and reintegration.

Within the developmental school, some seem to ally themselves with a scientific approach in support of Fordham. For instance, Knox (2003, 2004) presents Fordham as fitting well in the developmental models based on epigenesis, gene/environment interaction, and the self-regulating system – themes currently popular in developmental psychology. Knox argues that what has been suggested in cognitive science (i.e., concerning the concept of an image schema and the ways in which it is supposed to develop) and in attachment theory (i.e., concerning the concept of internal working models and how they might develop) supports the developmental explanation for the core concepts of analytical psychology (i.e., the archetypes and the complexes respectively) (2003, pp. 66–7, 102). Others seem to take a hermeneutic approach with a more critical view of Fordham. For instance, on the one hand, Hauke points out the similarities between the idea of the social construction of reality proposed by Peter Berger and Thomas Luckmann (1971) and Jung's explanations of a reality whose patterns are established and experienced by individuals' psyche by means of archetypal manifestations (Hauke, 2000, p. 199). On the other hand, Hauke challenges the approach of Fordham and the 'Developmental School' of analytical psychology for its use of fixed images of the child (Hauke, [1994] 1996). Criticising reductionism and questioning the use of the past for the future, he challenges the purpose of using the child as a metaphor in analyses and deconstructs the purely biological explanation and super-environmental paradigm of early experience. He adopts a cautious attitude to a hierarchical model of development in respect of child therapy: 'I do not think I am saying that some "growing" still needs to be achieved, or that a "stage" still needs to be passed, as the linear model of early development frames it' (ibid., p. 37). Hauke's stance resembles notions of 'the social construction of childhood' (Greene, 1997, p. 46). What matters is not the real childhood but the fact that the images and narratives of childhood construct meaning.

In this section I have not addressed various contemporary Jungians' accounts of the notions of recapitulation and development, though this area certainly needs further discussion. Recent work has especially been exploring the view of the psyche or its development as a self-organising or self-regulating system or as an emergent property or process (e.g., Cambray, 2006; Colman, 2006; Hogenson, 2004; Knox, 2003). With this view, Jung's idea of the autonomy of the psyche could be sustained and could even be linked with the views supporting the autonomy of the child or of the brain currently promoted in developmental psychology. However, the crucial question would be whether these arguments in Jungian psychology can be seen as compatible with the arguments in other disciplines that have inspired them, without distorting or losing the distinctiveness of Jung's theory.

Dialogues between the theories of Jung and post-Jungians and contemporary critiques of the idea of development

Jung's and post-Jungians' notions of development have sufficient similarities with critiques of developmental psychology for there to be a dialogue whereas before there was less possibility of this.

Challenging discourses of 'development'; questioning images of 'the child'

Like critiques of global parallelism, Burman regards modern accounts of the child–primitive comparison as 'single-minded masculine and Western forms of reasoning, stigmatising the irrational as inferior' by means of its emphasis on the roles of social environment and education (Burman, 1994, p. 160). She writes: 'What they indicate is that in its single-minded march to true maturity such a model is unaware of, and resistant to, recognising the cultural and historical origins and specificities of its own project' (ibid.). As we have seen above, any kind of dominant discourse has a danger of creating stereotyped images of children and their development; and we have to remember that this is so because its basic assumption lies in its one-sided or dichotomous explanations.

The question of dichotomies (in the form of opposites) could be raised for analytical psychology as a whole. More recent approaches to 'development' challenge the dichotomous debates about the causes of development. It has been pointed out that there are limits to causal, dialectic relationships, in which the two sides of a dichotomy together make the whole, and there is no other possibility.[26] As an alternative to dichotomous explanations of development, Richardson proposes dynamic systems theory and ecological thinking and points out its characteristic of self-organisation.[27] Similarly, Jung's notion of self-regulation could be seen in terms of a model which encompasses dichotomies (opposites/polarity) along with the other structures, contents, and functions of the psyche.

Fordham's and Giegerich's challenges to Neumann's idea of the development of consciousness and the ego could provide the bases for dialogues with more recent approaches to development. Morss criticises the way that developmental theory is made up into a kind of anatomy of human growth, something clean, polished, measurable, a perfect scientific phenomenon studied by psychologists (1996, p. 158). In Morss's view: 'The notion of development does not ignore the past, but it does violence to it' (ibid.).

Burman questions why developmental psychology is always presumed to be about 'the child', what the consequences of this are for the theory and practice of developmental psychology, and how this would be different from discussing 'children' or 'contexts in which people grow and change' (1994, p. 5). 'The child' also plays a significant role in Jung's theory of psychological development, the individuation process. Though not necessarily having the same connotation as in developmental psychology, when it is applied to actual 'children' or 'contexts in which people grow and change', the child as a symbol immediately raises questions as to its applicability to them. Deconstruction of the discipline seems much needed in both analytical psychology and developmental psychology.

When developmental psychology was all about child psychology and its betterment, the earlier state, i.e., the past, always meant something undeveloped, inferior, and primitive. This hierarchical ageing process produced the social framework of predictable development and certain expectations. However, having seen through the formerly unquestioned assumption of progress, the discussion of development could be opened to the possible distinctive contributions of Jungian theory. This is something that could be usefully explored in future studies.

Conclusion

As the aim of this chapter has been to bring Jung into the discussion of development in the wider context of developmental psychology, I have examined how the recapitulation theory adopted in psychology is related to the notion of development. I have also examined how Jung's use of recapitulation theory is different from those of other psychologists, and accordingly, how his notion of development is different from its use by other psychologists. Finally, introducing critiques of development, I have discussed how Jung and contemporary Jungians can have dialogues with the more recent criteria of development.

Some of the limitations in applying biological recapitulation to psychological development have been discussed. The assumptions of the notion of progress in the concepts of both recapitulation and development, of the unchangeable hierarchical model – whether linear or stage-like – in which the present is seen as the highest, and of the unquestioned parallel between mental functioning and observable physical change, in which the former is inferred solely from the latter, have been examined.

Some of the potential ways in which analytical psychology could open dialogue with developmental psychology were suggested. These include examination of some distinctive features of analytical psychology, focusing particularly on its notion of the collective unconscious, as well as comparison between analytical psychology and developmental psychology in terms of their agreement with models of development that are not necessarily progressive. Including issues which have not been covered so far, there exist many potential topics for discussion: for instance, how the spiritual dimension could be related to the nature/nurture debate; whether the continuity/discontinuity debate about developmental process could be seen as neither gradual nor stage-like; how archaic thinking could be linked with the active/passive roles of the child; how regression could be discussed in relation to the domain-general/specific debate about cognitive development; in what way the collective unconscious could be explained in relation to the impact of sociocultural contexts; and how psychic energy could be considered in terms of explanations for the mechanisms of how change occurs.

There seem to be two notions of progress in nineteenth-century thought. One is the idealistic, romantic notion of progress, according to which there is limitless progress in nature and every new change will become the step up to the next higher level. The other is the empirical, materialistic notion of progress, which presents an absolute hierarchy and explains progressive process as a mechanism. Nevertheless, for both, the present is the highest point so far attained in the hierarchy. Likewise, there seem to be two notions of development, which have influenced nineteenth-century developmental psychology: one is the idealistic, romantic notion, which regards change to produce something new as a uni-directional progress without any limit, and the other is the materialistic, empirical, positivistic notion, which reinforces the process of change by means of its mechanism. Both place the present human being at the top of the hierarchy in any kind of ongoing process over time, such as human evolution, civilisation, and individual development. What is problematic here is that the notion of progress in the nineteenth century in general and the notion of development in psychology in particular have been used as though they were equivalent. The individual is thought to develop (progress), as human beings are thought to limitlessly progress (develop). Nevertheless, the child is thought to develop only to the point which adults have reached. It is contradictory that the hierarchy of progress/development gives a limit or goal to the child (as an individual in the stereotyped collective human) but no limit or end to adults (as a representation of the most developed human). This picture apparently derives from recapitulation theory.

The assumption of progress having been questioned, 'development' is seen not necessarily as the process in which an individual infant comes to be a member of the progressed and still progressing community of human beings.

Development, as considered as the process of changes from lower to higher levels, reinforced by a certain notion of education and promoted from the present highest to an even higher level by the universal notion of civilisation – this picture of development has broken down. This opens the way to a reconsideration of what 'psychological development' means in analytical psychology.

Chapter 5

Methodological issues in developmental psychology and analytical psychology

Many studies with the title 'the origins and history of . . .' seem to have been once predominantly considered as 'developmental'. If not focusing on the causes of development as such, often these studies were concerned with chronological sequences or stages of development assumed to be universal facts. However, these kind of linear or reductive approaches now seem to be less dominant and there is a shift in the direction of exploring dynamic processes more deeply in the here and now. This includes the consideration of, for example, a person's subjectivity, intersubjectivity between people and in groups, the dynamic relationship between researcher and researched, both the conscious and the unconscious influence of various contexts of life, and the processes of continuous construction and reconstruction of, for instance, history or identity.

What has been called 'the new paradigm of psychology' (Reason and Rowen, 1981), i.e., the paradigm of co-operative experiential inquiry and research on people (Reason, 1988, p. 1) well illustrates the exploration of interpersonal relationships between the researcher and the researched. This paradigm arguably has been influenced by psychoanalytic thinking, particularly by analytical psychological theories. For example, Reason's account of 'the cycle of co-operative inquiry', which he presents in a figure (1988, pp. 4–6), looks very much like Jung's diagram of a psychological relationship (both conscious and unconscious) between two people, which he based on the diagram of the marriage of the King and Queen in an alchemical text (Jung, 1946). However, which influenced which is not really the issue here. For the origins and history of the qualitative stance do not matter so much as what qualitative approaches do in challenging the dominant images of development.

In this chapter I shall first discuss the methodological shift in developmental psychology from valuing mainly modern, scientific, quantitative research methods towards wider acceptance of postmodern, post-scientific, qualitative research methods. I shall discuss more specifically the quantitative–qualitative debate in order to illuminate the conflicts between the two methods as well as some more general controversies. For depth psychology has also been involved, to some degree, with both quantitative and qualitative methods. Considering the shift towards inclusion of qualitative psychology, I shall then examine the relevance of developmental research methods to depth psychology. I shall next examine how developmental research methods are conceptualised and used in analytical psychology. Finally, I shall consider how analytical psychology, given a favourable climate for open discussion, might contribute to the practice of qualitative research methods in developmental psychology.

Methodological shift in developmental psychology

Modern psychology and postmodern psychologies

Recent work has made direct connections between analytical psychology and postmodernism (e.g., Hauke, 2000; Jones, 2007). Here I shall examine the implications of postmodern perspectives for the contemporary practice of developmental psychology and potential connections between qualitative approaches to development and the methods used in analytical psychology.

Recent critical approaches to developmental psychology have enabled us to recognise varieties of discourses regarding the implications of psychological research methods. Erica Burman argues that developmental psychology is a *modern* discipline, since it shares its origins with psychology and the modern social sciences, particularly in the late nineteenth century (1994, p. 157). However, what is thought of as modern psychology has been challenged on the grounds that its underpinning ideas are linear, reductive, abstract, hierarchical, and patriarchal. Burman argues that in critical psychology circles, it is now commonplace to regard 'the rational unitary subject of psychology as rigid, incoherent, and shot through with racist, sexist, and heterosexist assumptions' (2000, p. 49).

Consequently, alternative perspectives have been suggested, and this has created dichotomous debates, that is to say, what Shiela McNamee calls 'the "either/or" logic of modernism' (2000, p. 180). Lois Holzman and John Morss explain this:

> Among the many grand narratives that comprise the discipline of psychology, the story it tells of static, stable things and objects (especially people) that fall neatly into dichotomous categories – an instance or identity of this or that (invariably some come to be accepted as 'normal,' 'good,' or 'right' and others as 'abnormal,' 'bad,' or 'wrong') – is one that postmodern psychology is attempting both to expose and transform.
>
> (2000, p. 13)

McNamee illustrates the kinds of dichotomies she has in mind, which are primarily presented in terms of good/bad (2000, p. 180) or right/wrong (ibid.,

p. 182): for instance, 'theory/practice', 'identity as given/identity as accomplished', 'politicized psychology/rampant relativism' versions of postmodern psychology, and 'reactionary/revolutionary' activities (ibid., p. 186). Likewise, Lenora Fulani challenges 'the dualistic traps of existing theories', referring to behaviourism and introspectionism, and 'the assumed bipolarities of individual-social, cognitive-affective, or biological-cultural' (2000, p. 156). Debates about other dichotomies, such as scientific/unscientific, quantitative/qualitative, objective/subjective, numbers/language, dominant/marginalised, and normal/pathological, have also been controversial.

However, the discourse of dichotomies, McNamee suggests, should be recognised as 'a *discursive* option and not a necessary form of argument'; for it 'does not attempt to reach agreement but attempts, instead, to open possibilities' (2000, p. 186). She writes: 'We strive to accept that we do not have an answer "now and forever", but that each new understanding gives birth to yet newer constraints which, in turn, provide the soil for further resources and elaborations, and so on' (2000, p. 184). She presents the views that both modernism and postmodernism are 'discursive options' (ibid., p. 181) and that postmodern psychology is about 'shifting the discourse completely' (ibid., p. 182). This view of postmodernism as a discursive option and its function of shifting the discourse lead to the trend of postmodern psychologies which aim at 'changing totalities' (Holzman, 2000, p. 88) – that is, totalities of the originally understood situations – and which remain in dialectic relationship with other points of view.

Postmodern approaches raise the question of psychology as a discipline, that is to say, the question of what psychologists do and what kind of impact psychologists can make on actual people and on human issues: individuals, culture, society, politics. The question is not only what kind of theories and methods psychologists can offer but also, through their practice, what kind of world-view psychologists can present. Some neglected facts about the paradoxical nature of psychology have been made explicit. For example, Peter Banister and his co-authors note that 'psychology is one of the disciplines in which subject (the investigator) and object (the investigated) coincide' (Banister *et al.*, 1994, p. 2) and that both the researcher and the researched are embodied human beings. He argues that 'we call people "subjects" but treat them as "objects", and we pretend to be objective but are still always deeply subjective' (ibid., p. 5).[1] Therefore, the activities and processes of psychological research could be seen as collaborative rather than a one-way study of physical substance. The foci of postmodern perspectives are on the practice of psychology and its process rather than on its results. Thus, psychological research methods have been questioned in parallel with the theoretical challenges in developmental psychology. As we have seen earlier, the dominant image of development as a linear, progressive change over time has shifted to a more diverse understanding of development (which does not necessarily follow fixed, predictable patterns or stages). Likewise, it is now clear that the dominant methods in mainstream psychology have shifted to more diverse methods which challenge the dominant methods and their underpinning assumptions about development. Both recent understanding of the notion of development and recent research methods in developmental psychology welcome alternative perspectives and such diversity.

With regard to discourses about the practice of psychology, there are arguments about method as practice, the practice of power, and theory as practice. Holzman proposes the concept of 'method as the practice of dialectics' and the idea of '*practising method* – an approach in which method is inseparable from the object to be studied' rather than '*applying*' any method (Holzman, 2000, p. 82). In this view, method and object are seen as 'a totality, a dialectical unity' (ibid., p. 82). The researcher's performance or activity is more important than knowing and theorising about epistemology. Vygotsky's practice of method is seen as a dialectical practice, since it engages with 'method as simultaneously tool and result' (ibid., p. 82) rather than with method as an instrumental tool for obtaining a result. This is what Fred Newman and Holzman call 'tool-and-method methodology' (1997). They claim that the underpinning idea of this performative psychology is Marx's notion of activity, i.e., 'revolutionary, practical-critical activity'. Holzman presents performative psychology and the non-epistemological approach for studying human life as 'a new kind of political-psychological practice' (Holzman, 2000, p. 81). Similarly, being aware of how methods are used as a 'disciplinary practice of power' and of 'the power of psychology as a method-as-theory' (2000, p. 52), Burman proposes a 'politics of psychology' as an 'unscientific psychology' (ibid., p. 73). By the term 'unscientific', she refers to the 'politically committed and scientifically sceptical attitude of psychologists and psychotherapists' (ibid., p. 49). McNamee calls such politics of method 'practical theory' or 'theory as practice' (2000, p. 182) in the sense that it illuminates 'the *process* of research as a relational *activity*' and, in particular, the 'political implications of research as a coordinate (relational) activity' (ibid., p. 183). Thus, both method and theory can be seen as dialectical practices of psychology. Mentioning 'Continuous process, interconnectedness, meaning-making, relationality, and activity' (Holzman and Morss, 2000, pp. 13–14) as some of many alternative concepts to the terms employed in the discourse of mainstream psychology, Holzman and Morss raise the question: 'how to create new human practices – given how hidden and/or distorted are the historicalness, the politicalness, and the interconnectedness between us by the seemingly objective scientific model of physical objects, particulars, and discrete ahistorical individuals' (ibid., p. 14). Psychology is presented here as the activity of embodied psychologists who use language with sensitive awareness of the historical and political implications of their own performance. Thus, this kind of postmodern approach seems to offer a holistic approach to the practice of psychology; that is to say, it requires the researcher's total involvement, focusing not only on the researcher's questions, claims, theories, methods, evaluation of evidence, and further questions that arise from the interpretation of evidence but also on the researchers themselves as individuals, their experience of their lives, and who they are as people.

There has been a particular emphasis on language in practice, participation, and ways of relating with others. John Shotter presents the idea of 'dialogically-structured' activity or 'joint action' (2000, p. 126, n. 5). He explains:

> Dialogically-structured activity can be understood neither in cause-and-effect terms nor in terms of logic or systems of calculation, nor reasons and interpretations. It is a *sui generis* realm of living activity with its own special, open, only partially specified or primordial nature, such that the reactions and responses occurring to us within it have the form of prototypes or candidates for all our more well-developed, separately characterized, deliberately conducted activities: all that we ever do or say in the special disciplines, in the arts, humanities, or sciences, has its origins in this ceaseless flow of dialogically-structured activity occurring between us.
>
> (ibid., p. 104)

This kind of approach places great emphasis on the researcher's participation in qualitative research and a kind of understanding gained from such an embodied researcher's relations to others. The implication of postmodern psychologies for the methods employed by developmental psychology is that, because there is no single 'correct' approach but multiple alternative options generated by the continuous practice of psychology, hermeneutic approaches focusing on interpretation, meaning-making, and subjectivity have acquired increasing value. This also applies to depth psychology in general and analytical psychology in particular, whose methods involve the interpretation of what is observed and listened to.

Language and psychological research methods: the quantitative/qualitative debate

'The language we use reproduces particular images of research, and of psychology' (Banister *et al.*, 1994, p. 15). The images of developmental psychology and of developmental methods have been reproduced by the discourses in the mainstream of empirical, scientific psychology until the discourses have gained more diversity. I discussed in Chapter 4 how particular images of development and of the child could have created the dominant discourses of developmental psychology. In turn, the language that developmental psychologists use could create particular images of what they do, what they approach, and what developmental psychology is all about.

The quantitative/qualitative debate illuminates the methodological differences between modern scientific psychology and postmodern unscientific psychologies and more general controversies about the 'duality of method' and a 'methodological pluralism' (Pearson, 1995, p. 760). It has been controversial whether the language used in modern scientific psychology is appropriate to account for psychological issues. The emergence of a 'new paradigm' in psychology in the 1970s and criticism of the 'old paradigm' and quantitative research have increasingly led to appreciation of qualitative research in the late twentieth century (Banister *et al.*, 1994, p. 4; Burman, 2000, p. 52; Pearson, 1995, pp. 760–1).

There are views that polarise quantitative and qualitative research as incompatible with each other. Quantitative research is usually seen as underpinned by a positivist conception of science and as operating by mathematical reasoning about human behaviour. In contrast, qualitative research is generally considered to be an interpretative study, to which the researcher is central, and as 'part of a debate, not fixed truth', so that it is incapable of being given a single definition (Banister *et al.*, 1994, p. 3).

Many instances of the quantitative and qualitative division can be described in terms of dichotomies. The quantitative/qualitative divide is described as behaviour vs meaning; artificial vs natural settings for investigation; emphasis on the discovery of scientific law vs interpretative hermeneutics; idealism vs philosophical realism;[2] logical positivism which seeks the facts or causes vs phenomonologism which is concerned with understanding; obtrusive and controlled measurement vs naturalistic and uncontrolled observation; objective vs subjective; the 'outsider' perspective vs the 'insider' perspective; outcome-oriented vs process-oriented;[3] and so on.

There are also views that quantitative and qualitative research are not necessarily located in opposition (Banister *et al.*, 1994, p. 1). Non-judgemental postmodern approaches apply to this dichotomous debate. On the basis of his understanding that 'No single method can be paramount' (1995, p. 94), David Krantz argues that the 'QQD [the quantitative–qualitative debate] needs to be shifted, if not resolved, by reformulating the issues' (ibid., p. 95). Both quantitative and qualitative research methods can be seen as discursive options available to our study of psychology, while the dichotomous debate moves forward to further questions about the implications of these researches. Burman agrees with Krantz that

> Qualitative research has been used to highlight the limits (and sometimes the abuses) of positivist research . . . by presenting alternative interpretations of the same phenomena, and also by demonstrating that there are arenas that positivist research does not know, cannot theorize, or fails to recognize.

(1997, p. 795)

By shifting the discourse, methodological issues enter epistemological, cultural and political dimensions. Geoffrey Pearson departs from describing quantitative research as 'hard' science and 'number-crunching', and suggests that a revolution is required in

> social attitude, which appears to be embedded in the culture of urban-industrial modernity, whereby the status of knowledge is privileged when it is large-scale and rests upon the assumption of mathematical (or quasi-mathematical) reasoning: that is, numbers rather than words.
>
> (1995, p. 760)

Likewise, Banister *et al.* point out that the logic of reduction and abstraction sustaining quantitative research could lead to disappearance of the context of the research (1994, p. 1). The tendency towards quantification is, they argue, a 'fantasy of prediction and control' (ibid., p. 3). They propose a 'turn to language in psychology' (ibid., p. 8), which might also be described as a 'turn to the text', in the form of qualitative psychology (Burman, 2000, p. 49). Moreover, looking at positivist research in psychology from a postmodern perspective raises the question whether the former is in fact unscientific in the way that it tries to ignore the power relations of human beings (Banister *et al.*, 1994, p. 9). Likewise, Burman draws attention to the power relations in and power of psychology itself, that is to say, 'the acts of privilege and exclusion psychology performs' and the 'notions of generalizability, standardization, replicability, and so on that permit the abstraction and decontexualization of human action into disembodied response or outcome' (2000, p. 52). She argues that both quantitative and qualitative research 'are actually potentially as "scientific" or "unscientific" as each other' (ibid., p. 73). In the quantitative account, qualitative research could be seen as unscientific for not meeting the criteria of traditional research methods which have acquired power in psychology. Conversely, in the qualitative account, quantitative research could be seen as unscientific for not considering the power relations of human beings which is one of the factors operating in psychology. Accordingly, the language used in postmodern psychologies not only differs from that used in conventional mainstream psychology but also raises the kind of questions that have never been asked in quantitative psychology.

Another relevant issue which should be addressed here is the problem of 'methodological reflexibility' (Cooper and Kaye, 2002, pp. 108–9) in various psychologists' approaches to language. That is, 'we must use language itself as the medium by which we investigate language' (ibid.). It is apparent that, whatever a particular psychologist's theorisation is, the whole process of research cannot be separated from the language which that psychologist studies. Likewise, it cannot be separated from the psychological issues which the psychologist studies. Therefore, the researchers must use their own psychological processes as the medium by which they investigate psycho-logical processes of human beings.

Moreover, there are views that the quantitative/qualitative debate cannot be resolved, especially on the philosophical level (Pearson, 1995; Rabinowitz and Weseen, 2001). When a question goes beyond methodological disputes, for instance, when asking 'what forms of knowledge are humanly useful and under what conditions?', Pearson argues that the conflict is to be lived with rather than resolved (1995, p. 761). Such philosophical questions as 'whether there is a necessary correspondence between "world view" and methodology' (Robinowitz and Weseen, 2001, p. 19) or 'whether qualitative methods qualify as science, good research, or even psychology' (ibid., p. 20) tend to dominate debates, Vita Robinowitz and Susan Weseen argue, 'because, as abstruse as the philosophical dimension can get, it is infinitely easier to discuss in the scholarly literature than are the political, social, and personal dimensions of the debate' (ibid.). As a consequence, rather than accepting the polarised images of the two kinds of research, the terms 'qualitative' and 'quantitative' have been stereotyped and even exaggerated (ibid.). Qualitative researchers are often seen as 'everything from trendy, left-wing, and politically correct to untrustworthy, soft-headed, hypocritical, and exhibitionist' and are criti-cised for 'a supposed lack of interest in truth, reality, reason, and anything else that stands in the way of advancing their social agenda or promoting their own careers' (ibid.). In contrast, quantitative researchers are allegedly thought of as 'uninterested in theory, understanding, context, getting close to the data, and respecting the integrity of research participants' or even as 'sexist, racist, homophobic' (ibid., p. 21). They are included in a general criticism of 'logical positivism' and 'positivists', terms which, according to Robinowitz and Weseen, 'are rarely defined, poorly understood, and prob-ably not applicable to anyone alive today' (ibid., p. 20). Nevertheless, they also identify quantitative and qualitative researchers' highly selective ways of questioning themselves: while the focus of the quantitative researchers tends to be on the practicalities of method with relatively little attention given to epistemology and ethics, the foci of the qualitative researchers are their epistemology and ethics (ibid., p. 24). Thus, discursive options as opposed to dichotomous debates do not answer but shed light on the fundamental problems in defining epistemology of science, psychology, psychological knowledge, and psychological methodology.

Furthermore, the social as well as disciplinary climate which sustains the quantitative/qualitative debate in psychology could be discussed in terms of the politics within the field of psychology. Krantz observes the factors which have been sustaining the debate: 'implicit, conflicting philosophical orienta-tions; intense intellectual and stylistic commitments; maintenance of group identity and resources; and variable criteria of research success' (Krantz, 1995, p. 89). Philosophical controversy could be a manifestation of the power struggle in psychology. Robinowitz and Weseen write: 'In large part, jobs, contracts, grants, journal space, and other forms of professional power and prestige have rested and continue to rest in the hands of traditional scientists' (2001, p. 21). The power relationship between quantitative and qualitative research is profoundly unequal. Therefore, they suggest that researchers 'study the studiers' and acknowledge 'the power disparities in our field and how those disparities affect the way people think and behave' (ibid., p. 25). In the political background of psychology, what Robinowitz and Weseen call 'professional power and prestige' (ibid., p. 21) seem to maintain psychology as a science in a traditional sense, but there are also continual challenges to this professional power and its underpinning epistemology of science. However, they also note that 'it is always easier to discuss metatheoretical issues than it is to change the practice of a discipline'.[4] They are of the opinion that 'the relentless disembodied philosophical critique of both qualitative and quantitative methods in psychology will deepen the divide between those at the poles' (ibid., p. 23) and suggest that researchers contemplate 'how the upstart debate in psychology can inform, promote, and liberate empirical research, instead of merely reproducing the swollen "QQD [quantitative/qualitative debate] industry" that so many have found abstract, sterile, and polarizing' (ibid., p. 23). Within analytical psychology such things could also be observed as the unequal power relationships between different methodological approaches, irresolvable philosophical debates, and attempts at making impact upon actual practice. The power relationships seem to affect not only the debates and dynamics within the Jungian circle but also how analytical psychology could be situated in different contexts. When particular kinds of theories and practice become preferred and dominant according to where power lies and the dominant power feeds on such theories and practices, it becomes a major challenge to discuss in what way existing research and practice of analytical psychology could be liberated.

Thus, various levels of the quantitative/qualitative debate have clearly shown the conflicts and controversies of different types of psychological research methods. The ongoing discourses contain the potential for shifting the existing images of research and psychology. In particular, discourses of qualitative research have shifted the images of developmental research methods and are still challenging the actual practice of developmental psychology.

Developmental research methods: their relevance to depth psychological approaches to early infancy

Some of the research methods employed by both developmental psychology and depth psychology involve the period of early infancy. Traditionally, developmental psychology and depth psychology have engaged in 'selective borrowing' of theories and practices from each other (Urwin, 1986, p. 258). For instance, the preoccupation with the mother–child dyad and the influence of Bowlby can be seen as a borrowing from psychoanalysis to developmental psychology, and yet Bowlby himself later elaborated his psychoanalytic theory by borrowing from psychology (ibid., p. 258). This suggests that, in spite of the apparent division between developmental psychology and depth psychology, they do share some epistemological and political assumptions and practical concerns. However, these kinds of selective borrowing were often adjusted to a form which would appear more scientific and less emotional, that is to say, to the form of modern scientific psychology, which assumes a biologically based core of normal development and privileges scientific reason. Urwin writes:

> many of the attempts to combine psychoanalysis and developmental psychology have explicitly or implicitly relied on these assumptions, producing normative accounts which reduce to the lowest common denominator and exclude fundamental aspects of psychoanalytic thinking in the process.
>
> (ibid., p. 275)

However, the methodological shift in developmental psychology, which takes more account of qualitative psychology than before, has made it possible for developmental psychology and depth psychology to have a dialogue about levels of emotional development, and about subjective experience in particular. Therefore, developmental psychology and depth psychology need no longer be seen as opposites: the one concerned with impersonal study of factual cognition and the other with introspective study of subjective emotion.

Daniel Stern's approach does not disregard the emotional dimension of the research process but borrows methods and findings from developmental psychology and combines them with insights from clinical practice. He distinguishes 'the *observed infant*, whose behavior is examined at the very time of its occurrence' by developmental psychology, and the *clinical infant*, who is 'reconstructed by psychoanalytic theories in the course of clinical practice' and therefore is 'the joint creation of two people' (Stern, 1985, p. 14), and yet he attempts to examine the 'way in which they together can illuminate the development of the infant's sense of self' (ibid., p. 15). Stern believes that both the observed infant and the clinical infant are relevant to understanding the infant's lived social experience and that each can contribute to the other in providing 'capacities that can be readily witnessed' and 'certain subjective experiences that are fundamental and common features of social life' (ibid., p. 17). For research on the actual experiences of the real infant involves both the observed infant, i.e., 'a description of capacities that can be observed directly' (ibid.) and the domain of the clinical infant, i.e., 'the subjective life of the adult, as self-narrated', which he considers as 'the main source of inference about the infant's felt quality of social experience' (ibid.). Stern believes that 'observable events . . . become transformed into the subjective experiences that clinicians call intrapsychic' (ibid., p. 18) and that the two perspectives create an interface.

Another example of the shift from selective borrowing in the form of quantification to exploration of qualitative psychology is an elaboration of attachment theory in the social context. Attachment theory, adopted from psychoanalysis by developmental psychology, 'relies on traditional quantitative research strategies rather than the interpretive methods of inquiry' (Bliwise, 1999, p. 43). The problem is that while attachment is defined as a behavioural system, in which attachment bonds are considered to be natural, self-evident and unequivocal outcomes of mothering, it is studied as a characteristic of individuals; that is to say, attachment behaviours and traits are seen as fixed and stable properties of separate, autonomous individuals (ibid., pp. 43, 44). Quantitative research has focused, for example, on the critical period when the child is of an age to form secure attachments, on the correlation between maternal deprivation in early infancy and later delinquency (e.g., Bowlby, 1944), and on the correlation between problematic behaviour and time spent at child care institutions (e.g., Goldfarb, 1947). However, critiques have been made that attachment theory does not have to be conceptualised with a narrow focus on the mother's responsibility for the child's social and emotional life or researched in terms of the child's individual capacity (e.g., Cowie, 1995). It has also been pointed out that the idea of the biological mother as the sole care giver, which fitted well in the social and political contexts of the post-war period, is no longer applicable to today's society (ibid.). Evidence has been presented which suggests that the child can form attachments with more than one person and that other family members can play an important role in attachment (e.g., Hinde and Stevenson-Hinde, 1988). There is increasing consideration of a 'multiple, systemic, and dynamic aspect of attachment theory' and 'the recognition of culture and social structure as important to interpersonal functioning across the life span' (Bliwise, 1999, p. 49). These emphases are not present in traditional quantitative psychology but have emerged out of questioning such dominant research.

Above all, contemporary psychological research does not cease with a mere criticism of modern psychology. Both the theoretical and the methodological shifts in psychology seem to be going in the direction of increasingly open, flexible, dynamic, interactive, transformative, mutual, corroborative, relationship-oriented exploration. In particular, qualitative psychology's emphasis on interpretation and the issue of the 'researcher-and-researched relation' (Burman, 1997, p. 792) seems relevant to the psychoanalytic approach in general and analytical psychology in particular, which I shall discuss later in this chapter. In view of this way in which psychology opens up discussions of methodology to the psychoanalytic approach, how could analytical psychology contribute to discussions of psychological methods?

Developmental practice in analytical psychology

Developmental methods and the Developmental School

I shall next explore the potential similarities and connections between methods of contemporary developmental psychology and those of analytical psychology, particularly of the Developmental School. I shall do so in as constructive a manner as possible, leaving my reservations and criticisms for later parts of the book. There seemed to be no developmental methodologies recognised in analytical psychology until the so-called 'Developmental School' emerged, that is to say, until Fordham's work at the SAP was called 'developmental'. Two prominent developmental methodologies with which Fordham was engaged will immediately be recollected. One is the reconstruction of childhood in analysis and the other is infant observation. Each of them is distinguished from modern infant research, and each method raises debatable issues.

Reconstruction of childhood in analysis

The clinically reconstructed child is different from the empirically observed child, as we have seen above. While the observed child is based on 'the most precise, often experimentally supported observations, with the least possible amount of presuppositions' (Jacoby, 1999, p. 32), the clinical child is psychoanalytically reconstructed by the therapist through the patient's childhood memories, dreams, and transference in analysis, in the course of searching for the origin of disorders in early childhood (ibid., p. 13). However, whether the process of reconstructing one's childhood in therapy is a process of searching for the origins of disorders or a process of exploring a situation here and now has been a debatable issue. In Stern's account, this clinical infancy is a story that is 'discovered, as well as altered, by both teller and listener in the course of the telling' (Stern, 1985, p. 15). Moreover, Stern also argues that 'real-life-as-experienced becomes a product of the narrative, rather than the other way round' (ibid. p. 15). Likewise, from the developmental psychological camp, Jerome Bruner proposes a notion of the self as situated within discourses (1986), and Dorothy Miell presents an account of creating a self by constructing narratives which change over time and in different situations and perhaps for different audiences (1995).

Also relevant here is the distinction between 'historical truth' and 'narrative truth' (Wetzler, 1985). While the former reflects factual reality which is fixed and therefore static, the latter reflects psychic reality which is never static. Scott Wetzler argues that psychoanalytic understanding of memory has been altered by Ernst Kris, for whom 'a memory was no longer seen as a trustworthy and *static* reproduction of an event' (Wetzler, 1985, p. 192; emphasis added). To verify whether meaning is based on the facts is almost impossible, because usually not all details of private facts in the past are available. Nevertheless, the kind of psychological impact one has experienced and is still affected by is a separate issue which cannot be neglected regardless of what historically happened in the past. Consequently, the status of recovered memories has become less important and less relevant analytically than narratives of subjective experience.

However, interpretation of personal memories could be split in two contradictory ways depending on contexts. Some might argue that memory is unreliable (since it cannot reflect precisely the historical truth), while others might argue that memory can tell us more about psychic reality than the mere events (since it reflects narrative truth).[5] Concentrating on historical truth might be considered reductive in the sense that the meaning of particular events is reduced to their generally agreed factual elements. This might prevent personal and emotional elements associated with the events from being voiced or listened to. For example, the Recovered Memory Movement, which resulted from mostly women speaking up about their traumatic experiences of abuse in childhood, and False Memory Syndrome, the diagnosis later given to those who recovered such memories, demonstrate how different interpretations of the same words can have different impacts on our understanding (Billig, 1999, p. 144).

There is a view that Jung and some of the classical Jungians were not involved with childhood analysis. Mario Jacoby writes that 'Jung himself, and the so-called "classical" orientation of analytical psychology, dealt hardly at all with reconstruction of the early childhood situation' (1999, p. 14). This is one of the main reasons that Fordham was concerned so much with childhood analysis, having experienced that his own childhood was not analysed in his analysis with Godwin Baynes and Hilde Kirsch. (I shall discuss Fordham's work and its context further in the following chapter.)

However, there is another view that Jung and some Jungians consider childhood analysis as retrospective and 'reductive', and therefore childhood analysis is not given as much importance as symbolic interpretation. Ellen Siegelman (1994) proposes to alter the terminology which refers to childhood analysis from one with negative connotations to one that is more constructive, that is, from 'reductive' to 'developmental' analysis. Jungian analysts basically believe that reductive analysis is 'to reduce the psyche to "nothing but" drives and defences, or to its infantile elements alone' (ibid., p. 479), which violates the complexity and richness of the psyche. However, what is actually dealt with is the present and future orientation of work with material from childhood (ibid., pp. 493–4). This process should therefore be called 'developmental', which appears to be more accurate and less pejorative (ibid., p. 494). Siegelman goes further, proposing that 'developmental' analysis is a stance rather than a specific school of Jungians, i.e., the so-called Developmental School. She suggests a possible solution to the conflict between analytical psychology and depth psychology by means of a new understanding of 'developmental' analysis in analytical psychology. Developmental analysis, in the sense she is proposing, seems to point to the changes in the images associated with the technique of reconstruction of childhood or the images associated with development. Whether altering a name for the method could change the attitudes of practitioners and the whole process of practice and the relationship with analysands would be a question to be further explored.

What we have seen above is a shift of the discourse: the meaning of reconstructing childhood could be different depending on its purpose and which perspective is taken. Accounts that place the main value on objective facts justify the search for origins and historical truth, but this does not seem to produce a satisfactory outcome when reconstruction of the inaccessible past is involved. However, for the kinds of approaches which take subjective experience seriously, what is more important seems to lie in one's actions (including narratives) and psychological states in the present as well as in the past.

Infant observation

Fordham set up the Child Analytic Training[6] at the SAP and, with the help of Gianna Henry from the Tavistock Clinic, introduced the technique of psychoanalytic infant observation with psychoanalytic theories into analytical psychology.

Psychoanalytic infant observation is distinguished from empirical infant research. This distinction parallels that between the clinical infant and the observed infant proposed by Stern, which we discussed earlier. Louis Zinkin writes that 'What emerges from current infant research is a totally different baby' from what is observed by analysts with their own analytic assumptions (Zinkin, 1991, p. 42). Coline Covington agrees with the difference between the infant observed by the researcher and the infant observed by the analyst, claiming that '*the findings reflect the method*' (1991, p. 69; emphasis in original).

Covington (1991) discusses the significance of infant observation as employed in the SAP in terms of its being: (1) a research tool; (2) a training tool; and (3) a part of analysis. First, infant observation as a research tool, Covington argues, is of limited value, because '*Infant observation does not provide supporting evidence, it provides evidence that corresponds with psychoanalytic theory*' (ibid., p. 68; emphasis in original). She explains:

> While infant observation can be used to illustrate developmental models and theories derived from adult analysis, it is no more useful to test certain theories than is our work with adult patients – and it can be argued that it is indeed less useful.

> (ibid.)

However, infant observation as a training tool, she argues, has much more to offer than infant observation as a research tool (ibid. pp. 71–3).[7] As a training tool, infant observation supports, according to Covington,

1   the value of learning how to observe;
2   the value of learning about the transference and countertransference;
3   the value of tuning in to non-verbal communication;
4   the value of learning that the thoughtful presence of the observer can be of considerable benefit in itself;
5   questioning developmental theories not only through highlighting the fact that there is a difference between the actual baby and what we refer to as 'the child within the adult' but also because their difference points to the need for different theoretical models or different styles of empathy;
6   witnessing change in the infant (and in the parents).

The points she makes touch upon several of the issues raised by qualitative, unstructured naturalistic observation, including the position of a participating observer, outsider and insider perspectives, influence by unconscious motivation, generating research questions, and making sense of what is observed in a given context. Infant observation may indeed be limited as a quantitative research tool or as a form of structured observation, but it could still contribute as a qualitative research tool or as a form of unstructured naturalistic observation. Accordingly, infant observation as a training tool could provide a qualitative research attitude as well as an analytic attitude.

Vygotsky's tool-and-result methodology is relevant here, in that infant observation can be 'simultaneously the tool and the result of the study',[8] that is, infant observation is not used as a tool which produces certain results but as a dialectical method in which the tool and the result are inseparable (cf. Ognjenovic, 2000, p. 211).

I have suggested that the developmental methods used in analytical psychology, i.e., reconstruction of childhood in analysis and infant observation, could be useful as qualitative research methods, even if they are not useful as quantitative research methods. Once it might have been the dominance of quantitative methods in psychology that led to a devaluation of the psychoanalytic perspective, but there now seems to be more scope for discovering the value of analytic methods, including the relevance and contribution of analytical psychology to qualitative methods.

Can analytic practice inform and contribute to discourses of developmental psychology?

In this section we shall discuss how analytical psychology, with its method-as-practice and theory-as-practice, could contribute to the discourses of qualitative methods in developmental psychology.

Can analytic practice be totally translated into the language of qualitative research methods?

So far I have examined analytical psychology and qualitative psychology in parallel by focusing on their common features. But is it possible to be an analyst and a researcher at the same time? The question could be asked not just of analytical psychology but of depth psychology as a whole. Of course, psychological research and psychotherapy have different aims, for, as Stephan Frosh argues, psychoanalysis, unlike conventional psychology, has its roots in the consulting room where a patient's distress is to be helped or resolved (1989, p. 1). However, this is not a simple question about the aims of analysis and research but a question about the language used in each practice and the potential discourses between them. In other words, can the analyst–analysand relationship be seen as comparable with the researcher–researched relationship?

There seem to be many contentious issues, if we compare an analyst (analysis) with a researcher (psychological research), whether quantitative or qualitative. First, for instance, there is the issue of how upset and distress are dealt with. As Frosh argues, in the course of analysis, whether during the actual consultations or outside of those hours, an analysand could re-experience trauma, and experience further psychological turmoil and suffering beyond the level of psychological pain likely to occur in the context of everyday life. However, in psychological research, participants should be protected from any risk, including psychological stress. Second, whose needs are being served? In the case of analysis, it is the patient who needs to come to the analysis, while in psychological research, it is the researcher who needs to obtain data from participants. Connected to this is the question, who is paying? It is the patient who pays the analyst a fee for the analysis, while it is usually the researcher, often supported by research funding, who pays the participants of his or her project (unless the researchers use unpaid volunteers or observe people in public places).

To the question of whether it is possible to be an analyst and a researcher at the same time, the answer would be a definite 'no', if we compare an analyst (analysis) with a quantitative researcher (quantitative psychology). With regard to the issues about confidentiality, it seems to be more straightforward to separate the identity of those who are involved from the data themselves in the quantitative research than in analysis. The analytic case should be confidential but can be easily identified and therefore, when it is presented to the public, is often disguised and not accurate. Likewise, information obtained about participants during psychological research should normally be confidential, and should be anonymous in publication, so that an individual or organisation will not be identified. However, unlike analytic data, quantitative research data themselves are usually objectively recorded and accurately presented, often because it is easy to separate the data in question from other details which can reveal the participants' identity. Also, there are issues about evaluation. It is debatable what should be regarded as the objective of an analysis. Some people might say that it should be cure, others that it should be the patient's satisfaction, for instance. Though increasingly an outcome-based evaluation seems to be applied to the results of therapy over limited timescales, there still remain difficulties with defining and identifying progress as well as problems. Apart from the issue of whose definition and evaluation are to be followed, there is an issue of where the progress and problems are to be located – not just in the observable behaviours and conscious attitude but as unconscious processes deep down in the psyche. In the case of analysis, the objective of an analysis seems to remain an open question. However, in quantitative research, the research question is usually a closed question, and the investigation is aimed at testing the hypothesis. The significance in the statistics, which indicate whether the result is meaningful or due to chance, will provide a clear-cut answer regarding whether or not the hypothesis is sustained, though of course interpretations are left open to some extent to the researchers. In addition, analytic techniques could vary according to each analysis, and what aspects of the patient are to be dealt with are not specified but left open. Quantitative research, however, should use standardised and reliable methods to ensure replicability and should clarify in advance the validity of its experimental designs. There seems little ground for arguing that the analyst–analysand relationship is comparable with the traditional quantitative researcher–researched relationship.

However, the analyst–analysand relationship could, in a sense, be seen comparable with the researcher–researched relationship, if we compare an analyst (analysis) with a qualitative researcher (qualitative psychology). The questions of whose needs are served and of payment still remain, but analytic practice and qualitative research might share the same kinds of conflicts and controversies in comparison with quantitative psychology. Qualitative psychology pays attention to issues of mutuality in the relationship between the researcher and the researched. As I discussed earlier, in qualitative psychology issues of subjectivity and objectivity are unavoidable. The use of the terms 'subject' and 'object' could be explored in terms of the language of analytic practice, e.g., transference and countertransference, projection, introjection, and projective identification. The subject of transference (projecting) is the object of transference analysis (interpreted), the subject of countertransference (projecting back) is the object of countertransference analysis (interpreted). The subject–object relationship could also be examined in terms of the Jungian concept of the ego–self axis (in terms of the relationship of both observer–observed and container–contained), or of the diagram of the mutual conscious–unconscious relationship between analyst and analysand. Moreover, qualitative psychology raises further issues which are relevant to analytic sessions, for instance, concerning the 'psychology of the research setting', 'the struggle to make sense of what is going on', and 'a continual tension between "personal reactivity" (the attempt by the "subject" to understand and control the research) and "procedural reactivity" (the ways in which the demands of the situation limit their room for manoeuvre)' (Banister *et al.*, 1994, p. 5). These issues could also be addressed in analytic sessions. The setting and the process of analysis are as a matter of course considered on both objective and subjective levels, and there is an inevitable conflict between the analyst's receptive attitude and the time limit of each session. Furthermore, it is worthwhile considering whether the postmodern view of research as collaborative work between the researcher and the researched can apply to the analyst–analysand relationship. Harlene Anderson, on the basis of 'the notion of research as part of everyday practice' (2000, p. 205), thinks that a patient can be a 'coresearcher' just like any other client who might be in the position of student, community, agency, or colleague. She refers to the psychiatrist and clinical scholar Tom Andersen's work as encouraging 'therapists to be collaborative researchers – coresearchers with their clients rather than hierarchical ones' (ibid.). Andersen himself argues that his focus is on *therapy as relationship* (Andersen, 1997, p. 126) and emphasises the 'process of researching together with clients' (ibid., p. 132).

Thus, on the one hand, when 'analysis' is concerned with data and results, there seem to be significant differences between analysts and (quantitative) researchers, and they might be incompatible. Frosh argues that unlike in conventional psychology, the way the data are obtained from a dialogue between a patient and an analyst is highly reactive (1989, p. 1). On the other hand, when the practice or the process of 'analysis' itself is the matter of concern, both analysts and (qualitative) researchers are involved in similar issues which are particular to practising psychology, and therefore their perspectives could be comparable and could even contribute to each other. Even though *analytical data* cannot contribute to quantitative psychology, an *analytical method* seems to have much to offer to qualitative psychology. Therefore, the analyst could be a qualitative researcher in the limited sense that the analyst can provide insight into qualitative methods, though without providing concrete data from the analysis. In this way, the analyst–analysand relationship in the consulting room could be seen in parallel with the researcher–researched relationship in qualitative psychology, and the language of analytic practice could enrich the language of qualitative research methods.

Analytical psychology and postmodern psychologies

Looking at analytical psychology from the viewpoint of postmodern or post-scientific psychologies, many shared concerns can be observed, but the distinctiveness of analytical psychological practice can also be observed. Both postmodern psychologies and analytical psychology seem to disagree with some aspects of modern psychology, but their reasons for this disagreement seem to differ. Postmodern psychologies emphasise the need to recognise methods for studying psychology (the human mind studying the human mind) as different from methods for studying the physical world. But from the viewpoint of analytical psychology, any one-sided method is inappropriate for studying whatever the subjects are, whether physical or psychological worlds, or in its view, the objective world where psyche and matter are connected. Moreover, while postmodern psychologies favour diversity over universal laws and subjectivity over objective facts, analytical psychology maintains the view of the universality of the objective psyche.[9] There also seems to be an emphasis on language in postmodern psychologies whereas analytical psychology prioritises symbols over language.

Like analytical psychology, contemporary approaches to psychology, which some might call postmodern or post-scientific psychologies, move away from such traditional notions as cause-and-effect, numerical logic, and monological reasoning. However, entering the realm of dialectical practice and open discussions, the explorations of language in these have become politically engaged and sensitive to multiculturality, diversity, and equality. Analytical psychology, by contrast, has focused on the realm of symbols beyond language and, as a result, has produced its distinctive perspectives in psychology. This focus on symbols might in itself have alienated others. Debates concerning the social and cultural implications of Jung's work, particularly the political implications have been pioneered by Samuels (e.g., 1993; 2001) and furthered by him and others (e.g., Adams, 1996). But in order to communicate more actively with those outside of the Jungian circle (and to make impacts on actual people's lives), there might be further work required for analytical psychology in this area with the kind of political awareness one finds in postmodern psychologies, that is to say, awareness into the question of what kind of impact analytical psychology can make on clients, analysts themselves, those who are not involved in analysis, the field of psychology as a whole, other disciplines, and issues in interdisciplinary areas.

Traditionally the language of analytical psychology, in line with the theory of individuation, has been often used for self-encounter and self-understanding but rarely as a means for having discourses with others, while postmodern psychologies explicitly invite open discussions with other individuals, disciplines, and professions, and are willing to listen to those others' voices. When symbolic meanings are prioritised, the meaning of language could be lost and this may lead analytical psychology to fail to offer a clear discursive option.

It seems critical for analytical psychology to maintain some kind of balance when attempting more dialogical relationships with other disciplines while remaining true to its focus on symbols. One of the challenges would be not to lose sight of such symbolic meaning as its distinctively Jungian contribution. For it is tempting and seems easier to adapt to popular discourses and modify Jung's thought so that it fits well into them. The seeming weakness of analytical psychology may indeed present challenges, but it could also be seen in a positive light, if we liberate it from any particular framework – not attempting to ally it with any existing trends in psychologies but instead viewing it as possibly operating with a different epistemology from both modern and postmodern psychologies.

The contemporary methodological shift in developmental psychology has opened the ground for discussion of shared psychological issues. Analytical psychology has a continuous contribution to make by connecting its understanding of symbols via language with diverse ways of questioning the world and human beings.

Conclusion

There is scope for considering analytical psychological methods in terms of qualitative psychological methods. As we saw in Chapter 4, the notion of development has been questioned and the debate still continues. Accordingly, the ways in which development is studied have changed and will continue to change.

This chapter has suggested that analytical psychology could be associated with postmodern, post-scientific psychologies when it comes to its challenges to modern, scientific, old-paradigm psychology. With this association, analytical psychology could appear to be more accessible and less alienating, and the potential relationships of analytical psychology with other fields of studies, including developmental psychology, might seem more promising than before. It could also be seen that analytical psychology could gain stronger credentials for participating in the continuing debates in wider social, cultural, and political contexts. How much capacity postmodern psychology has for inclusion of analytical psychology is another issue for discussion. But analytical psychology has certainly something to offer in terms of its methods as well as its theories.

Nevertheless, a question remains as to whether analytical psychology can totally fit with postmodern psychologies. There may be limitations in borrowing the acquired recognition of postmodern psychologies when presenting analytical psychology as one of many discursive options, even though the two approaches seem to make some common claims that have been marginalised by the dominant modern psychology. Having identified some features shared by analytical psychology and postmodern psychologies, we shall later explore possible limitations in the comparison between them. Specifically, the final chapter of this book will explore whether it is possible to view Jung as a qualitative psychologist. In doing so we will try to identify the distinctiveness of analytical psychological approaches to development as well as some features shared with other approaches. After looking closely at the Developmental School of analytical psychology in Part III, in Part IV we will explore the question of the qualitative approach with a specific focus first on Jung and then on the Developmental School and analytical psychology as a whole.

The Developmental School of analytical psychology

Chapter 6

Jung, Fordham, and the 'Developmental School'

In analytical psychology, the word 'development' tends to be connected to the Developmental School of analytical psychology. The connection between the Developmental School of analytical psychology and the images and narratives of development with which I am concerned largely rests on the diversity and ambiguity of the meaning of the word 'development'. As in Jung's work, so in the work of subsequent analytical psychologists there seems to be no clear-cut definition of the word 'development'. Nevertheless, Michael Fordham and his followers at the Society of Analytical Psychology (SAP) are called the Developmental School and this classification is widely accepted. It is therefore debatable in what way the words 'development' and 'developmental' are connected with the Developmental School. This chapter will look at the formation and characteristics of the Developmental School and, in relation to them, attempt to identify some elements and rhetoric of development in analytical psychology. I shall examine the images and narratives of development which might be specific to analytical psychology and may be distinct from the general images of development which, as I have discussed earlier, largely imply progressive change and betterment over time. I shall also examine how the general images of development are adopted in the theories of analytical psychology and whether these images are explicitly connected with their theories, are repudiated and therefore hidden as the shadow of their understanding of development, or are accommodated through some kind of compromise.

When and how did the 'Developmental School' emerge?

The name 'Developmental School' first appears in Andrew Samuels' *Jung and the Post-Jungians* (1985, pp. 15–19). Samuels suggests that there are three main schools of post-Jungian analytical psychology, distinguished in terms of both theoretical and clinical aspects, i.e., the Classical School, the Developmental School, and the Archetypal School. He notes that his classification overlaps with others' earlier classifications: his 'Classical School' with Adler's 'orthodoxy' and Fordham's 'Zurich School'; his 'Developmental School' with Adler's 'neo-Jungians' and Fordham's 'London School'; and his 'Archetypal School' with Goldenberg's 'third generation Jungians' (ibid., p. 16). It seems that differences among Jungians have been a long-standing issue for discussion. Samuels presents the Developmental School in terms of its theoretical emphasis on the development of personality, compared with the Classical School's emphasis on the concept of the self and the Archetypal School's emphasis on the definition of archetypal (ibid., pp. 15–19). He also characterises the Developmental School in terms of its clinical emphasis on the analysis of transference–countertransference, compared with the Classical School's emphasis on symbolic experiences of the self and the Archetypal School's emphasis on examination of highly differentiated imagery (ibid.). In *Post-Jungians Today* (1998, pp. 21ff), a new classification[1] of four schools of post-Jungian analytical psychology appears: fundamentalist, classical, developmental, and psychoanalytic.[2] Nevertheless, Samuels' account of the Developmental School remains consistent. The Developmental School is characterised by its focus on 'the importance of infancy in the evolution of adult personality and character' and its equally stringent emphasis on 'the analysis of transference-countertransference dynamics in clinical work' (ibid., p. 20). Therefore, the notion of a 'Developmental School', which emerged in Samuels' classification, has drawn attention to the diversity of both theoretical focus and clinical practice in analytical psychology, and the political tensions among post-Jungians.

Within analytical psychology, the identification of a 'Developmental School' has been broadly accepted. Whether this name is agreeable or not, it is certainly often used. Nevertheless, it appears that the Developmental School has not been seen only in terms of Samuels' original characterisation, as post-Jungian understanding of what 'developmental' means could vary. Additional images seem to have accrued in the use of the name of this school.

It would be worthwhile considering the history[3] and background of the 'Developmental School' of analytical psychology, in order to explore what the word 'developmental' signifies and what kinds of images are projected onto the 'Developmental School'. I shall look at the history of the SAP,[4] though I am aware that this is not the only possible way of describing its history.

As previously noted, it is Michael Fordham, one of the founders of the SAP, and his followers at the SAP that are called the Developmental School. (Nevertheless, it should immediately be noted that not all members of the SAP agree with this naming.) We then have to alter the question of how the Developmental School emerged to the question of how the SAP emerged.

When, how, and why did the SAP emerge, and what did its position in the Jungian world come to be? After World War II, a new Jungian institution was established in the UK, in which Michael Fordham was largely involved. There were geographical and political as well as personal factors involved in its establishment. First, due to the difficulty of getting personal analysis with Jung or with his close associates in Switzerland, there was a need for people outside Switzerland to have a training institution. Fordham was frustrated at not being able to have analysis with Jung himself, while others in the UK, such as H. G. Peter Baynes (Fordham's first analyst) and E. A. Bennet (Fordham's colleague at the SAP) not only were analysed by Jung but also had a close personal relationship with him. In order to make it possible to have Jungian analysis in the UK, a training institution was established in 1945 and named the Society of Analytical Psychology. Fordham became the first practising analyst from any institute of analytical psychology outside Zurich.

The difference between London and Zurich became more recognisable. In 1962, at the Second International Congress of Analytical Psychology in Zurich, Murray Jackson (a member of the SAP) presented a paper on 'The Nature of Symbols'. Esther Harding (a founder of the Analytical Psychology Clubs in Zurich and New York) criticised Jackson, maintaining that he did not understand what Jung meant by the term 'symbol', and most analytical psychologists supported the Zurich viewpoint (Kirsch, 2000, pp. 42–3, 63). Consequently, the SAP established in London was called the 'London School' in contrast to the 'Zurich School'. (Originally, the members of the Zurich Psychoanalytic Association founded in 1913 were called the 'Zurich School', as distinct from the 'Vienna School' [Kirsch, 2000, p. 32].) The 'London School' would eventually be called the 'Developmental School' (ibid., p. 43).

There seems no clear answer to the question of why the 'Developmental School' is so called. The first classification of different schools was geographical (Vienna, Zurich, and London). Recent classifications have focused more on theoretical and political differences (Classical, Developmental, Archetypal; Fundamentalist, Classical, Developmental, Psychoanalytic). Samuels points out the confusion in the geographical naming of schools (Samuels, 1998, p. 19). For the four current Jungian trainings in London (i.e., Society of Analytical Psychology [SAP], Association of Jungian Analysts [AJA], Independent Group of Analytical Psychologists [IGAP], and the Jungian section of the British Psychological Society [BPS]) can no longer simply be portrayed as the 'London School', and the traditions of theory and practice that are associated with 'London' and 'Zurich' are now disseminated all over the world. Besides, there is a so-called umbrella group in London which aims to represent all UK Jungian analysts by containing the diversity of the above four London groups. Papadopoulos argues that societies do not split or form exclusively for theoretical reasons (personal communication, 2001). More likely, it is a question of a mixture of different perspectives, such as personality, theory, politics, and other circumstances, that are involved in the institutionalisation of Jungian analysts in various places and in various contexts (ibid.). For instance, there are many Jungian groups in the world, not only in

Zurich and London, but also in New York, Los Angeles, San Francisco, Berlin, Rome, Paris, Basle (Casement, 1995, p.328; see also Kirsch, 2000), and Japan. Although all fundamentally started as institutes of Jung's analytical psychology, beginning with the Zurich Psychology Club founded in 1916, there are slightly different emphases in each institution.

The 'Developmental School' emerged from the need for a training analysis to become a Jungian analyst. Since the SAP was the first to establish a training analysis outside Zurich, it became the focus for various conflicts about the institutionalisation of Jungian analysis. These centred around the issue of whether, in view of its regulations and policies as well as its theories and practices, the SAP was or was not Jungian. When the split occurred between the SAP and the AJA, the question became in what way the SAP was Jungian. In what way the SAP is developmental also matters here, partly because it is another way of asking in what way 'Jungian' psychology is developmental. The *new* elements and *changes* that the Developmental School introduced into Jungian psychology provoked controversy. These innovations and modifications led to some of the dominant images of development that I have addressed so far and such images could obviously or less obviously have an effect on analytical psychology.

What does the 'Developmental School' do?

What distinctive aspects of the work of the SAP, particularly of Fordham, lead to their being called the 'Developmental School'? What are their agreements and disagreements with Jung? It might not be appropriate to equate the 'Developmental School' entirely with the SAP, given that, as already noted, there are some members of the SAP who do not agree with this naming. Rather, as the naming originates in Fordham's theoretical and practical emphases, it seems more appropriate to focus specifically on Fordham and his agreements and disagreements with Jung.[5]

First, with regard to Fordham's position in London at that time (Miyagi, 1998), it could be noted how different Fordham's professional and political contexts were from Jung's. His colleagues included not only Jungian analysts but also other analysts who had a background in medicine or in psychoanalysis, especially Object Relations Theories. Fordham was a medical doctor, who had read biology and physiology at Cambridge and was interested in scientific medicine and neurology (Fordham, 1985b, pp. 1–2). He worked for the Child Guidance Clinic before the war and came to be influenced by Melanie Klein's practice in her child analysis, especially by her use of play technique as a method of communication and her interpreting transference which she believed the child developed in play. Fordham found similarities between Klein's notion of unconscious phantasies and Jung's concept of archetypes (Fordham, 1993b, p. 66), and later found no difference between Susan Issac's definition of unconscious fantasy, which Klein had accepted in her metapyschology, and Jung's definition of the archetypes (Fordham, 1985b, p. 215). Fordham had belonged to the Medical Section of the British Psychological Society, and had opportunities to discuss topics such as 'Archetypes and Internal Objects' (1949) and 'Countertransference' (1960) in relation to psychoanalysis and analytical psychology with other psychoanalysts (for instance, John Rickman, Michael Balint, Clifford Scott, Wilfred Bion, and Donald Winnicott). Fordham observed their agreements on the relation between archetypes and internal objects and on the viewpoint of transference and countertransference (Fordham, 1985b, p. 213). At this time he also elaborated on his theory of autism, arguing that autism was a disorder of what he termed deintegration (Fordham, 1993b, pp. 101–2). He became the first chairman of the SAP, as the chair of council was required to be a medical person (Kirsch, 2000, p. 41).

On the practical level, Fordham introduced some innovative techniques in the SAP. First, he started a training analysis. As mentioned earlier, Fordham was dissatisfied at not having had analysis with Jung himself. He was also unsatisfied with his own analyses with Baynes (for seven months) and Hilde Kirsch (from 1936 to 1939), which did not take much account of transference or childhood. Consequently, analysis of childhood and transference and countertransference came to be emphasised in the training analysis at the SAP. Fordham contributed to it with such concepts as syntonic transference and countertransference, and countertransference illusion.

Second, Fordham made innovations through his work on children. His work on children began in 1933, the year his first son Max was born. He also initiated the Child Analytic Training at the SAP in 1974 (see further Davidson, 1986). During the war, Fordham served as consultant for evacuated children and that experience made him realise the necessity of child analysis. He also thought that Jung avoided analysing the unconscious processes of children (Fordham, 1993a, p. 631). He adopted Klein's play technique,[6] Object Relations Theories, and infant observation as part of the training. What Fordham introduced from psychoanalysis to analytical psychology still remains an integral part of the tradition of the SAP.

On the theoretical level, Fordham challenged not only Jung's notion of the child but also some of Jung's key concepts, such as the self, the archetype, and, accordingly, the individuation process. With regard to the concept of the self, Fordham disagrees with Jung's idea that the self is to be achieved only in adulthood (see, e.g., Fordham, 1971, pp. 83–4, 1976, p. 14; also Astor, 1995, p. 45), curiously, in the form of the eternal child. What is more, Fordham maintains that if the self is the whole psyche, it cannot be observed 'as such', for the ego that would observe it is actually contained within the self (1963, p. 25). He argues that 'in Jung's general theory of the psyche, a part of it, the ego, is specifically differentiated from the archetypes' (ibid., p. 28). However, it is arguable whether the concept of the self as the whole psyche is as problematic as Fordham believes. It could be argued that there is no inconsistency between Jung's theory of individuation and the concept of the self as totality. If the self is to be only worked towards in the process of individuation rather than be something actually achieved, then the ego being part of the self, would naturally not be able to realise the whole self. A possible exception might be if the psyche somehow were to achieve a non-ego status, perhaps through a temporary domination by the unconscious which might be attainable, for instance, in dreams and fantasies, or as a result of enlightenment, extreme creativity, or some noticeably unusual state of mind which might often be labelled as pathology or insanity, where the person who regained eco-consciousness might only be able to reflect on the temporary experience of wholeness. (We shall revisit this problem in the final chapter of this book.) Opposing the concept of the self being both an archetype and the totality, Fordham also points out that Jung's definition of 'the self as an archetype began after the idea of it as the totality of the psyche' (ibid., p. 29). Fordham thought that the self cannot be the totality and an archetype at the same time, since the self as an unknowable archetype should be differentiated from the ego which is supposed to be contained in the whole psyche (ibid., p. 28). Accordingly, Fordham concluded that the images of the self are not theoretical but metaphorical or hypothetical (ibid., pp. 25–6).

With regard to the notion of the child, Fordham disagrees with Jung's understanding of the child's psyche. Jung claims: (1) the child's psyche is different from the adult's psyche; (2) the child's psyche is mostly related to the parent's mind; and (3) the child's psyche has no centre and no boundary between consciousness and unconsciousness (see Jung, 1928a, 1927/1931a, 1934a, 1910/1946, 1940, 1926/1946). To analyse the unconscious of a child is thought to be inappropriate in classical Jungian practice. This is because Jung believes that a child's pathology is based on its parent's unconscious pathology and, moreover, that the child, who has not yet acquired adult language, could be overwhelmed by the archetypes, which carry too much mystical material for its mind. Fordham's view is that the child's mental structure is not all that different from an adult's (Fordham, 1985a, p. 3) and that the child's psyche is separate from the parent's mind from the beginning (e.g., Fordham, 1985b, p. 90). He claims that the child's experience of the self is essentially the same as adults' experience (1965, p. 106) and that archetypal images function in much the same way as in adult life (1985a, p. 2). Therefore, with his understanding of the concept of the self and of the child's psyche, Fordham believes that the individuation process is relevant to childhood as well as adulthood.[7] However, Fordham did not pursue the implications for wider social contexts of claiming that a child's mental structure is not dissimilar to an adult's. This will be further discussed in Chapter 7.

Based on his points of disagreement with Jung, Fordham formulated his theory of individuation in childhood, with his concepts of the primary self, deintegration and reintegration, and the state of identity. An important agreement of Fordham with Jung would be that both were concerned with what was normal as well as pathological and considered the self as essential, as opposed to the ego. However, in relation to the individuation process, a further crucial difference of Fordham from Jung seems to lie in Fordham's understanding of the self at the beginning of one's life. Fordham defined the self as 'both an integrator and also a system which could deintegrate' (Astor, 1995, p. 79). Elizabeth Urban observes that while the self for Jung was 'the individuating self', the self for Fordham was 'the pre-individuating self' (Fordham, quoted in Urban, 1992, p. 414), which is what Fordham calls the primary self (Urban, 1992, p. 414). As we have seen above, Fordham regarded Jung's concept of the self on one level as an archetype, and on another level as the total psyche, which is the unification of the ego and the archetypes. However, Fordham's understanding of the self was beyond the archetypes and the ego (Fordham, 1988, p. 24). He suggested a formula, 'self = ego + archetypes' (1963, p. 25), to represent 'union or combination of the conscious with the unconscious'. However, it is arguable whether Fordham's formula of 'self = ego + archetypes' (ibid.) is any more helpful than Jung's attempts to theorise the psyche in terms of these concepts. The formula could be disputed in various ways. For example, it immediately seems unsatisfactory when presented as 'ego = self – archetypes' or 'archetypes = self – ego'. Fordham's formula of the relationships between the self, the ego, and the archetypes may raise further questions about the crucial differences between Jung's and Fordham's understanding of the psyche. There needs to be further discussion on Fordham's challenge towards Jung's understanding of the child's psyche, his concept of the self, and his theory of individuation.

The innovations and elaborations that Fordham bequeathed to the SAP are considered to be 'developmental'. His work is often characterised by images relating to the child, transference, and psychoanalysis. These images also carry another kind of image of development, i.e., as something involving what is new and changed. Fordham's ambivalent status as a Jungian could be seen as a consequence of his exploration into non-Jungian areas. However, Fordham's ideas did originate from Jung, and he could have simply been exploring different aspects of the same essential issues as Jung. Fordham's contribution could perhaps also be seen as developmental in the sense of nurturing and deepening Jung's concepts of archetypes, the self, and individuation.

To what extent and in which aspects is the Developmental School 'developmental'?

Fordham shows ambivalence towards the term 'Developmental School'. He accepts 'developmental' as a fundamental characteristic of both Jung's and his own approach (Samuels, personal communication, 2000). However, he does not accept the 'developmental' as a characteristic that distinguishes his own approach from Jung's. Rather, Fordham considers the 'developmental' as a positive feature of Jung's work that connects with and was elaborated by Fordham's own work. According to Casement, Fordham responded to Samuels' naming of the 'Developmental School' with the view that 'it is plausible but quite false, as Jung's whole approach is developmental in, for instance, opening up therapy to older individuals so that they too can go on developing' (Casement, 1995, p. 329). Likewise, James Astor explains:

> Fordham's objection to these categories is that they create confusion by claiming to make distinctions which Jung himself did not make . . . All Jung's work, in Fordham's view, is developmental, since this is the core of his concept of individuation, which concerns the growth of the personality.
>
> (Astor, 1995, p. 36)

However, Casement also argues that Fordham favoured the term 'Developmental' inasmuch as Jung's psychology essentially is developmental (Casement, 1995, p. 330). She reports: 'it was a way of linking the study of infancy and the infantile transference with a particular Jungian perspective on psychology' (ibid.). When it comes to the characterisation of him as 'developmental', Fordham's emphasis seems to have been on his work as an extension of Jung's work rather than as contra to it.

Fordham's conflict may have been that he wanted to become closer to Jung, like Jung's assistants in Zurich, but was unable to become one of them. This may have produced in him an ambivalent feeling towards 'them', i.e., the idealised people, in Fordham's mind, near Jung. For instance, the year before the SAP was founded in 1945, Fordham proposed a centre for analytical psychology, considering this proposed centre 'as part of the Analytical Psychology Club and not separate from it' (Kirsch, 2000, p. 40). However, Fordham was ambivalent. He writes: 'I insisted on calling our society the Society of Analytical Psychology and not the C. G. Jung Institute', partly because he was sufficiently accepted by the Jungians and others in England, and also because he thought: 'we were serving a science' (Fordham, 1993b, p. 94). He found himself alienated from other Jungians in and from Zurich, but at the same time, he also identified 'our society' with the SAP. He seems to have enjoyed his independent position, as he later acknowledged: 'in spite of all this my position as leader seemed just to come about and I enjoyed the power of it' (ibid.). He further states that 'I had not studied in Zurich nor did I intend to' (ibid.). But at the same time, he seemed unable to shake off the feeling of being rejected. He writes: 'My "defect" was partly felt by myself but was also used by "authentic" Jungians (Gerhard Adler, Culver Barker and Erna Rosenbaum), who . . . felt that I did not have the true Jungian spirit' (ibid., p. 95). Fordham's feelings of otherness, of longing and even of competition seem to have been experienced in relation to the people around Jung at least as much as to Jung himself.

Here we need to make a distinction between two questions: in what way Fordham is 'developmental' and in what way Fordham is 'Jungian'. There have apparently been political conflicts within analytical psychology regarding Fordham's innovative work. So long as we are concerned with the question of what is 'Jungian', we only see the political tensions among the various schools of analytical psychology, that is to say, not only the conflicts between Classical (Zurich) and Developmental (SAP, London), but also the conflicts within the UK, between Developmental (SAP) and Archetypal (AJA), and between Archetypal (AJA) and Symbolical (IGAP). However, even within the SAP, some agree that they are developmental, while others disagree, and, as Papadopoulos points out, the differences *within* the various schools of analytical psychology can be greater than the differences *among* them (Papadopoulos, 1998b, p. 169). Still, the question remains of what post-Jungians identify by the word 'developmental'.

There are obvious and less obvious links between the images of the Developmental School and what is thought to be 'developmental' in analytical psychology. Obviously, development is often understood in terms of child development. Child development is a 'developmental' issue, and the approach to the child is a form of 'developmental' work. Less obviously, development is also understood in terms of scientific or technological development. An empirical approach to the early period of life could be understood as a 'developmental' technique. First, as pioneering work, Fordham's approach to child development represents a *new* element and a *change* in the tradition of Jungian psychology – newness and change being some of the dominant images of development. Second, because of its resemblance to biology and physics in terms of choosing smaller, younger, and more fundamental subjects and implying a natural law of origins, the empirical approach to the early phase of life might be considered as more highly sophisticated or more *advanced* or *progressive* – advancement and progress being some other dominant images of development.

Discussion of child development brings us immediately to the question of whether infancy is important or relevant to Jungian psychology, which in fact Fordham himself questions (Fordham, 1985b, p. 2). The child could be understood in analytical psychology in terms of both the actual child and the child archetype. Therefore, child development could be understood literally as well as metaphorically, i.e., in terms of both the development of the actual child and psychological processes involving the child archetype. For some, 'developmental' work might mean to focus on the development of the actual child. However, for others, 'developmental' work might not necessarily mean this. For instance, numerous themes of life might be focused on as 'developmental' facts, in which the child archetype and other associated archetypal images are involved (e.g., parental imagos, the Great Mother, the senex archetype, the God image, etc.). Consequently, the 'developmental' approach could be understood both literally and metaphorically, both as knowing 'better' about the actual child and as deepening one's understanding of the symbolic connection with the child archetype. Within analytical psychology, both approaches are scientific in different ways, that is to say, both are based on the observation of empirical facts which could involve different kinds of reality.

The naming of the Developmental School has raised an essential issue which has not been addressed, i.e., how the dominant images of development appeal to Jung, to Fordham, and to various schools of analytical psychology, and what kinds of reactions occur in analytical psychology to these dominant images. Child development; progress, advancement, betterment; change, and the appearance of a new element, which I presented earlier as among the dominant images of development, seem to be constellated in analytical psychology. However, what is particular to analytical psychology seems to be the symbolic or metaphorical use of the word 'development', which always allows for other, more flexible, often marginalised meanings of development which are not necessarily progressive.

What are the elements and rhetoric of development in analytical psychology?

I have discussed when, how, and why the 'Developmental School' emerged in Britain, and why Fordham and his followers in the SAP are called the 'Developmental School'. I made a distinction between the questions of in what way Fordham is 'developmental' and in what way Fordham is 'Jungian' and discussed the question of in what way the 'Developmental School' is developmental. Here I shall not discuss development in terms of the politics or organisational aspects of what it means to be 'Jungian'. Rather, I shall focus on the rhetoric of 'development', which might be categorised as a 'concept', an actual 'process', a 'metaphor', and an 'emblem' (Papadopoulos, personal communication, 2001). In this respect, development could be considered as

1   a concept which has not been clarified in analytical psychology but implies Jung's and Jungians' understanding of psychological development;
2   the actual process of development, whatever it means, which goes on autonomously and might be what Jung tried to understand through his experience of life as well as his work;
3   a metaphor, according to which, in addition to the literal child, the metaphorical child plays a significant role in understanding psychological development; and
4   an emblem, a flag, a trademark, a brand name, a label, which may carry positive as well as negative images of 'development' and therefore can provoke feelings of superiority and inferiority. (Political debates may be unavoidable when discussing this category.)

Different authors in different contexts refer to different facets of development. However, I shall refrain here from providing examples of various authors' statements that could be identified as belonging to each of the above categories. To conduct textual analysis according to the four categories suggested above could be a future project but is beyond the scope of this book. Here I shall restrict this section to raising questions for future study and exploring issues on the theoretical level.

In line with the concepts of the collective unconscious and the archetypes, symbolic meanings of development could be applied to all the different levels above and could be presented as comprising a further specific image of development within analytical psychology. However, when development is used as a metaphor, symbolic and literal meanings are explicitly intertwined, and the split between them could create confusions as well as conflicts in terms of the duality or even diversity of their potential meanings. Likewise, when 'development' is used as an emblem, the emblem could convey some kind of conscious as well as unconscious value which creates confusions and conflicts in identifying the quality of what is developmental.

As a concept, the meaning and implications of the word 'development' contain underpinning assumptions and expectations of its use. Various concepts co-exist, but the processes of conceptualisation involve mainly rational, often causal thinking and explanation. As a process, development can be approached in a more amplificatory way without seeking a definition. Processes of development, even if not defined as such, reveal certain aspects of psychology and a particular author's viewpoint.

As a metaphor, child development signifies a pattern of development. Using a child as a metaphor for development could be seen as a child-centred approach. When interpreted as an actual child, some might question why the locus of development has to be a child and not anyone at any age. When perceived in relation to one's own childhood, some might argue that focusing how a child develops could help an adult understand his or her origin, beginning, and basis of their lives. Taken either as human or individual development, others might argue that child development has nothing to do with the process of psychological development but the child archetype does. It might be seen as a threat to the child archetype to concentrate at the concrete level on the actual child, losing sight of the symbolic, spiritual, mythical realm by focusing only on something visible and inevitable. However, in relation to developmental themes, the child, whether literal or metaphorical, does not seem to stand on its own but is surrounded by a network of relationships with others in various contexts (Papadopoulos, 2006, p. 32). For even a symbol-centred approach would have to rely, to some extent, on the connections between the self, the child archetype, and the notion of the parental imago, which are based on the notion of the child. Samuels observes that there are many connections as well as discrepancies between the literal and metaphorical aspects in descriptions of personality, giving as an example the 'interconvertible' links between the real infant and the metaphorical infant (Samuels, 1989, pp. 27–8). He writes: 'Metaphor cannot be divorced from the roots of its content even though those contents have been absorbed into a wider and less literal understanding' (ibid., p. 47). Nevertheless, even though the literal child (the actual child) and the metaphorical child (the child archetype) co-exist, sharing many similar features, the literal approach to understanding development (through knowing more about the actual child) and the metaphorical approach to understanding development (through appreciating the child archetype symbolically) seem to stand in a complex relationship. The problem remains of how a connection can be made between the two approaches.

Commonly used within analytical psychology, the name 'Developmental' has become a kind of emblem of the SAP. As an emblem, 'Developmental' implies a certain value with *new* characteristics and it could be understood in both positive and negative ways. It should be noted that value judgements are involved here, but I am not suggesting which, if any, is the correct understanding. I shall only discuss the possible implications of the term 'Developmental' serving as an emblem. Again, the focus here is on asking in what way 'development' is developmental rather than whether 'developmental' is Jungian, as our aim is to engage with the notion of development rather than to enter political debates. However, because of the sense of superiority/inferiority potentially being provoked by an emblem, it seems particularly difficult to separate the above two issues. Seeing 'development' in the light of scientific, technological advancement and betterment, 'developmental' work may be regarded as a useful approach to knowing more about the actual child, or even as a threat to the child archetype and its symbolic expressions. The emblem can be understood as implying something either 'advanced' or distinctive (with a positive identification or superior feeling) or merely 'different' or idiosyncratic (with a negative identification or inferior feeling), depending on the conception of the *new* element brought by *change*. Accordingly, technical development could cause feelings of superiority as well as inferiority, depending on whether the identification is with an advanced or an excluded status. There could be dual responses to the label, which carries the general, dominant, and positive images of 'development', i.e., 'progress', 'advancement', 'betterment', 'change', 'evolved', 'more scientific', 'more civilised', 'more technological', 'more social', and the like. Use of 'Developmental' as a label could invite agreement but could also provoke disagreement concerning these dominant images. On the one hand, the 'Developmental' could be seen literally, that is to say, as implying a progressive approach to psychology, and on the other hand, it could be seen metaphorically, that is to say, as altering these kinds of progressive images of 'development' into a different kind of understanding of development, one recognising progression and regression, compensation of opposites, change and stability, separation, recognition, integration, transformation, symbol formation, self-regulation, and probably other important themes in Jung's psychology.

From the history of analytical psychology in Britain, it could be assumed that the word 'development' was first equated with child development. But what was not obvious in this connection was the association of the idea of development with an empirical approach to the earlier phase of life. This empirical approach might be considered more scientific, or more advanced or 'developed'. The shadow of the name which the Developmental School carries might stem from a particular conception within analytical psychology at that time of an empirical approach to the human being. (It is a kind of 'physics envy' [Rose, 1997, p. 9], where it is assumed that the smaller the scale of consideration, the stronger the proof of the associated laws.) There might be a kind of feeling of inferiority within analytical psychology regarding its image of being preoccupied with myth which makes it difficult to have dialogues with other scientific disciplines. The 'Developmental School' has in a way achieved what was longed for, i.e., other kinds of methodologies, explanations, or vocabularies to communicate with other scientific disciplines. The SAP emphasised the scientific as it was understood from a specific perspective at that time. What is scientific here seems to consist of an empirical, quantified, and positivistic approach. This is one definition of science. However, this definition does not apply to all forms of science. Papadopoulos argues that the images and concepts of what is scientific have shifted and 'there has been a change in the perception of what constitutes evidence in many academic spheres' (1997, p. 299). For example, human and social sciences, due to 'the limitations of the reductive models of causalistic determinism of nineteenth-century science', have been taking more account of 'the merits of qualitative research which includes designs emphasizing, *inter alia*, the constructivist meaning of narrative, discourse analysis, and creative ways of connecting the individual to wider structures of meaning' (ibid., p. 299). Therefore, we have different contexts for understanding Jung's work in the light of this new paradigm of science. The 'scientific' aspect of the Developmental School is no longer 'scientific' within this paradigm. It has come to be considered that reducing human psychology to child psychology is neither specifically scientific nor an advanced way of proceeding.

'Science' can gain power from its connection with the idea of 'development' or vice versa. Scientific development, that is, when a new form of science points out what was lacking in older forms, arouses feelings of superiority and inferiority both within and between these old and new forms. The 'developmental' emblem once seemed to signify a 'scientific' (empirical) approach, which was seen as more 'advanced' than a non-scientific (archetypal, symbolic, and mythical) approach. The emblem seemed to signify not only a technical achievement in scientific infant research but also a threat to the world of symbols, which includes the archetype of the divine child. However, the emblem might also be the result of another kind of threat at the level of epistemology. Presenting SAP as 'scientific' might have been a way for Fordham to obtain status within analytical psychology. Rather than focusing on 'symbolic', which is usually deemed essential to analytical psychology, emphasising a 'scientific' approach in relation to 'the child' can be seen as a striking and powerful attempt on the part of Fordham to present himself in terms of new images. The 'scientific' and 'the child' both have strong implications in relation to development, so for the SAP to be associated with them might have helped Fordham to assume the image, or emblem, of the developmental.

The 'scientific' approach was in fact used as a supporting image of the SAP. When the tension between Fordham and Adler increased within the SAP, most Jungians outside of the UK sympathised with Adler, and when Adler (AJA) split from Fordham (SAP), Fordham was seen as the deviant from the Jungian approach (Kirsch, 2000, p. 57). Then, after 1962, the *Journal of Analytical Psychology* (which was founded and first edited by Fordham in 1955 and is still sponsored by the SAP) shifted its editorial policy from embracing a wide range of viewpoints and subjects to a more scientific and clinical approach that excluded some traditional Jungian themes (ibid., p. 43). The Developmental School thus seems to have become emblematised as 'developmental', gathering to itself powerful images of scientific development as well as child development. Astor views Fordham's tendency to emphasise the scientific as 'an antidote to the cult of personality' (1995, p. 36), saying that 'it seems as if he [Fordham] was trying to ground the analytical psychologists who were starting to work in England in a method which had a firm empirical base' (ibid.). However, in the light of the new paradigm of science, the narratives of any schools of analytical psychology are equally deserving of consideration, and 'scientific development' will be only one of many underpinning images of different narratives of what development means. In analytical psychology, there have been 'two opposing strategies' (Papadopoulos, 1997, p. 298) which connect Jung with the academy: one is characterised by 'omnipotent expectations that academics accept the Jungian "wisdom" unquestionably' and the other is characterised by 'inappropriate efforts to fit Jung within an unsuitable paradigm of science' (ibid., p. 297). The former might be seen as a cult of personality and the latter as the removal from Jung's psychology of its distinctive character. Both attempts have failed to connect with academic discourses, and neither of them has obtained status within the academy. For this reason it could be suggested that a more beneficial way for analytical psychology to proceed could be to enter interdisciplinary debates, where no single approach has authority over others, and every approach could potentially make an equally valuable contribution to the debates through bringing its own expertise and value.

Still, one of the remaining problems would be that analytical psychology as a whole does not seem to have a unified identification with what is scientific, any more than with what is developmental. But for the purposes of interdisciplinary discussion, presenting analytical psychology as scientific may not be as important as conveying its unique perspective and connections with other perspectives. Showing how scientific or unscientific analytical psychology is in both old and new paradigms might connect its view with other discourses to deepen particular debates. But it often does not matter how an approach is labelled, for what matters is the content of the discussion, what analytical psychology can actually contribute theoretically and how it can change the ways the issues are dealt with.

Conclusion

This chapter has looked at some historical aspects of the emergence and continuation/extension/activities of the Developmental School. It has discussed the extent to which and the ways in which the Developmental School is developmental. It has also discussed what elements and rhetoric of development can be observed in analytical psychology.

Above all, in the work of the Developmental School, the word 'development' seems to stand for both 'child development' and 'scientific, technological development'. Child development is thought to be 'developmental' work, or work with children is thought to be pioneering work, involving a new approach, change, and scientific, technological development. However, because of the element of the *new* in the Developmental School, development as a metaphor and as an emblem seems to have dominated attention, and this makes it difficult to consider development as a concept or as an actual process.

There seems to be a tension between the ways in which images of development manifest in the theories and practices of analytical psychology. On the one hand, there seems to be a clear opposition to the dominant images of development, often represented as one-sidedness and mass-mindedness in Jung's understanding of the self and the individuation process. As discussed in Chapter 4, due to Jung's understanding of development which was distinctive and different from other psychologists in his time, it could be seen that in a way he cut himself off from others. On the other hand, in Fordham's approach there seems to be a welcoming inclusion of dominant images of development, frequently presented as much needed tools and methods. This has opened the doors of analytical psychology to many other fields by enabling it to present itself as more powerful than before through having acquired a dominant position – instead of remaining in an isolated position. Thus, in Jung, because of his strong disagreement with the dominant views, there is scope for exploring what is specific to analytical psychology in its understanding and approaching development other than in terms of its dominant images. However, it is more difficult to find such scope in Fordham especially when he embraces the dominant images of development as strengths in his work.

Chapter 7

The children's rights movement and Fordham's work with children

Compared with Jung's theory of the individuation process, Fordham's theory of individuation in childhood has not been scrutinised in wider contexts outside analytical psychology. Jung's psychology involves and has been discussed in terms of natural science, social science, and the humanities: biology, physics, phenomenology, epistemology, politics, gender, feminism, racism, theology, philosophy, alchemy, Gnosticism, religion (Christianity, Judaism, Buddhism), mythology, Eastern thought, the arts, literature, and many other disciplines and issues. Jung's theory of individuation has been discussed in the above contexts independently or in combination with other disciplines. In contrast, Fordham's theory has been discussed in very few contexts and in a narrow range of ways.

This chapter explores connections between Fordham's theory and an interdisciplinary issue related to children's rights, which involves not only psychology but also law, sociology, politics, economics, education, and many other academic disciplines as well as various kinds of practical work with children.

In analytical psychology, a one-patterned narrative of children and childhood seems to have been predominant. Fordham's critical account of Jung's view of children and childhood, that is to say, that Jung neglected actual children in favour of the child archetype, has been widely accepted in analytical psychology. Fordham subsequently drew attention to actual children through his own understanding of such concepts as the self and individuation. (This is not to deny that there were some who disagreed with Fordham's departure.) Fordham's concept of the primary self could be explained biologically or metaphorically and his idea of individuation in childhood could be demonstrated clinically as well as theoretically. The primary self is described through an analogy with DNA (Astor, 1995, p. 147) or with a fertilised egg (Urban, 1992, pp. 414–15), which, on the one hand, has all the potential for becoming what it will be, and, on the other, is deintegrating and reintegrating from the beginning through interaction with the environment. Many followers of Fordham at the Society of Analytical Psychology elaborated on primarily theoretical and clinical explanations of individuation in childhood, which contributed to the establishment of child therapy within analytical psychology (for instance, Astor, 1995; Sidoli and Davies, 1988; Urban, 1992, 1994, 1998).

Fordham's theory has been invoked almost exclusively in relation to Jung's view of children and childhood, but there has not been much discussion which critically reviews Fordham's account. The implications of Fordham's theory for various interdisciplinary areas have yet to be explored. Some post-Jungians, such as Samuels and Hauke, have made connections in terms of historical or social contexts. Samuels (1994) considers Fordham's model of the infant in relation to the relationship between individuals and states. Hauke ([1994] 1996) considers Fordham's as well as Jung's models of the child in relation to the image of children in the modern world. I shall here attempt to examine Fordham's theory in relation to the children's rights movement, an area in which there seems to be some significant correspondences. The children's rights movement is one of many potential contexts in which Fordham's theory could be examined.

The children's rights movement is relevant in the way that it reflects images of children and childhood, which is a controversial issue in both Jung's and Fordham's work. Specifically, comparable issues arise from consideration of children's rights and of children's individuality, the latter of which is the keynote of Fordham's theorisation. I do not attempt to make any definite statements about the value of Fordham's theory in social or historical contexts. Rather, I shall simply suggest an aspect of Fordham's work which could be seen from a new angle and in relation to debates about children and childhood in wider social and historical contexts.

The aim of this chapter, then, is to discuss the implications of Fordham's emphasis on individuation in childhood in the light of the children's rights movement. Specifically, I shall focus on the implications of Fordham's claims about the individuality of children. I shall discuss similarities not only in the kind of contributions they can make but also in the controversies to which they give rise. I shall also discuss the strengths and weaknesses of Fordham's work for the discussion of the images of children and childhood in comparison and contrast with the narratives that have emerged from the children's rights movement. Finally, I shall look at Jung's view of children and childhood and how this might reflect the images examined through children's rights.[1]

What does Fordham mean by the *individuality* of children in his theory of individuation in childhood?

The significance of Fordham's work with children is widely recognised: generally, his pioneering a marginalised field in both the theory and practice of analytical psychology, and specifically, his bringing actual children into the picture. Before his own work, Fordham argued, there was no Jungian analyst who was interested in children, and therefore he was working on his own for a long time (Fordham, 1994, p. vi).

In analytical psychology, Fordham was also a pioneer in claiming that children have *individuality*. He writes: 'The unity [the primary self] of the infant expresses his *individuality* and . . . it could provide the motivation for individuation' (1985b, p. 90; emphasis added). Fordham formulated his theory of individuation in childhood in terms of his concepts of the primary self and the action of the self, that is to say, deintegration and reintegration. He describes here the primary self as 'a state of unity', 'a primary unity of the self', and the 'primary integrated state', out of which the new-born baby comes into relation with his mother by means of deintegration (ibid.). However, what is the individuality which motivates individuation in Fordham's account?

Fordham sees children as, psychologically, separate individuals. Accordingly, his claim for the individuality of children could be explained in terms of:

1   subjectivity (as opposed to having no distinction between subject and object, or as opposed to being an object of an other's psychology);
2   independence or separation from parents (as opposed to dependence on or fusion with parents);
3   personality or individuality (as opposed to not being separated from collective or archaic aspects).

All these characteristics are intertwined.

Concerning the subjectivity of children, Fordham sees children as the subjects of their needs, relationships, and environments, while, in Fordham's view, Jung and many other psychologists see children's needs on the basis of their dependence on their parents. Fordham states:

> almost from birth, they [babies] seem to create conditions for a good feeding experience. Some also [seem] to have a capacity, by giving remarkably precise signals, almost to show a hesitant mother how to establish a good feeding relationship by supporting and drawing out the capacities of a mother uncertain of her mothering functions.
>
> (1985b, p. 49)

Fordham regards these actions as 'actions of the self' and not as the ego adapting the infant to the infant's physical and emotional conditions (ibid.).

Concerning the independence of children, Fordham sees children as persons separate from their parents, while, in Fordham's view, Jung and many other psychologists see children as integrally and psychologically connected with their parents. Frieda Fordham argues that Michael Fordham's 'discovery that self symbols were to be found in early childhood' (1969, p. 117) is opposed to 'Jung's view that child and parent are as one', just as it is to Winnicott's emphasis that 'There is no such thing as a baby . . . A baby cannot exist alone, but is essentially part of a relationship' (Winnicott, 1964, p. 88).

Concerning personality, Michael Fordham questions: 'Is it going too far to state that a baby is, in the sense of self, acutely personal from the start and later on develops a non-personal relation to objects needed for ego development?' (1985b, p. 49). He writes that it does not seem 'the collective unconscious . . . becomes a significant element in a child's life until his psychic structures have developed sufficiently for him to become related to the wider society outside his family' (ibid.). This contradicts Jung's view that children are in a state of mind characterised by primitive identity, what Lévy-Bruhl calls *participation mystique*, that is to say, non-differentiation between conscious and unconscious, between subject and object, between 'I' and other. For 'Jung did not think that a child could be a personality . . . before the fourth or fifth year' (F. Fordham, 1969, p. 116). Fordham does not believe in a stage of primitive identity and maintains that 'Being an individual from the start, individuation becomes realization of his condition through the development of self representations' (M. Fordham, 1985b, p. 54).

Fordham's claim about the individuality of children certainly introduces new elements into analytical psychology. As we have seen earlier, it has generated debates about Fordham's deviation from Jung and subsequent political tensions within analytical psychology, on the one hand, and the narratives of Fordham's success and significant contribution to analytical psychology, on the other. However, the meaning of 'individuality' within Fordham's model is yet to be explored in a wider context outside analytical psychology.

In what way is the children's rights movement useful for the discussion of Fordham's work with children?

Children's rights issues are often closely linked with images of children and childhood. Looking at both the change and continuity of images of children and childhood could help us review Fordham's and Jung's views of children and childhood. An approach to Fordham's work in contexts wider than the comparisons between Fordham and Jung might enrich the ongoing debates in analytical psychology as a whole.

First, the children's rights movement could be seen as a reflection of images of childhood. Philip Veerman argues that 'The way children are conceptualised in society creates what we call the *Image of Childhood* of that particular society' (1992a, p. 398). In his systematic study, Veerman attempts to demonstrate that 'ideas concerning the rights of children are strictly dependent on the prevailing "Image of Childhood" ' (ibid., p. 398), in other words, 'ideas on children's rights are expressions of an image of childhood of the beholder' (ibid., p. xv). Likewise, could we consider that ideas on children's individuality are an expression of the image of childhood of the beholder?

Veerman reports as the major finding of his study that *'there has been a change in the image of childhood as reflected in ideas of children's rights'* (ibid., p. 398; emphasis in original). Could we consider that changes in the image of childhood are also reflected in ideas of children's individuality? Freeman also writes about change in the history of childhood:

> Children's rights have been argued about for well over a century, and by a variety of different professionals with different perspectives. A century is a short time span in the history of childhood but even within the last century or so we can observe the different values that have attached to children at particular historical moments.
>
> (1992a, p. 3)

There is also the view of childhood as a relative concept. Geraldine Van Bueren argues that 'the international law on the rights of the child reflects a variety of cultural traditions' (1995, p. xxi). She asks 'whether the specific nature of children has been consistent over a period of time or whether the concept of childhood has changed dramatically' (ibid., p. 5). She argues that 'Childhood is a relative concept which changes according to local culture, the geographical environment and the prevailing social and economic conditions' (ibid., p. 6). Moreover, Veerman refers to the first International Interdisciplinary Study-Group on Ideologies of Children's Rights, which reflected upon the children's rights movement (1992b, p. 357). The group argued that the concept of childhood is 'both historically and culturally relative' (ibid.), complementing the view of the Scandinavian School of Legal Realism that ' "rights" are merely beliefs of people and expressions of feelings' (ibid.). Could we then consider that 'individuality' as conceptualised within analytical psychology is a relative concept insofar as the concept of childhood is relative?

However, not only changes but also continuity in the history of childhood are observed, and some argue that continuity is more significant than changes. Hugh Cunningham (1995) observes continuity as well as patterns of change in both the conceptualisation and the experience of childhood, as these interact with economic developments and public policies. Likewise, Veerman argues that 'Although Children's Rights documents often reflect temporary political and economic circumstances . . . some issues in the field of Children's Rights are of an enduring nature' (1992a, p. 397). Linda Pollock (1983) takes much more account of continuity than of change in the history of childhood as well as in the lives of actual parents and children. She writes: 'There have been very few changes in parental care and child life from the 16th to 19th century in the home, apart from social changes and technological improvements' (ibid., p. 268). Could we then consider that children's individuality similarly has some persisting characteristics?

There is a parallel between the rights of children and the individuality of children. The children's rights movement has raised precise questions about our images of childhood and attitudes toward children, some of which have not been, but usefully could be, asked by those working in analytical psychology. Veerman writes: 'The concepts "right" and "child" are themselves subject to change, and we need the participation of philosophers of law and historians of childhood to explain to what extent this has influenced our present thinking on children's rights' (1992b, p. 358). He continues: 'An important input has to be made by developmental psychologists, since their insight in developmental stages and needs of children is essential. Other disciplines are equally important' (ibid.). Narratives of the children's rights movement involve many controversial issues regarding child development and human development, to which analytical psychology could contribute.

Discussion: Fordham's work with children in the light of the children's rights movement

In order to examine the implications of Fordham's claims about the individuality of children, I shall examine the significant similarities and differences between Fordham's work and the children's rights movement. In this section, I shall discuss seven issues:

1   the rights of children and the individuality of children;
2   the wall between children and adults, the wall between childhood and adulthood;
3   public and private lives of children and childhood;
4   needs and rights, needs and individuality;
5   ideology and profession;
6   universality and diversity;
7   relativity of children's rights, and relativity of children's individuality.

The discussions aim to identify debatable issues and articulate questions rather than provide immediate answers.

The rights of children and the individuality of children

One of the significant contributions could be that both Fordham and the children's rights movement reacted to the marginality of children from adult society, and they both brought children into the picture. It might be useful to look at some of the historical background.

The Declaration on the Rights of the Child, known as the Declaration of Geneva, was adopted by the League of Nations in 1924.[2] This was the first international human rights Declaration adopted by any inter-governmental organisation (Van Bueren, 1995, p. 6). The Declaration reflected the effort of an English teacher, Eglantyne Jebb,[3] who established the committee of the Save the Children Fund in 1919, and then, with the assistance of the International Committee of the Red Cross, the Save the Children International Union in 1920. She had had prior experiences of and had taken actions on behalf of children victimised during World War I.[4] In 1959, the Declaration on the Rights of the Child was passed by the United Nations General Assembly. In 1989, the Convention on the Rights of the Child was adopted by the United Nations General Assembly, and since then has been signed by all countries in the world apart from the USA and Somalia. The Convention asserts the equality of the child as a rights holder and views children's rights in terms of what was to be called the four Ps, i.e., protection, prevention, provision, and participation (Fottrell, 1999). The inclusion of participation rights signalled the newly emerged image of children as competent and autonomous individuals whereas before they were seen mainly as vulnerable and in need of adults' protection.

Since 1934, Fordham had been working as a psychiatrist for several child guidance clinics and he continued to do so during and after World War II. He published his first book *The Life of Childhood* in 1944 (revised as *Children as Individuals* in 1969), which included his experiences and some cases at these clinics. He produced numerous articles and books on the theme of individuation in childhood until his death in 1995. He also set up the Child Analytic Training and infant observation at the SAP (see Chapter 6). Arguably, through his work with children, he rescued their psychological state from its passive status in relation to adults, and through his theory of individuation in childhood he encouraged children's active participation in their own psychological lives.

The children's rights movement made children legal subjects. Likewise, Fordham made children psychological subjects. Freeman argues that children became legal subjects, while they were previously objects of intervention (1992b, p. 30). Veerman also argues that children became subjects of rights, whose opinion is voiced and asked for, while they were previously objects of rights in need of protection (1992a, p. 396). Likewise, Fordham's model shows that children are subjects of their own psychology, which is to be seen as separate from their parents' psychology. Formerly, they tended to be seen as objects of psychotherapeutic treatment, or rather, objects of parental problems which were in need of treatment.

The wall between children and adults, the wall between childhood and adulthood

Fordham's work and the children's rights movement make both similar contributions and display similar contradictions. It seems that both Fordham and Jebb reacted in a similar heroic way to the marginality of children and childhood. However, did their claims about the individuality and the rights of children share an underlying ideology? Michael King observes two types of supporters of children's rights. The one is 'child-savers' and the other is 'kiddy-libbers' whose aim is to set children free (1985, p. 49). According to King, child-savers see children as 'weak innocents in need of protection from the superior strength and experience of adults and from corruption and exploitation at their hands' and try to preserve the wall between children and adults and between childhood and adulthood, or even to build a new wall between them (ibid.). Cunningham observes, in support of King, that ' "saving the child" came to take on a dominant meaning of preserving for the child what was thought of as a proper childhood; and this implied a childhood separated from the adult world in innocence and dependence' (1995, p. 188). Cunningham illustrates one way of 'saving the child' as rescuing children from the labour market, which became the aim of innumerable voluntary organisations in the nineteenth and early twentieth centuries. Like child-savers, in King's terms, or like child protectionists, then, did Fordham try to keep the distinction between children and adults, and between childhood and adulthood? Did Fordham primarily consider children as innocent and vulnerable, and in need of adult protection?

On the other hand, kiddy-libbers, as King calls them, or child liberationists try to break down the wall between children and adults, and between childhood and adulthood. Although they see children as being incompetent, they agree that, liberated from adult domination, they could become responsible and competent at a much earlier age than is the case at present (King, 1985, p. 49). Veerman also writes that they want not only to grant children more rights but also to wipe out all borders between childhood and adulthood (1992a, p. 133). Their work is usually seen as part of the children's liberation movement, whose primary concern is with autonomy and self-determination, for which age is irrelevant. Cunningham supports this:

> Children have begun to acquire rights which bring them closer to adults rather than separate them from them ... Statements of the rights of children now put the emphasis not only on protection of children, but also on children's rights to a degree of self-determination, an emphasis which thoroughly muddies the earlier attempt to separate out the worlds of adults and children.
>
> (1995, p. 189)

Did Fordham, like child liberationists, attempt to break down the distinction between children and adults, and between childhood and adulthood?

Moreover, critiques point out the limits of the distinction between children and adults. Freeman argues that those who regard children as different, having lesser abilities and capacities, being more vulnerable, and needing nurture and protection, could justify the double standard in our social practices and laws with 'one set of rights for adults (providing them with opportunities to exercise their powers) and another for children (providing them with protection and at the same time keeping them under adult control)' (1992b, p. 34). However, Freeman also argues that the same double standard could be unjust in cases where age is irrelevant. Nevertheless, the problem is that any line drawn between children and adults is arbitrary. He writes that 'no one can seriously believe there is a real distinction (in powers, competence, etc.) between someone of 18 years and a day and someone of 17 years and 364 days' (ibid., p. 35). He points out that the law dislikes uncertainty and tends to think in dichotomies of guilty/not guilty, liable/not liable, male/female, and categorises persons into adults and minors; the former with full capacity and the latter with little or none (ibid.). Was, then, Fordham aware of the limits of attempts to make a clear distinction between children and adults, and between childhood and adulthood?

It seems that Fordham was not entirely a child-saver or child protectionist, because he does not seem to agree with the child-savers' view of the distinction between children and adults, and between childhood and adulthood. For in some respects he attempted to break down the wall between them, maintaining that individuation is not only for the second half of life but also for childhood. He states: 'the basic underlying process of individuation in infancy, childhood, adolescence, and adulthood is identical' (1985b, p. 92). However, he was not entirely a kiddy-libber or child liberationist either, because in some respects he accepts the distinction between children and adults, and childhood and adulthood. He writes:

> Though it is true that infants and small children can take part in and influence the formation of their environment, it is not until adolescence that children are sufficiently independent to make much impact on society; then it is their identity conflicts that become dynamically acute as they struggle to find their place in society.
>
> (1994, p. 115)

Fordham admits that a small child or infant is different from adults, pointing out that children are involved in different forms of identification which are based on their parents (ibid.). For this reason, he argues, individuals in later life do not become children again when social identifications break down but become childlike through establishing a relation to the child archetype by means of regression (ibid.).

Moreover, Fordham does not explain when and how the primary self turns into the self. This could be understood either as a clear distinction between childhood and adulthood, the primary self belonging to the former and the self belonging to the latter, or as implying no distinction between childhood and adulthood inasmuch as the self remains throughout. (In the latter case, however, Fordham says that the self is found in childhood as well as in adulthood, but he does not say that the primary self is found in adulthood as well as in childhood.) Therefore, Fordham seems inconsistent in the way he viewed the distinction between children and adults, and childhood and adulthood. In one way, emphasising the importance of children's *individuality* seems to imply that children shall be taken as seriously as adults, while emphasising the importance of *children*'s individuality suggests that there should be special category of individuality applied to children. Consequently, a question remains: is children's individuality the same as adults' individuality?

Public and private lives of children and childhood

Fordham's theory has not provided an equivalent vocabulary for each of the well-established discussions in the children's rights movement. However, it is at least useful to apply the debates on images of children and childhood to Fordham's theory in order to point out its strengths and weaknesses. I shall begin by identifying the specific emphases of Fordham's interests and discussing his possible purpose in arguing for the individuality of children.

Cunningham makes a distinction between 'children' and 'childhood', with the former referring to 'human beings' and the latter to 'a shifting set of ideas' (1995, p. 1). Likewise, Pollock makes a distinction between 'attitudes to children' and a 'concept of childhood' (1983, p. 4). Fordham, in contrast, did not make such a distinction. What he distinguished was primarily Jung's and his own views of children and childhood. Fordham did not explicitly take account of childhood as a general, public set of images, even though he might in part have been influenced by these images.

Cunningham also makes a distinction between the histories of the private life and the public life of children and childhood (1995, p. 187); that is to say, between the 'emotional quality of the lives of children' (ibid., p. 2) and the 'public policies toward children' (ibid.). In the 1960s and early 1970s, he observes, 'the history of childhood consisted far too exclusively of a study of public policies towards children' (ibid., p. 187), while in more recent years 'anything outside the private sphere' has been ignored (ibid.). He suggests examining the history in terms of interactions between 'economic developments, public policies and ways of imagining the world', on the one hand, and 'thinking about childhood and the experience of being a child', on the other (ibid.). For both 'ideas about childhood' (as a set of ideas) and the 'experience of being a child' (as a phase of life) 'have been primarily economic and demographic, and, in the second place, political' (ibid., p. 3). Fordham, in contrast, was not concerned with the public life of children and childhood. His work was not concerned with the economic or political conditions of children under any kind of authority, power, control, or regulations other than those of the parents.

However, Fordham's strengths lie in his account of the private lives of children. He was concerned with both parents' and children's emotional life. Astor writes that Fordham's approach was 'thinking about and working on emotional experience', an approach which Fordham regarded as 'scientific' (Astor, 1996, p. 22). It should be noted here that emotional life does not always mean the same thing in different narratives. What historians of children and childhood mean by that predominantly concerns parental love. There are criticisms that 'recent historical writing about children has actually been more to do with parents than with children' (Cunningham, 1995, p. 2). However, Fordham's concern with emotional life was not solely about love, i.e., parental love or children's love toward their parents. As a psychoanalyst, he offered a richer vocabulary for describing emotional life, and therefore has much to offer to the discussion about psychological aspects of children's lives. In debates about the children's rights movement, 'quality of life' has been discussed much further in terms of not only physical conditions but also non-material conditions including psychological aspects, and its meaning has been extended accordingly.

Fordham was interested not only in other children's private lives but also his own. Adults' experiences, memories, and images of their own childhood could play a part in forming the view of contemporary children and of childhood in general. However, this is not usually an issue in the children's rights movement. The major difference of Fordham from the children's rights movement here would be in the degree of their self-reflective attitudes. The general rule for professionals not to mix any private childhood issues with public interests in children seems to apply both to those who are concerned with children's rights issues and to Fordham who was concerned with children's psychological well-being. However, the level of awareness and insight gained from attending to one's own psychological process can make a significant difference. In analysis or therapy, the analyst or the therapist is trained to be aware of his or her own issues and therefore might be able to distinguish the analysand's or the client's issues from his or her own. But in other circumstances, even though people have their own issues and these issues are not supposed to interfere with their professional acts, they do affect them and yet are not attended to, as though they do not exist. Having said that, it is of course still possible that unconscious processes can affect anyone, even analysts or therapists in relation to their clients or analysands. Astor points out the shift of Fordham's work from 'demonstrating the impact of archetypal images on child development' to emphasising 'more the affective state of the child in the consulting room in relation to him' (1996, p. 16). Fordham writes of the value of continuing analysis of the delusional transference:

> In health, the creative and destructive deintegrates of the self are required for growth, so even when we deal with pathology there must be a question as to whether it is empathic, in the deeper sense of the term, to repair the good aspects of the self at the cost of leaving the bad ones untransformed. So it is not enough to act as a reflector (mirror transference), it is necessary to take in (projective identification) and metabolize the

material by digestion until it can be returned to the patient in the form of interpretation usable by the patient.

(1985b, p. 160)

Although Fordham speaks only in relation to delusional transference, where a patient has a very rigid and fixed idea about the analyst, delusional counter-transference could also be possible. Fordham might have been successful as an experienced analyst in distinguishing the patient's childhood issues from his own. But as his personal materials are always there in the unconscious, it is quite possible that he developed delusional countertransference, where the analyst's personal issues are projected onto the patient in the session.

To what extent might Fordham's attitude towards his own childhood have contributed to or affected his work with children? Fordham often expressed his frustration with his personal analysis with Godwin Baynes and Hilde Kirsch for not gaining understanding of unresolved childhood issues (see Chapter 6). Fordham's analysis with Baynes was published in Baynes' *Mythology of the Soul* ([1940] 1969) (Fordham, 1993b, p. 71). In Baynes' book, the reader might hope to find reference to some of the unresolved elements of Fordham's childhood. However, no such references are apparent, since Baynes does not touch upon Fordham's personal life apart from his paintings. What Baynes is concerned with are the mythical themes that appeared in Fordham's paintings and what Fordham said about the paintings, rather than Fordham himself. Baynes' interpretation does not deal with transference and counter-transference. Perhaps Fordham was right to be dissatisfied with these deficiencies of transference analysis and the analysis of his own childhood by Baynes. One gets the impression that Fordham's case as presented by Baynes is not about two persons' communication but about Baynes' attempt to make Fordham's paintings mythically alive in his interpretation. For instance, Baynes frequently refers to nail-biting, which the reader might expect must refer to Fordham's behaviour in the analysis. However, it emerges that this refers to motifs identified in the paintings and associated with 'onanistic libido frustration' ([1940] 1969, p. 232) or an 'infantile fantasy of self-fertilization' (ibid., p. 282). Joseph Henderson writes in the preface to this book that 'two main themes of special interest to which Baynes seemed always to return' were 'how the methods of depth psychology could be applied to the treatment of schizophrenia and to the interpretation of schizophrenic-like products of modern art' (ibid., p. xii). It could be understood, then, that what Baynes wanted to approach with the methods of depth psychology was the 'schizophrenic Fordham' and his 'schizophrenic-like products'. Baynes accepted Fordham's material in place of payment for the analysis, since Fordham was not able to pay much at that time and Baynes wanted to use the material in a book he was writing (Fordham, 1993b, p. 71). Fordham writes: 'It was not a satisfactory solution: one disadvantage was that I felt obliged to keep on producing pictures to keep up payments!' (ibid.). Baynes, in contrast, argues:

> In so far as the intruding factors often have the character of archaic contents actually belonging to the remote childhood of the human race, they cannot be dealt with as mere personal belongings. Such factors are best expressed in the universal idiom of the myth, just because they are universal psychic elements. And because of their universality they also contain a superior energy-content or value, which demands a special kind of treatment.
>
> ([1940] 1969, pp. 509–10)

It appears that Baynes' focus was on the archaic sphere of the psyche rather than the personal sphere. Moreover, Baynes presents Fordham's attitude in analysis as evidence of the conscious resistance brought about by his immediate experience of the unconscious (ibid., p. 510):

> While the patient [Fordham] was producing these pictures he understood little of their psychological content. Being in a highly reactive, almost mediumistic condition, when I tried to provide him with a theoretical standpoint from which he might be able to view his experience from a more detached position, he was unable for a time to make use of it. It is indeed often the case that the activation of the primordial, myth-making psyche is liable to produce a temporary intellectual eclipse.
>
> (ibid., p. 509)

According to Baynes, full conscious reception of symbolic experience such as Fordham's may take many years (ibid., p. 511). However, Fordham's evaluation of this analysis shows no sign of having changed when he came to write his autobiography, published two years before his death. For Baynes, it seems, Fordham remained a schizophrenic, and for Fordham, Baynes' analysis remained mythic. Their aims and foci were different and, accordingly, the place of childhood in analysis was missing in their views. As Baynes writes, 'however the methods may differ in form, the reintegration of the total personality is the fundamental goal of every effective treatment' (ibid., p. 510). For Baynes, the analysis was a treatment, but for Fordham it was not. Fordham's interest in childhood analysis in terms of transference and countertransference does involve normal cases as well as pathological cases. Above all, while Fordham sought to understand his childhood, Baynes did not. This might provide us with a perspective for understanding why Fordham came to show such passion for exploring the psyches of children; for he would also have been gaining understanding of his own childhood issues.

What both Fordham and the literature on the children's rights movement acknowledge is the view of children as subjects, and, accordingly, the private or emotional life of children. Children are not seen as mere passive entities in any sense: they do not have to be victimised or pathologised. The view of children as agents is central in child psychotherapy and more and more the inclusion of children's own views and voices is encouraged in children's rights discourses.

However, whereas children's rights are concerned with children's relationships with both parents and state policy, Fordham saw children predominantly in relation to parents and did not explicitly register state policy as a wider social factor in children's lives. What seems needed in Fordham's account is, on the one hand, a view of childhood as a set of ideas and, on the other, a perspective on children in connection with state policy both as a form of authority, power, and control and as a representation of social, economic, and political phases of life. Nevertheless, what Fordham was particularly concerned with while the children's rights movement was not, is the view of childhood as adults' experience, memories, and images of their own childhood. Of course, Fordham's account of childhood will need to be explained more fully outside the context of analytical psychology, for instance, in terms of its difference from the views of other psychoanalysts such as Freud and Klein – though this is not a task that can be taken up here.

Needs and rights, needs and individuality

There have been many discussions about the similarity between children's rights and developmental needs.[5] Veerman writes that 'Rights are based on some "quality of life" notion conceptualised in different terms, such as lists of needs or end results' (1992a, p. 57). Likewise, could the individuality of children be explained in terms of developmental needs?

Discussions about children's rights and needs offer at least two different kinds of narratives. One kind concerns different levels of rights and needs. Veerman argues that 'in regions and times of poverty the [Children's Rights] Movement focuses mainly on the physical aspects of life, whereas more wealth results in demands for non-material rights for children' (ibid., p. 398). Freeman writes that the distinction between the two approaches to children's rights, between the 'nurturance' and 'self-determination' orientations, has now been widely recognised (1992b, p. 30). It appears that there are different emphases on children's rights and needs in terms of their survival or their social and psychological well-being. As a consequence, some might interpret individuality as part of human rights.

Generally, Fordham talks about deintegration and reintegration of the primary self in a physical sense as well as psychological sense. But they are not necessarily placed at the opposite ends of a spectrum; rather, they are seen as occurring in parallel. For Fordham, there is no distinction drawn between physical and psychological deintegration and reintegration: even though children's individuality is primarily a psychological concept, it does not need to be separated from physical experiences, whether at the level of survival or self-realisation. Nevertheless, to what extent his idea of children's individuality overlaps with children's needs remains arguable. Speaking about both biological and psychological needs, Fordham touches upon biological needs as well as needs of the personality in relation to individuation. He writes: 'Family life can be understood as a means not only of satisfying biological (instinctual) needs, but also as a way of realising individuating processes in the personalities of the parents' (1994, p. 113). He explains the need for further individuation in terms of the need for parents to understand each other's needs by withdrawing certain archetypal images, and claims that the adolescence of children is a testing time for the parents. Fordham's concern with the needs of personality here is expressed only in relation to parents' individuation and not children's individuation. However, he is also concerned with psychological needs from the children's viewpoint. He writes:

> in many cases the force of the child's needs impels him to seek out the failures of his parents, and raise them to monstrous proportions and if, later on, it becomes apparent that his family was not worse than others, then it can be the structure of society that is at fault.
>
> (1985b, p. 158)

In this way Fordham does include society as part of children's environment, but for him, what kind of impact society makes upon children is not an issue.

The other kind of narratives about children's rights and needs concerns the connection between personal and public interests of children. The rights of children to be protected fitted well in the efforts of both child-savers, whose interests were in providing children with a 'happy childhood', and states, whose interests were in securing the future of society as this was projected onto children (Cunningham, 1995, pp. 159–62). There was an 'investment motive'[6] behind children's rights, that is to say, society's concern was with children's usefulness to society (Freeman, 1992b, p. 30). The notion of children's rights has also shifted from being a charitable towards being a political concept (Veerman, 1992a, p. 396). For instance, the public activities of Jebb started with her founding the Save the Children's Fund, which was a voluntary organisation and therefore viewed as a charity, and ended with her involvement in drafting the Declaration of Geneva, which was adopted by the League of Nations (ibid.). Veerman argues that 'in the beginning of the Century concerns concentrated mainly on *physical safety and security*, whereas nowadays *inter-actional processes* between the individual child as carrier of a social role, and adult institutions are in focus' (1992a, p. 398; emphasis in original). Freeman agrees that whereas the child-saving movement was concerned with individual children in terms of salvation and protection, the issue of the children's rights movement has now moved from a shortfall in parental or other adult behaviour to institutional discrimination (1992b, p. 30). The body of advocators of children's rights has become institutionalised and internationalised, and therefore a greater social and political dimension has been added to individual interest (Veerman, 1992a, p. 396). Having shifted from individual efforts to protect individual children to institutional efforts to uphold the rights of children in general, a situation has arisen in which this global range of rights is 'beyond a child's perception' (ibid., p. 396) and the scope needs to be narrowed down, again, to 'an individual level' (ibid., p. 397).

In Fordham's theory, children's individuality is not something to be fulfilled by adults or parents. So individuation in childhood remains a personal issue as much as a universal phenomenon. In analytical psychology, the individuality of children was first seen as Fordham's personal interest. However, his personal interest has survived as a profession. Earlier, I connected Fordham's interest in children's individuality with his unsatisfactory experience of his personal analysis, in which his childhood was not properly analysed, but it is hard to distinguish what is personal and not professional. Another question arises as to whether and in what respect there were any kinds of support which reinforced Fordham's interest in children and helped to establish his interest as a profession.

Connected with the link between personal and public interest in children, it appears that the needs of children are often defined by various interests of individuals or groups of adults which are not necessarily the interests of children themselves. I shall discuss this further in relation to ideology and profession in the next section.

Ideology and profession

From the literature of the children's rights movement, we can learn about the danger of popular narratives becoming *fashion*. Veerman writes:

> Never in history has so much attention been paid to Children's Rights as in our own times ... This growing recognition and popularity of Children's Rights, however, is not free from the danger of becoming *a fashion*. It may well be in the spotlight for a certain period but be left in the dark again when the spotlight switches to another subject. It is therefore the task of the children's rights movement to provide a secure foundation for its work.
>
> (1992a, p. 400)

Fordham's interest in and work with children might have been just a fashion and not have survived, if his personal contribution was not integrated in an institution, that is to say, the SAP. The question is: what helped Fordham's work to survive as a profession? The answer could be sought in terms of timing, environment, and connections. First, Fordham's first step in analytical psychology seemed to be timely: he was working with children in the post-war years when there was widespread concern about children's welfare. Second, the general climate and its atmosphere could have been supportive for any work concerning children's conditions and their lives. Viewed in wider social and political contexts, his personal interests might have connected with others' interests in children: those in other professions such as child psychologists, child psychotherapists, social workers and educators as well as the general public. Third, Fordham also had good personal and professional connections with other doctors and psychoanalysts whose expertise was in work with children. Fordham, together with Klein, Winnicott, Bowlby and other child analysts and child therapists, might be seen as partly representative of the prevailing post-war concern about both 'our' future society and 'our' children. There must have also been many Jungian analysts who felt the necessity of focusing on children and childhood. Fordham always tested what he found in his work against Jung's theory, and he was keen on producing 'Jungian' narratives. His connection with the Tavistock Clinic also helped establish the child training at the SAP. What is distinctive about Fordham's work as a profession would be the combination of these various connections. However, the Child Analytic Training (CAT) at the SAP ceased in 2006, due to the difficulties brought about by the linking of child psychotherapy training with NHS training posts.[7] Accordingly, the Children's Section at the SAP has been discontinued, though infant observation seminars will continue (Urban, personal communication, 2007). The question now is whether the idea of the individuality of children will continue to be appreciated in analytical psychology or might gradually cede to other ideas.

Not only is there a danger of children's rights becoming a fashion, there is also a danger of professions defining a particular ideology under the name of children's needs, rights, individuality, and the like. Critics see this kind of assertion as 'a political statement masquerading in the guise of a psychological truth' (King, 1985, p. 51). The underlying message is that only the professionals have the 'expertise to identify and spell out for the benefit of the world what children of all ages and cultures needed in order to become "psychologically sound adults"' (ibid.). The same argument may apply to child psychoanalysts and psychotherapists. It is arguable to what extent, in the context of therapy, the whole psychoanalytic and psychodynamic approach based on the unconscious allows the therapist to interpret what goes on in the child's mind. In fact, some psychotherapists and clinical psychologists do carefully consider children's rights specifically in psychotherapy (Halasz, 1996; Seagull, 1978). This is effectively an acknowledgement of the limits of the authority of the child analysts or therapists. However, it is questionable whether Fordham was aware of this danger for his profession of making a statement from an ideological position and locating it in a political context. What critics maintain is that the discourses about the psychological or emotional needs and rights of children make 'ideological assumptions about (a) the sort of adults these children ought to grow up to be and (b) the sort of society and the sorts of values they, the advocates of children's needs and rights, wish to promote' (King, 1985, p. 51). This could also apply to the individuality of children. However, Fordham's ideology or his professional position in relation to public views about children are unclear, unlike many other psychologists who have been the targets of these critiques. He did not attempt to clearly define the individuality of children. This leaves us with the question: what kind of ideology or principle supports today's work of the Developmental School of analytical psychology? Could exploring this question weaken or strengthen Fordham's approach to children's psyche and individuality?

Universality and diversity

Let us now look at Fordham's model of a baby in terms of his assumptions about a child. In Fordham's model, a baby has neither gender nor ethnicity (Samuels, personal communication, 2000). Questions arise as to what kind of political impact Fordham's model of a baby made and what discourses it has generated in analytical psychology. Does the same kind of debate concerning the universality of children's rights and the diversity of ideas about what children should be apply to Fordham's model and Jung's theory?

Some feminists and anti-racists might support Fordham's model of the baby, if we take a perspective that it assumes development proceeding regardless of the baby's gender, sex, race, and ethnicity. There is an argument supporting Kohut's model of ego-development from a feminist point of view, which could apply to Fordham's model of the baby. Christiane Brems sees Kohut's theory as a 'nonsexist' as well as a 'genderless theory of human development' (1991, p. 147). She explains: 'though Kohut proposed his theories in an upper middle class, male setting, he focused on a reexamination of basic human needs and values that was highly compatible with feminist values' (ibid., p. 146). She refers to nurturance and security as basic human needs which both feminists and self-psychologists value (ibid., p. 145) and argues that these characteristics have been perceived as feminine traits which are unnecessary and socially undesirable, because masculine traits, represented by scientific, logical, and rational endeavours, were believed to solve all human problems (ibid., p. 146). She presents self-psychology as 'a gender-free conceptualization of human mental health', since it does not deny unique individual difference among human beings (ibid., p. 158). Nevertheless, she cautiously recommends further exploration of self-psychological theory within the context of feminist thought, in order to clarify the full potential of self-psychology not as a gender-blind theory but an alternative genderless theory. This is also a crucial issue for Fordham: whether his theory is genderless or simply gender-blind.

The children's rights movement is concerned with issues of both universality and diversity, that is to say, the issues of applying universality to diversity and of recognising diversity universally. Veerman argues: 'The issue of *universality* of Children's Rights is important but complicated because it is difficult to reach consensus with many representatives of different ethnic backgrounds, nationalities and religions' (1992a, p. 397; emphasis in original). He points out that 'the' child, conceptualised in the Western World, especially in a Western monopoly of pedagogics, does not apply to a 'global village' of the whole world, which also includes children living in the so-called 'Third World' (ibid.). Adam Lopatka writes from a different perspective: 'It is worth stressing that the right to be different from others is now becoming recognised as a universal human right, and that respect for the rights of ethnic, religious and linguistic minorities is acquiring an ever greater importance'.[8] In attempting to achieve universality, diversity becomes an obstacle. But diversity can be universally recognised and respected, and this can universally sustain the diversity. Hence, children's rights have various implications for concepts of children, childhood, development, education, and other concepts involving issues of universality and diversity.

Likewise, Jung was concerned with both the universality of the collective unconscious and the diversity of the individuation process. However, his concern with both universality and diversity has also been controversial. When his statements about differences turn to women, primitive tribes, and Jews, Jung is sometimes seen as racist, sexist, and anti-Semitic.

Fordham, in contrast, escaped such critiques. However, his model does not specifically resolve the critiques of Jung as sexist or racist, though Fordham himself focused on the aspects of the human psyche which are common to everybody. Was Fordham sensitive to these political issues or merely negligent? Could his model of the baby be approved by feminists and anti-racists for implying that there are equal opportunities of development for women and any ethnic minority? Or, could Fordham's model be criticised by the children's rights movement for its one-sided claim to universality, not acknowledging the diversities of gender, sex, race, colour, ethnicity, religion, national or social origin, economic conditions, property, birth or other kinds of status?

Fordham is sometimes seen as so innovative as actually to be non-Jungian, because his interests reached beyond the traditional Jungian field. However, Fordham's uncertainty seems to lie in the same area as Jung's struggle, that is to say, the tension between the individual and collective. Jung's key theory of the collective unconscious and the archetypes is often characterised by universality and totality. This theory postulates a deeper layer of the psyche in all human beings, in addition to the personal unconscious and personal conflicts and complexes, which show only part of the psyche and not the whole psyche. Accordingly, when Jung comes to speak of individual differences, some critiques see this as problematic. In contrast, Fordham's major concern was with the individuality of children. However, his argument was not sensitive to the diversities that I have mentioned above but emphasised the actions of the self (the process of deintegration and reintegration) as universal characteristics of the baby whoever it was. Asserting the individuality of children, Fordham did not seem to be involved deeply in the discussion of individual differences, though he acknowledged, to a certain extent, that children have different backgrounds in terms of external environment. While Jung spelled out his view of differences as well as of universality and therefore laid himself open to criticism, the ideas underpinning Fordham's theory remain unclear. If Fordham had started discussing such diversities, he might have been challenged by the same kind of critiques as Jung. However, discourses about Fordham's work do not seem to explore the implications of his theory in this regard.

Even though attempts are made to deconstruct both Jung's and Fordham's theories in terms of their underpinning ideologies, there seem to be difficulties in doing so for different reasons. Jung's theory presents many aspects which are contradictory and paradoxical, while Fordham's theory does not seem to reveal much about where he comes from. Is there a possibility that the difficulties lie also in the fact that both Jung and Fordham point to objective facts or the objective psyche? Issues relating to subjectivity and objectivity will be explored further in the final chapter of this book.

Relativity of children's rights, relativity of children's individuality

In the children's rights movement discourses, concepts such as children's rights are often regarded as relative. This is considered to be problematic, when universal legislation tries to determine what children's rights should consist of, and yet diverse opinions keep suggesting the need for more flexibility and diversity. Does this apply to the concept of children's individuality held in analytical psychology?

When it comes to the concepts of children or children's rights, a dominant position in the debate seems to be taken by the social constructionist perspective that these concepts are the products of human meaning-making. For instance, Anna Davin argues: 'Ultimately childhood can only be defined in relative terms. The question "What is a child?" must be followed by further questions – in whose eyes? When? Where? What are the implications?' (1999, p. 33). Emphasis is often on the diversity of cultural practices and social values at particular times, which are seen to deeply underpin personal beliefs and ideology and to contribute to the human construction of meaning. For instance, Veerman argues: 'Concepts like "child", "rights" and "society" are tied to place and time. Therefore the concepts "children" and "children's rights" allude in fact to one specific interpretation of these concepts' (1992a, p. 398). Likewise, King argues that there is no universal consensus about the psychological needs of the child nor general agreement about the meaning of justice for children, which is a relative, not an absolute concept. He maintains that 'It depends for its interpretation on the particular ideological position held by its interpreters' (1985, p. 53). The same arguments may apply to the concept of children's individuality.

Others argue for relativity based not on personal or cultural views but on the changeability and dependence experienced in actual interactions with nature and other human beings in everyday life. Speaking of development, for instance, Lopatka argues:

> The life and development of each human being [are] conditioned by the development of other human beings with whom he or she has a direct or indirect relationship. This concerns both that person's contemporaries and the past generations to which the present one is heir. Like other living things, human beings live in the natural environment but they also have their own human environment, which they create.
>
> (Lopatka, 1992, p. 47)

Again, this may also apply to children's rights and individuality, where one's rights and individuality are involved in others' rights and individualities.

The claim that children have unconditional rights seems to be similar to Fordham's claim that children have individuality from the beginning of their lives. However, that the relativity of the concept of children's rights gets in the way when collective agreement is to be reached in the form of international legislation may not apply to children's individuality. Whereas rights require universal/collective agreement, individuality has no need to be agreed collectively. In Jung's view, in particular, individuality should go against unanimous ideas and mass-mindedness (1957). Whereas rights matter to society as much as to individual children, individuality should matter only to each child but not necessarily to others or to society. In other words, for determining the meaning and judging what is appropriate, while the outsider view matters to rights, the insider view matters to individuality. Therefore, unlike the relativity of rights, the relativity of individuality should not in itself cause any conflict between cultures.

Even though these concepts are relative to some extent, they seem, in some cases, to have acquired absolute power over the conscious mind, albeit such power itself may still be part of a social construction. In contemporary society, the word 'human rights' seems to hold a particular, irresistible power in itself, to which you cannot say 'no' (Kawai, personal communication, 2002). The word 'individuality' could have the same effect when used along with such terms as one's 'rights', 'autonomy', and 'quality of life' – particularly, when it comes to children. Dominant discourses about rights seem to carry a sense of being justified because they are based on a moral consensus. It seems ironic that the concept itself, which is considered to be the product of human meaning-making, could potentially take over our thinking process. Instead of accepting these concepts as socially constructed, exploring their archetypal qualities from an analytical psychological viewpoint might introduce a more challenging perspective into the debate.

Can Jung's view of children and childhood be updated?

Was Jung open-minded in his ideas about children, considering that he had flexible ideas about how the individuation process can take place differently for different persons? Or, were his ideas about children rigid and fixed? Jung's view of children and childhood could be seen in the context of the history of childhood, which also provides a perspective on some of the ideologies behind the children's rights movement. Jung's alleged lack of concern with children might be seen as his sharing a perspective with the world-view of the Middle Ages. Pollock writes: 'The history of childhood is an area dominated by myths . . . The worst of the myths have no substance and also provide a surer foundation on which to base more research on this topic' (1983, p. viii). The historian Philippe Ariès triggered off a discussion by saying that the idea of childhood did not exist in medieval society (1962, p. 463).[9] Some historians have taken up and elaborated his argument, but most have been sceptical of Ariès' claims (e.g., de Mause, 1974; Sears, 1986; Shahar, 1990). In particular, some recent scholars have pointed out that there are both continuities and differences between medieval and present views of children and childhood (Cunningham, 1995; Pollock, 1983). Because Jung did not write about children's individuation, it has been assumed that he did not have a notion of the individuality of children or of individuation in childhood. Indeed, this assumption has not been challenged.

Let us suppose that Jung had ideas about the individuality of children. How could these ideas be elucidated for discussion? I suggest that we can look at how the medieval views of children and childhood are discussed and then reflect this back on Jung's ideas.

Contrary to the view that the idea of childhood did not exist in medieval society, many images of children and childhood in the Middle Ages have been revealed. But these images, which appear to be ambivalent, raise further complex issues. Cunningham observes that 'the middle ages did have a concept of childhood, not perhaps the same as in later centuries, but a concept nevertheless' (1995, p. 30). He proposes that the impact of Christianity was a significant factor in causing the Middle Ages to accord more importance to young children than had the ancient world[10] (ibid., p 40), for instance, by making young children a subject of their soul, and also by making infanticide categorically a crime.[11] He observes:

> The Christian belief in the need of every human being for salvation immediately implied a higher status for young children. They needed to

be brought, as early as possible, into the Christian family of God . . . there was a perceived need to make young children aware that they had a soul, and that their life in the hereafter as well as on earth was dependent on the state of their soul; they could not be treated as of marginal importance to society as a whole until they had achieved adulthood.

(ibid., p. 27).

However, Shulamith Shahar points out the ambivalence of medieval Christian thought (1990, p. 9) and argues:

Just as medieval culture displayed ambivalence over procreation, so it fostered two conflicting images of the child, which may be defined, simplistically as the negative and the positive approaches. Like the different attitudes to procreation, they too reflected both conscious and unconscious emotional ambivalence.

(ibid., p. 14)

The idealised images of the child are seen as the archetype, connected with a saint or Christ. Shahar gives the example of 'an exceptional child – a future saint' whom medieval authors described as having skipped childhood (ibid., p. 15). The 'archetype of the sainted infant', namely, the *puer senex*, is described as one of the most prevalent archetypes in the Lives of saints (ibid.). In medieval sources the *puer senex* 'is old in everything but years', while in classical literature and myths, *puer senex* 'combines the freshness and charm of youth with the maturity and wisdom of old age' (ibid.). Moreover, the child was depicted not only as 'the symbol of purity and innocence' but also 'as the embodiment of Christ' (ibid., p. 18). Shahar observes:

Worship of the infant Jesus flourished in the twelfth century, together with worship of the Holy Mother: Christ is depicted as a human child, small, weak, laughing, weeping, eating an apple given to him by his mother, innocent, and pure, the archetypal child.

(ibid.)

Likewise, the Holy Mother was depicted as 'the archetypal devoted mother', being 'pictured in pregnancy, suckling her son, playing with him, and caressing him – as an example to all mothers' (ibid., p. 13). Furthermore, in the medieval world the child was considered to be 'a trust from God', whereas in the Roman world it was considered legalistically as the property of its parents (ibid.).[12]

In contrast, the negative images of the child, Cunningham argues:

stemmed in large part from Augustine's stress on original sin, combined with a high valuation of those who either never had sexual relationships or who were willing to give up their children for the sake of dedication to God, a common theme in the lives of female saints.

(1995, p. 37)

Shahar writes that while Augustine described the infant born in sin, emphasising its drives, 'Medieval authors shifted the emphasis from instincts to helplessness, lack of reason, and pathos of the infant born in sin' (1990, p. 14). Consequently, she argues that, 'Whether the view of childhood was positive or negative, there can be no question but that, in the Middle Ages, childhood was perceived as a separate stage in human life, with its own quality and characteristics' (ibid., p. 20). The irony, according to Shahar, is that both the concept of childhood innocence, which was so popular in the Romantic era of the nineteenth century, and 'the belief that children were ruled solely by their drives, which anticipated Freud's theories of childhood sexuality' were derived from different medieval Christian scriptural commentaries on the same texts (ibid., p. 6).

Historians have argued about when the radical change occurred in the history of children and childhood, but a further controversy concerns the extent to which there may be continuity as well as change. Shahar argues that, 'The authors of medieval didactic literature divided childhood into stages',[13] describing this as 'Reminiscent of the classifications of Piaget or Erikson' (ibid., p. 6). She writes: 'Views and customs which were unpopular in western industrial society for lengthy periods but were rife in medieval society (and other societies) are now gradually gaining acceptance again' (ibid.). However, as discussed in an earlier part of this book, stage models of development, including those of childhood, have been questioned due to their implication that development is linear, predictable, progressive and hierarchical. Further examination is necessary to establish whether the underpinning ideas of the medieval and recent stage models imply the same thing.

Coming back to Jung, his images of children and childhood are often understood not literally but metaphorically, that is to say, as images associated with the archetype of the child. It now becomes apparent that there is a parallel between the medieval views of children and childhood and Jung's concept of the child archetype. The main difference would be that while the medieval view of the child as an archetype is described only in terms of positive images of the infant Jesus as opposed to the negative images of the human child born in sin, Jung's concept of the child archetype contains both positive and negative images within itself. Nevertheless, both Jung's concept of the child archetype and the medieval views of children and childhood seem to contain contradictory images and, consequently, could imply both positive and negative interpretations of the same attitude towards children. As Shahar writes: 'Theories on the child and attitudes toward him in medieval culture were undoubtedly marked by ambivalence' (ibid., p. 20). It seems that children in the medieval view and the child in Jung's view were both seen as unimportant and beloved at the same time; they were marginal-ised and treasured at the same time; and they were mortal and divine at the same time.

While the medieval authors explicitly spelled out the stages of childhood, distinguishing 'features of each stage and the characteristic signs of devel-opment therein and dwelt on the status, rights, and duties of the child and adolescent' (ibid., p. 22), Jung did not. It is sometimes not clear whether Jung idealises or undermines the status or the individuality of children. Jung's concept of the child archetype has both positive and negative images, which can be projected onto actual children. The child archetype also has a complex and sometimes ambivalent relationship with the parental imagos, which can be observed in actual relationships between a child and parent. The ambigu-ity of Jung's discussions of children and childhood could be a reflection of the nature of the child archetype, which, as an archetype, contains the oppos-ites. Or we could speculate that the paradoxical images of the child archetype reflect Jung's ambivalence towards Christianity, which, it has been argued, contains not only ambivalence about procreation and therefore images of children and childhood but also about other elements with which he strug-gled personally, including his ambivalence towards his own father.

Children's rights involve contradictions and ambivalence of different images of or attitudes towards children. An example of this is the debate about protectionist and participatory approaches. If one overemphasises one approach, then another approach could be totally subjugated. For instance, if one insists that children should be protected in all circumstances, critiques will say that children are deprived of the right to make choices, e.g., 'choice not to attend school', 'choice to refuse or accept treatment', 'choice of where to live', etc. (Veerman, 1992a, p. 51). If one insists that children should be given choices, critiques will say that children will be deprived of their 'happy childhood' and risk being exploited by the world which is mainly operated by adults' interests. Solutions might be sought in various ways, but the point is that this is a matter of the conflict of opposites, which Jung elaborated throughout his work. Jung, instead of proposing his own definition of the individuality of children, could be understood as drawing attention to the difficulty of attempting to define an issue such as the individuality of children at all. His concept of the child archetype could be understood as offering a ground on which to lay out all the problems in narrating a history of children and childhood and describing particular images of and attitudes towards them.

Can the view on children and childhood in analytical psychology be updated?

Is it appropriate to perpetuate the view which locates Jung at one end and Fordham at the other end of the spectrum, in terms of their images of and attitudes towards children and childhood? For instance, could the view be justified that Jung's approach was old or traditional, while Fordham's approach was new or radical? In favour of Fordham's approach, Jung might seem to have taken less account of actual children or was even negligent of them with his focus on the second half of life, while Fordham took more account of actual children and understood them better, focusing on early childhood. On the other hand, in favour of Jung, his approach could be seen as archetypal and metaphorical with its use of the concept of the child arche-type, and therefore more meaningful and useful, while Fordham's approach was literal and reducible largely to his perception of actual children.

There could be a parallel between the followers of Jung who do not believe in the necessity of children's individuality and those who do not believe in the necessity of children's rights. Freeman presents the two myths which tend to be employed by those who do not believe in the necessity of recognising children's rights: one is the idealisation of child–parent relationships, and the other is the view of childhood as 'a golden age, as the best years of life' (Freeman, 1992b, p. 30). The former 'emphasises that adults (and parents in particular) have the best interests of children at heart' and the latter sees childhood 'as synonymous with innocence', 'a time when we are spared the rigours of adult life', and 'a time of freedom, of joy, of play' (ibid.). By idealising parents or the time of childhood, non-believers in children's rights and non-believers in children's individuality could be sharing the same kind of ideology and underlying images of children and childhood. Therefore, not only the developmental school but also other schools of analytical psychology, which hold views of childhood either as essentially dependent on parents or as a golden age too special to be interfered in by adults, could incorporate images of children and childhood which reflect those in the children's rights movement.

The same myths might underpin the ideas of non-supporters of children's rights and of children's individuality. Nevertheless, the same myths could also be supporting child-savers, who try to define the needs of children and to provide rights to them from an adult's point of view. The difference is the emphasis on the attitude of adults. By viewing adults, parents in particular, as the ideal people to make decisions for children, and viewing childhood as an idealised phase of life free from any elements of adult life, non-supporters of children's rights and child-savers could be emphasising different aspects of the child–adult relationship. Based on the same ideology, non-supporters of children's rights value what *adults* can do for children, e.g., the role of parents in children's lives, adults' knowledge, experience, authority in decision-making, and interventions, whereas child-savers focus on what adults can do *for children*, i.e., the ways in which children can be rescued by means of, e.g., adults' help, protection, and resolutions about children. Could the same apply to Jung, if we consider Jung as a non-believer of children's individual-ity or as a child-saver? Is it possible that Jung attempted to address parents' psychological problems where problems were observed in their children's psyche, because he did not believe in children's individuality or wished to protect the children's psyche from parental invasion?

There are many issues related to children's rights to which contemporary Jungians might be able to contribute in addition to Jung himself. A Jungian perspective could be compared with the social constructionist perspective which has been making the most significant recent contribution to debates about images of children and childhood. Comparisons between the social constructionist perspectives on child images and Jung's concept of the child archetype in particular are discussed elsewhere (Main, 2008). It is acknowledged that both approaches suffer from the weakness of favouring child images over embodied children, but suggested that Jung presents a significant challenge to social constructionism by offering an alternative way of conceptualising the universality and diversity of child images, and by highlighting the potential to realise our unlimited imagination beyond social constructionism. Further discussions of this issue could include Fordham and other Jungians who are concerned with children and childhood.

Conclusion

In this chapter I have made some comparisons between issues relating to children's rights and Fordham's ideas about children's individuality. I have examined the images of children and childhood underpinning the children's rights discourses as well as Fordham's and Jung's theories.

It has been believed that Fordham's work was innovative because he worked with children, an area with which Jung did not appear to be very much concerned. However, it could be argued that Fordham's work was also and even more innovative because his claim for children's individuality seems to connect with the newly established discourse about the concept of children and the rights of children. Particularly relevant are the recently emerged images of children, that is, of children as autonomous individuals, which underpin the participation rights introduced in the CRC in 1989 and have since caused heated debates about their conflict with protection rights.

If we apply some of the issues identified in the children's rights movement, the significance of Fordham's work and the differences between him and Jung could be looked at from a fresh angle. Fordham might seem to be in accordance with the rise of the children's rights movement in the way he draws particular attention to the psyche of children and takes children's psychological processes seriously. Jung might be viewed as a non-believer in children's individuality, sharing the kinds of images of children and childhood held by non-believers in children's rights. Alternatively, the current debate about protection and participatory rights could be applied to the views of Jung and Fordham: Jung being protective of children by seeing their psyche as vulnerable and in need of adults' care, and Fordham empowering children by viewing their psyche as competent and resilient. However, it may not be so straightforward, as there are ambiguities about both Jung's and Fordham's views about children.

Although Fordham's work is significant in opening up the field of child analysis in analytical psychology, its theoretical and practical implications need to be examined further in relation to the newly emerged images of children as capable, knowledgeable, competent and autonomous individuals. It is also unclear whether Fordham and Jung were aware of the limitations of or at least difficulties in distinguishing between childhood and adulthood. Other remaining questions are, to what extent analytical psychology as a whole might have comparable aspects to the debate about children's rights issues, and what distinct contributions analytical psychology could make to this interdisciplinary debate. The comparison and contrast between the children's rights movement and Fordham's work with children show us a particular significance of the psychological approach to children's individuality, and at the same time raise the question as to its further implications. It seems that Fordham's claim for children's individuality needs to be updated in relation to contemporary images of childhood and other related issues. Moreover, there is an impact of declaring the individuality of children which connects to other developmental issues, even if this was not intended, and this impact should at least be acknowledged.

The word 'individuality' has different meanings and connotations in analytical psychology and the children's rights discourses. So do the words 'autonomy', 'competence', and 'quality of life' which are frequently used in children's rights discourses. To what extent Fordham's as well as Jung's psychological perspectives on 'autonomy' and 'individuality' could be made relevant to children's rights discourses needs to be further explored. Jungian terminologies may not necessarily be comparable with general uses of the same terms. For instance, the meaning of the term 'identity' is quite different in Jung's view from general views (Jung, 1921, para. 741; see also Samuels et al., [1986] 1991, p. 71) (this will be discussed in Chapter 8). Likewise, the meaning of 'individuality' could be unique in both Fordham's and Jung's view and therefore incompatible with other views. Like the difference between Jung's and Fordham's concepts of the self which Urban observes as 'the individuating self' for Jung and 'the pre-individuating self' for Fordham (Urban, 1992, p. 414, quoting Fordham, 1969, see Chapter 6), there seems to be a difference between Fordham's and Jung's use of the word 'individuality'. From Jung's point of view, individuality is the goal of individuation, to be achieved through the individuation process, whereas for Fordham, individuality is the pre-condition of individuation, given from the beginning of life. Nevertheless, they would agree that individuality is an absolute quality of the psyche which is as objective as much as it is subjective.

Above all, seeing Fordham's work in relation to the children's rights movement has helped us to identify in his theory the same newly emerged images of children and childhood which have captured the world's interest especially in the area of international legislation. It has also generated many potentially fruitful questions about the social and political as well as theoretical and clinical implications of viewing children as individuals.

Part IV

Towards a Jungian developmental psychology

Chapter 8

Jung as a qualitative psychologist

I have discussed so far in this book: (1) how one could understand the notion of development in Jung's work; (2) what kinds of notions of development have been held and what kinds of approaches have been sought by developmental psychology as well as by analytical psychology; and (3) what kinds of images are associated with the Developmental School of analytical psychology and how the Developmental School could contribute to wider interdisciplinary issues and debates about development.

Here I shall consider which aspects of analytical psychology could be particularly useful to mainstream developmental psychology. As we have seen, various images and narratives of development co-exist within analytical psychology. It would therefore be too complex to present analytical psychology as a whole. It would also be over-ambitious to formulate a Jungian developmental psychology as such in this limited space. Nevertheless, we could make a cautious start with Jung's own work, which even by itself is quite complex enough. We could identify the issues addressed in developmental psychology with which Jung was also concerned and the debates to which he could possibly contribute. I shall narrow down the question for investigation: What could be a useful way to introduce Jung's psychology to developmental psychology? How could Jung's perspective be understood and in effect be helpful to enrich today's debates on developmental issues?

Jung's psychology is usually absent from or plays very little part in histories of psychology and psychoanalysis. Likewise, Jung's contribution to discussions about development is not addressed in textbooks of developmental psychology. Jung's psychology, with its specialist vocabulary and in particular its emphasis on symbolic and archetypal meaning, may not be comprehensible to those who are not necessarily familiar with it. Perhaps identifying and then using the vocabulary and discourses established within developmental psychology to make explicit the relevance of Jung's psychology to current debates on development would be more beneficial.

One way of introducing Jung to developmental psychology could be by looking at Jung as a qualitative psychologist. As discussed in Part II of this book, the recent challenges to conventional, modernistic, positivistic, quantitative psychology, including the concept of development as a linear or stage-like progress in the field of developmental psychology, seem to support both Jung's understanding of psychological development and the recent increasing recognition of the methodological value of qualitative research. I shall discuss how Jung's work could be introduced to developmental psychology as a form of qualitative psychology and then to what extent this way of introducing Jung could be useful.

In short, the aims of this chapter are:

1   to introduce Jung to developmental psychology (because Jung is absent from this area and yet very relevant);
2   to propose how Jung's psychological approach might be articulated using language which reflects contemporary debates in developmental psychology;
3   to suggest future studies on Jung, Fordham and perhaps other practitioners of and researchers on analytical psychology in terms of their possible further contribution to developmental psychology.

On the one hand, more consideration of what goes on in contemporary developmental psychology is necessary for our discussion of a possible Jungian psychology that is developmental, and on the other, more consideration of developmental themes within analytical psychology is necessary for our discussion of a possible developmental psychology that is Jungian. Nevertheless, this chapter will not attempt to cover an extensive range of issues debated in developmental psychology. Rather, it will focus on assessing the way in which Jung could be presented as a qualitative psychologist to developmental psychology and links between his qualitative approaches and some of the topics involved in the field.

Could Jung be introduced to developmental psychology as a qualitative psychologist?

Presenting Jung as a qualitative psychologist could be a first step in recognising that Jung's stance has important areas of agreement with contemporary challenges to conventional, modernistic, positivistic and often quantitative psychology. We could then explain why Jung does not hold a linear, one-patterned, stage-like model of development, where progressive changes are normalised and predicted. Qualitative approaches to development, whether they are seen as conflicting with, compensating, or even incomparable with quantitative approaches, do not remain mere criticisms of conventional developmental psychology. Their value is as much in the continual challenges they present to the practice of developmental psychology. Viewed in this light, Jung's perspectives could contribute to today's debates by providing yet another discursive option and enriching the field as a whole with its unique perspectives on the human psyche. Our attempt to present Jung as a qualitative psychologist could also help to identify the distinctiveness of Jung's psychological approach.

From the perspective of qualitative psychology, I shall address the issues of language, diversity, subjectivity and reflexivity, and make links between Jung's perspectives and today's debates in developmental psychology. From Jung's work, I shall specifically look at his word association test, theory of psychological types, and more generally, his concept of the objective psyche and theory of archetypes. From among many areas of developmental psychology, I shall consider those of emotion, personality, sense of self and relationships, in all of which Jung's perspective could be introduced.

Jung's qualitative stance: language and meaning, diversity, and subjectivity

Jung's qualitative stance could be explored in relation to the characteristics of qualitative psychology which were discussed in Chapter 5. We have looked at qualitative researchers' emphases on or openness to:

1   an interpretative stance, the use of language, and the process of meaning making (to some extent in contrast to numerical data and mathematical thinking);
2   diversity and multiplicity (challenging generalisation and standardisation);
3   subjectivity, subjective standpoints, and the co-existence of subject and object (challenging what is thought to be objective psychological research).

Further points could be made through combining the above points. For example, accepting the subjectivity of both the researcher and the researched leads us to the more mindful use of language and conceptualisation: for instance, research could be viewed as the researcher's action and performance, or as the participation and collaboration of the researcher and the researched. Considering diversity and the ways in which we make sense of the world leads directly to alertness to ecological validity and consideration of social and cultural contexts in the process of psychological research; and indirectly to political awareness, awareness of social hierarchy, inequality and power relationships in the social world and professional circles.

Jung's qualitative stance in his practice of psychology can be observed from the beginning of his work. In his MD dissertation, 'On the psychology and pathology of so-called occult phenomena' (1902), he was a participant as well as an observer in his research. In this research he explored the role in producing mediumistic phenomena of certain psychopathological conditions and the altered states of consciousness brought about by mediumistic trances.

He observed for at least two years the phenomena exhibited during seances by a medium, who was in fact his cousin, a teenage girl.[1] During the seances, he asked questions to the medium and commented on the phenomena that occurred. The other participants were mostly Jung's and his cousin's relatives and family, including Jung's mother and sister. He concluded that certain psychological phenomena, which appeared to be occult, were the result of heightened unconscious performance.

Jung's use of language often demands modifications in the way we conceptualise psychological matters. His serious concern with both rational thought processes and irrational psychic processes, the latter of which are not easily categorised or expressed in language, requires expanding the vocabulary of psychological explanations. He also frequently notes the limit of language where meaning cannot be understood literally. In the research with his mediumistic cousin, the process by which Jung attempts to make sense of the apparently occult phenomena reveals his commitment to clarifying the 'irrational' by means of the rational medium of language.

Concerning diversity, Jung's theory of individuation could be understood in terms of individual diversity as opposed to conformity with the mass. His concern with cultural diversity could also be observed in his remarks on the differences between Swiss and Germans and other Europeans, and between Europeans and Africans, Indians, Native Americans, and Chinese. Though largely based on reading, this concern did also involve him in trips to Africa, India, and New Mexico.

Concerning his subjective standpoint, also relevant is Jung's account of his decision to go into psychiatry which was at that time generally held in contempt, and not internal medicine, which would have promised him a stable career ([1963] 1995, pp. 129–32). He was inspired by a psychiatry textbook in which the author makes a subjective inquiry into the subjectivities of human beings. When Jung was preparing for the state examination he was least interested in psychiatry, but, having read the line in the textbook where the author, Krafft-Ebing, called the psychoses 'diseases of the personality', Jung realised that psychiatry was the only possible goal for him (ibid., p. 130). Jung writes:

> Here was the empirical field common to biological and spiritual facts, which I had everywhere sought and nowhere found. Here at last was the place where the collision of nature and spirit became reality ... My violent reaction set in when Krafft-Ebing spoke of the 'subjective character' of psychiatric textbooks. So, I thought, the textbook is in part the subjective confession of the author. With his specific prejudice, with the totality of his being, he stands behind the objectivity of his experiences and responds to the 'disease of the personality' with the whole of his own personality.

> (ibid.; emphasis added)

In this passage, Jung's awareness of the role played by the subjectivity of the researcher in the whole process of research is clearly illustrated. Indeed, Jung's self-reflexive and participatory stance can be observed throughout his work: from his early work to his autobiography. His concern with such issues as language, diversity, and subjectivity also reveals his agreement with qualitative research and the compatibility of his perspective with contemporary debates. I shall now discuss three topics of developmental psychology, namely, emotion, personality, and sense of self and relationships as some of the areas in which we could address Jung's qualitative stance. I shall then discuss the level of political awareness in Jung's psychology, which seems to need further research. I shall also explore the limitations of presenting Jung as a qualitative psychologist and the distinctiveness of his approach.

Emotion: an approach from the perspective of language and meaning

Jung's study of the word association tests[2] (1904–7, 1910) is well known as a form of quantitative research which demonstrates the statistical significance in the delay of the participant's reaction time to particular stimulus words and suggests a relationship[3] between longer reaction times or other disturbances and the incidence of the feeling-toned images and memories that he calls 'complexes'. He studied both adults and children and found complexes in both. However, Jung's investigation could also be seen as a form of qualitative research, in the way that the whole process of the tests raises the question of the meaning of the delay in the participant's response to particular words. Jung explores the meaning of the participant's associated reactions to the particular words verbally presented. This could be seen as Jung's qualitative investigation into 'the gap between objects and representations' (Banister et al., 1994, p. 4), a gap which conventional psychology often finds intolerable.[4] Banister et al. argue:

> Quantification all too often fuels the fantasy of prediction and control, but qualitative research in psychology takes as its starting point an awareness of the gap between an object of study and the way we represent it, and the way interpretation necessarily comes to fill that gap. The process of interpretation provides a bridge between the world and us, between our objects and our representations of them, but . . . interpretation is a *process*, a process that continues as our relation to the world keeps changing. We have to follow that process and acknowledge that there will always be a gap between the things we want to understand and our accounts of what they are like if we are to do qualitative research properly.
>
> (ibid., p. 3)

Jung explores the gap that appeared to him in his association test, that is, between *what is unsaid* and *what is said*. He writes that though the original purpose of the word association test was to study mental association, 'One can study nothing of the sort by such primitive means. But you can study something else when the experiment fails, when people make mistakes' (1935b, para. 99). As an indicator of psychological complexes, he noted that 'the prolongation of the reaction time' is of the greatest practical importance, as are other disturbed reactions such as

> reaction with more than one word, against the instructions; mistakes in reproduction of the word; reaction expressed by facial expression, laughing, movement of the hands or feet or body, coughing, stammering, and such things; insufficient reactions like 'yes' or 'no'; not reacting to the real meaning of the stimulus word; habitual use of the same words; use of foreign languages; defective reproduction, when memory begins to fail in the reproduction experiment; total lack of reaction.
>
> (ibid., para. 100)

Jung approaches the material both quantitatively and qualitatively. His data are the participant's measured reaction times and observed reactions to disturbances, but he not only presents the results in terms of statistical significance but also explores, even more extensively, the underlying psychological processes that may be concealed within the quantifiable results of this study.

Jung's argument could be invoked in the debate on the unconscious aspect of emotion: his word association test suggests that there are feeling-toned complexes in the unconscious, which seem to be related to unexpected reactions to particular stimulus words. Jung writes: 'There is no one who has no complexes, just as there is no one who is without emotions' (1906a, para. 736). To summarise some of the characteristics of the complexes: (1) they constellate, as revealed in the way that they influence thinking and behaviour (ibid., para. 733); (2) they have distressing characteristics ([1911] 1913, para. 1351); (3) they refer to personal and private matters (ibid., paras 1350, 1351); (4) they are usually not consciously recognised and occasionally are even disapproved of by the person who has such complexes (ibid., para. 1351); and (5) they have autonomy, in the way that they can break through the participant's self-control and self-intention (ibid., para. 1352). Moreover, Jung distinguishes the complex, which is usually distressing and of a personal nature, a content of the personal unconscious, from symbolic contents of the unconscious, which he later refers to as symbols, archetypes, and the contents of the collective unconscious. The problem is that since complexes involve the sphere of the unconscious, they cannot be totally clarified. However, Jung points to elements which we are to struggle to make sense of by using language and, instead of dismissing them, seriously explores ways of understanding these non-verbalised elements in our psychic processes. On one level, Jung examines the effects of the unconscious complex from early on in one's emotional life and relationships with others. His study of the word association tests applied to families (1910b)[5] also reports a tendency to agreement in the reaction type between relatives, between children and their mother (more than their father), and between unmarried sisters. On another level, Jung explores the gap between objects and representations, and suggests that we try to understand it in terms of such emotional elements as complexes, rather than through the conscious use of language. His theory concerning these non-verbalised elements could be considered as yet another discursive option for making sense of our emotional process. Jung does not claim that complexes or symbols could fill the gap. Rather, he suggests that there are elements which we cannot make sense of by using language consciously but which affect our psychological process. He seems to propose a creative aspect of experience where language does not immediately react or function.

Jung's work in this area arguably has some methodological drawbacks. For example, the experimental setting of his study could be seen as lacking ecological validity. However, Jung argues that the spontaneous reactions to the stimulus-words observed in this study would also occur in everyday life (see Jung, 1906a, para. 895). He also observes patients' reactions to particular words in his therapeutic practice (see e.g., Jung, 1906c; [1963] 1995, p. 170). This could be seen as confirming his research findings through his clinical practice, and vice versa. The fact that the same words do not mean the same thing to all participants could be seen as another methodological limitation. However, this does not affect the results of Jung's study, because which response words indicate the presence of the feeling-toned complex is not the focus of concern. What is of interest is the participant's reactions themselves to any of the stimulus words given. Jung considers words as 'really a kind of shorthand version of actions, situations, and things' and explains that 'we must content ourselves with the linguistic surrogates for reality; at the same time we must not forget that the stimulus-word will almost without exception conjure up its corresponding situation' (Jung, 1910a, para. 944). He goes on to say:

> the stimulus-words have an excessively strong effect, that they are taken absolutely *personally*, as if they were direct questions. The subject entirely forgets that he is faced with mere words presented in print. He looks for a personal meaning in them, tries to guess the meaning and defend himself against it, altogether forgetting the original instruction.
>
> (ibid., para. 952)

Thus, Jung observes this effect, and instead of eliminating it as a meaningless phenomenon, he takes it seriously and explores the meaning of such unconscious, emotional responses to particular words. He presents the unexpected reactions of human beings as something meaningful. He could have more explicitly addressed not only the personal level of such emotional reactions but also the social and cultural contexts of the use of language and particular words, which now receive greater attention from many psychologists. However, he does not approach the social context in a causal, reductive way, by investigating which emotional reactions might be affected by what kind of social and cultural elements. Rather, he prefers to draw our attention to the unconscious sphere of the mind and possible interactions between conscious perceptions/representations and unconscious actions/reactions. Connected with this, there is also scope for longitudinal studies in order to ascertain whether and to what extent, or in what way, the amounts or the contents or the manifestations of complexes remain or change. It also raises a question about emotion and its relation to cognitive capacity or ability. Unlike developmental psychology, where links between emotion and cognitive capacity have been increasingly discussed, Jung does not make a clear link between emotion and cognitive abilities.

Emotional development for Jung cannot be explained without considering personal complexes in the unconscious and symbolic contents of the collective unconscious. This also raises the questions as to how the complexes might develop and the role of the personal complex in one's emotional development. Likewise, it could also be asked how the collective unconscious might affect one's emotional development. Approaches to these issues require an understanding of the meaning and impact of personal and symbolic images which language does not necessarily convey. In this respect, Jung's qualitative stance, with its exploration of language and meaning, may be no longer sustainable. Symbolic meaning seems to be prioritised over the meaning of language. Yet Jung still has to engage with language in order to express his enquiries into symbolic meaning. Consequently, his approach could still be seen as part of qualitative research, insofar as he continually struggles with language and displays this process in trying to express the aspects of the psyche where language does not make sense.

Personality: an approach from the perspective of diversity

Jung's account of diversity found in his theory of personality could provide another link between his approach and qualitative psychology. Unlike psychometrics, Jung's work on 'Psychological Types' (1921) does not build and test a theory through measurement of behaviour: it does not aim to establish categories for individual differences in terms of measurable aspects of people or measuring behaviour by reliable means. Jung's typology has in fact been elaborated into experimental research, psychometrics, and personality tests (e.g., the Myers-Briggs Type Indicator [MBTI]). However, Jung's reflexive analysis seems to indicate that his interests lie somewhere else, that is, in understanding different theoretical formulations of psychology from the viewpoint of personality; more specifically, in accounting for the differences between Jung's perspective and Freud's and Adler's (see Jung, [1963] 1995, p. 233). Jung presents a way of understanding, rather than measuring, individual differences and their potential effects on conducting psychological research as well as on everyday life. Again, Jung argues that his theory is supported by the evidence that he collected in his therapeutic practice (see Jung, 1921, p. xiii). He takes not only the outsider viewpoint by focusing on his observations of others but also the insider viewpoint by considering his patients' self-reports and his inner experience of his own personality.

The distinctiveness of Jung's theory of psychological types seems to lie in its consideration of the unconscious aspects of personality in relation to the opposite manifestations of consciously recognised personality. Jung's typology presents 16 types of personality (a combination of either introverted or extraverted attitude-types with one of four basic functions [thinking, feeling, sensation, intuition], which appears as the primary function-type, and another of the four basic functions, which appears as the secondary function-type). Introverted-extraverted (attitude-types), thinking-feeling (function-types in terms of judgement), sensation-intuition (function-types in terms of perception) are presented as bipolar features of personality, and one is considered to be superior, being recognised consciously, while the other is considered to be inferior, being largely unconscious. In his account, these antitheses operate dialectically: one is conscious while the other is unconscious, one is laid in the foreground while the other is in the background; they compensate each other, and conflicts emerge when there is excessive one-sidedness (Jung, 1923). Nevertheless, Jung is open to other possible classifications (Jung, 1921, para. 848).

Though Jung makes claims for the biological foundations of psychological types (Jung, 1921, paras 558ff), his view does not seem to be as rigid as the view that personality is biologically determined and unchangeable. He talks about adjustment, which he considers to be achieved more easily than adaptation. According to Jung, through adjustment one can fit oneself without much difficulty into existing conditions, the style of one's environment, which includes the social demands that coincide with the moral laws governing one's action (ibid., para. 564). However, this could cause in a person a certain 'loss of equilibrium' (ibid.). Jung also suggests that there can be spontaneous, situational, unconscious manifestations of personality. For example, one's inferior function, which does not usually manifest on the surface but remains hidden in the shadow side of the social persona, could manifest negatively on the conscious level and could also manifest symbolically in dreams, fantasies, and in other situations where unconscious contents emerge. Moreover, the spontaneous manifestations of the unconscious aspects of personality could actually affect one's dominant personality on the conscious level. This could be seen as states, which are thought to be transient and dependent on situations, rather than traits, which are thought to be relatively constant over time (Thomas, 2002, p. 295). However, from Jung's point of view, such personal aspects as appearing to be transient and dependent on situations could be more significant than one's relatively constant aspects. What should be added here, from Jung's perspective, is the continuous effects and influences on one another of the conscious, dominant aspects and the unconscious, auxiliary aspects of personality.

Jung's view could be seen as in agreement with the interactionist view that, although traits and temperament are relatively fixed and coherent over time, the expressions of personality are not totally determined and unchangeable but could be changeable and situational, corresponding to the interaction between nature and nurture. However, Jung would add another dimension: the autonomy of the psyche and the world. He believes that the world we live in and the psyche which experiences the world are autonomous. As discussed in Chapter 1, Jung uses the words *nature* and *culture* in a way that is different from how nature and nurture are widely talked about. In this context, for Jung, culture means the unnatural or spiritual aspect of human beings as opposed to the natural, biological or physical aspect, and therefore culture does not necessarily mean environmental influences or social context. Taking this into account, in Jung's view, the conscious, dominant personality seems to be relatively consistent but could be changeable in the interactions between consciousness and the autonomous psyche or the autonomous world. These interactions include phenomena and psychological processes which are not necessarily recognised consciously but could autonomously make a powerful impact on what goes on in consciousness. Thus, Jung's theory of psychological types is deeply concerned with the unconscious aspect of the psyche, which is autonomous and not totally known to us. In one sense, his theory might be seen as loose and unclear, but it could also be seen as challenging the limits of psychological studies of personality and our account of personality which so far have mainly focused on conscious manifestations of the psyche and observable behaviours.

However, this leaves us with a question as to the extent to which Jung considers the influences of socio-cultural contexts on personality. Again, his engagement with social factors is not often explicit. Critiques have pointed out that his theory lacks the kind of evidence for its relevance in other cultures and language groups that might be provided by cross-cultural examination (e.g., McGowan, 1994). However, Jung's notion of the persona, the mask we use for social confrontation, does concern social roles in which we have relationships with other individuals in the same or different social groups. Jung notes that an individual can wear more than one mask at the same time, depending on the social or cultural demands in a particular society. Nevertheless, Jung gives the impression that he generally has a dismissive attitude towards such identification with social requirements.

It should be noted here that Jung's use of the word 'identity' appears to be different from the concept of identity that is widely held in psychological discussions. Jung's particular use of words which might cause confusion has to be explained, in order to introduce Jung's notion of the self. Jung's use of the word 'identity' is to be understood as referring to an unconscious identification between subject and object, where there is no differentiation between the two (Jung, 1921, para. 741). In that sense, identity, for Jung, does not refer to an individual characteristic but to personal identification with the collective and the consequent loss of individuality. Instead, Jung's notion of the ego could be described as what we generally understand as personal identity (Samuels *et al.*, [1986] 1991, p. 71) or, to some extent, what Henri Tajfel calls social identity (e.g., Tajfel, 1972, 1978; Tajfel and Turner, 1986). Jung postulates the self as both the totality of the personality and the whole psyche, which includes the ego, as the centre of consciousness, observing the psychological process and expressions of personality.[6]

Having theorised the collective unconscious as a universal characteristic of the psyche, Jung writes that 'every individual is an exception to the rule' (Jung, 1921, para. 895). He argues that approaching the psyche from the standpoints of uniformity and diversity are 'two contradictory and mutually exclusive theories' (ibid., para. 853). He explains:

> Everything which in that view [the uniformity of the psyche] was left out of the picture as an individual variant now becomes important as a starting-point for further differentiations; and everything which previously had a special value on account of its uniformity now appears valueless, because merely collective.
>
> (ibid.)

Therefore, although Jung considers the social context of personality, this seems to mean 'merely collective' in his approach to the diversity of the psyche. What interests him in this approach seems to be the diverse patterns of expression of and reaction to such collective identification rather than the collective factors in the social context. It could be that, however societies and cultures vary, what one identifies with are such collective factors as, for example, authority, ideology, expectations, inhibitions, morals, common sense, etc., and consequently, social and cultural diversity are irrelevant to his theory of personality.

Yet, Jung still seems to retain flexibility in his approach, being aware that taking only a one-sided approach could weaken not only the other but also itself. Jung's theory of psychological types could be viewed as an inquiry rather than an outcome: an inquiry into the diversity of the psyche. Jung is concerned not only with 'laws of reason' (Jung, 1921, para. 775) but also with exceptions: on one level, not only the general/universal but also the specific/diverse, and on another level, not only the rational and reasonable but also the irrational, perhaps symbolic, '*beyond* reason' (ibid.). In relation to diversity, Jung emphasises the difficulties in accepting other views or personalities that differ from one's own (ibid., paras 847, 849). He inquires into the relationship between a researcher and the psychology studied by the researcher. This perspective keeps us aware of the subjective equation and the diversity of such subjectivities which are crucial for studying and understanding psychology. In this respect, Jung seems to agree with the idea that 'Subjectivity is a resource, not a problem, for a theoretically and pragmatically sufficient explanation' (Banister *et al.*, 1994, p. 13). However, Jung might add another dimension to the necessity of reflexivity. He emphasises the incompleteness of rationality, which avoids or excludes what it cannot comprehend. Instead of labelling such factors as irrational and putting them aside, Jung suggests that we consider seriously what appears to us as irrational and remain open to alternative approaches to, means of making sense of, and ways of understanding the marginalised aspects of the psyche. In this respect, his theory of psychological types could also be seen as a critical theory of different ways of doing psychological research. The criticism of the lack of clarity and reciprocity in his methods due to the heavy reliance upon self-reports and self-assessment if not observation, could be turned around as honest and subjective enquiry with awareness of human limitation in making judgements. The development of personality for Jung could be explained as the continuous process of coming to recognise one's own subjectivity in different contexts, recognising others' subjectivities, and realising the diversity of subjectivities.

Sense of self and relationships: an approach from the perspective of subjectivity

Jung's perspective on subjectivity could be the most significant aspect of his work for illuminating his qualitative approach and at the same time could also be the most controversial in terms of methodological value. In this section we shall explore Jung's account of subjectivity (intersubjectivity between people and intrasubjectivity within oneself), its relationship with objectivity in research, and its methodological value. Jung's ideas of subjectivity seem to cover much greater breath and depth of subjectivity than other psychological theories, since his approach involves the conscious and both the personal and collective unconscious within and between individuals.

Jung's perspectives on subjectivity could be introduced to debates within developmental psychology on topics such as the sense of self and relationships with others. We have just looked at how Jung's notion of identity, unlike our general understanding of the notion, does not refer to a continuous sense of 'who I am', such as emerges in relationships or in seeing oneself as belonging to or not belonging to particular social categories. It should also be recalled that his notion of the self does not refer to the conscious identification of 'who I am'. For Jung, realisation of the self refers to the goal of psychological development, in his language, the individuation process, i.e., realising the totality of the personality and the whole psyche which includes both the conscious and the unconscious. His theory of individuation concerns the *process* towards this goal, which is a never-ending task. As discussed in Part I of this book, Jung does not hold that there is a uniform pattern or law of the individuation process.

Jung's theory could be and often is interpreted in a chronological sense according to which the second half of life, after the mid-life crisis, is important for the individuation process. However, as is made clear in earlier parts of this book, this view poses a question. An alternative interpretation of Jung's theory is that the tensions, conflicts, compensations and other kinds of relationship between consciousness and unconsciousness persist, and therefore age is mostly irrelevant to individuation. Jung's writing does often concern the second half of life, but he is also concerned with adolescence and expresses the need for future research on childhood (Jung, 1910b). Jung's theory is not simply chronological. It is difficult to obtain clear-cut explanations for the development of the sense of self and relationships with others in Jung's account, but we can examine Jung's potential contribution to psychological approaches to these topics without aiming at defining the patterns of the processes.

An implication of Jung's distinctive perspective for the debates on self and relationships goes beyond subjectivity: he considers both *intersubjectivity* between people and *intrasubjectivity* within a person. These considerations apply to the unconscious as well as on the conscious levels. Jung's theory of archetypes postulates both *intersubjectivity* and *intrasubjectivity* in the way that one relates with others as well as with the images of others within oneself. On this point some similarities between Jung and other psychological approaches could be noted. For instance, Jung's account of intrasubjectivity addressed by archetypes might be seen as similar to Bowlby's concept of the internal working model (e.g., Bowlby, 1969).[7] This concept supposes that an infant comes to build up an internal working model of his or her relationship with the attachment figure, usually the primary caregiver, which is based on the quality of the infant's experience of that relationship and persists later in life as an expectation of the quality of his or her relationships with others and the self (Cowie, 1995). Both Bowlby and Jung consider the impact of the unconscious process or images on relationships and the sense of self. Jung also believes that the first relationship becomes the basis for later relationships with others (Jung, 1910b, paras 1007, 1008). However, Jung's account seems distinctive because he holds a unique way of understanding subjectivity as well as objectivity which I shall discuss later.

The images of others[8] and the self which Jung proposes are not merely constructed through one's own experience of relationships with the primary caregiver and other people, but are also rooted in both the personal unconscious of an individual and the collective unconscious. On the personal level, therefore, these images could actually be unrecognised aspects of one's own being, and, on the collective level, could manifest in any culture and society. These images, what Jung calls archetypal or symbolic images, could be regarded as universal expressions or manifestations of both personality and social roles. The archetypal images that Jung postulates are, for example, persona (expressions of personality to meet social requirements), shadow (unconscious aspects of personality, the opposite of the conscious, dominant aspects of personality), anima (unconscious feminine), animus (unconscious masculine), the self (the totality of personality), the great mother, the child, the wise old man (each of which is a package of both positive and negative, expected and unexpected images associated with existing characteristics of a mother, a child, and an old man), and so on. These images can be observed in many fairy tales and myths, can manifest in individuals' dreams and fantasies, and can be projected on to other people. Therefore, the process towards the realisation of the self and being in relationship with others are inseparable, in the sense that persons have to work with their own images of others and of themselves in relation to themselves. In one sense these images are acquired over time through experience but in another sense they can emerge spontaneously from the autonomous psyche at any point in life regardless of age and experience. This notion of the autonomous psyche makes Jung's perspective particularly distinctive from other depth psychological perspectives.

We shall next consider the relationship between the embodied researcher and researched in psychology. In doing so we shall consider the potential contribution of Jung's perspective on subjectivity to future qualitative research.

Jung's use of the term 'subjective' and his understanding of the notion of subjectivity could be explored in various ways. In Jung's account, subjectivity seems to be involved in the study of psychology in at least the following ways:

1   The researcher makes a subjective inquiry into the subjectivity of the researched.
2   The researcher makes a subjective inquiry into the intersubjectivity between the researcher and the researched.
3   The researcher makes a subjective observation of his or her subjective inquiries (i.e., a subjective inquiry into the intrasubjectivity of the researcher).
4   The researcher makes a subjective inquiry into the objective psyche and the objective world, which consists of objective facts (this includes the subjectivity, intersubjectivity, and intrasubjectivity described in 1, 2 and 3, which are only in part known to us).

In all four, the researcher cannot escape from his own subjectivity to make a purely objective enquiry – Jung agrees with qualitative psychologists on this point. The key to understanding Jung's unique contribution to qualitative psychology seems to be his engagement with *intrasubjectivity*, or a deeper layer of subjectivity observed by the subjectivity within oneself, and its relationship to the objective psyche (3 and 4), which qualitative psychologists seem mostly not to believe in. These certainly add an extra dimension to psychology that is concerned with subjectivity and intersubjectivity, and raise a question as to how subjectivity stands in relation to objectivity.

Here we also need to pay particular attention to Jung's use of the term 'objective'. What subjectivity and objectivity mean can be an endless philosophical debate, but in this restricted space we shall focus only on Jung's use of these terms. In the first place, Jung does not seem to believe in the so-called 'objectivity' adopted in conventional psychological studies, that is to say, the 'objective' research which is presented as though it is detached from subjective and personal interpretation and inference. Instead, he presents his notion of the 'objective psyche',[9] which cannot be perceived or experienced subjectively but remains unknown to us.

The relationship between subjectivity and objectivity seems to be consistent in Jung's thinking, but his emphasis seems to differ in different places. Sometimes he seems to emphasise that subjective experience is, at the deepest level, connected with the objective psyche, and other times that subjective experience cannot reach the objective psyche. In the former, he seems to present subjective experience as a means of getting a hint of understanding of the objective psyche, while in the latter, he seems to present subjectivity as our limit, the limited framework that we can have of the objective psyche which is never totally known to us.

In his 'Two kinds of thinking' (1911–12), Jung connects subjective thinking with the unconscious, as opposed to logical or reality-thinking which is totally conscious. As I have discussed in Chapter 2, Jung presents subjective thinking as equivalent to archaic thinking, dream-thinking, fantasy-thinking, non-directed thinking, as opposed to logical thinking, reality-thinking, directed thinking, adapted thinking, thinking in words. Subjective thinking is 'guided by unconscious motives' (1911–12/1952, para. 20) and, although much of it 'belongs to the conscious sphere, at least as much goes on in the half-shadow, or entirely in the unconscious' (ibid., para. 39). Logical thinking, meanwhile, is 'an altogether conscious phenomenon' (ibid.).

However, in a letter to Jolande Jacobi, in 1948, Jung defines objective psyche as opposed to subjective psyche, explaining that the former is not always conscious but the latter is (Jung, 1973, p. 497). It seems contradictory that Jung views subjectivity first as partly unconscious and later as totally conscious. However, this could be understood as his struggle to explain the relationship between subjectivity and the objective psyche, the latter of which is different from what is often thought to be objective in old paradigm research. In his 'Freud and Jung: Contrasts' (1929c), Jung argues that subjective ideas emerge out of the objective psyche (ibid., para. 769). He then explains that subjective ideas are in fact the closest to the objective psyche (ibid., para. 770). He considers that taking subjectivity seriously is the way of most closely approaching the objective world, which, however, cannot be totally known to us (ibid., para. 771).

For Jung, the target of our subjective inquiry is represented as conscious objects. But this is different from what he calls the objective psyche, which belongs to the unconscious. When objective facts become known to us, this happens only through subjective observation. The objective facts that become known to us by subjective observation therefore become subjective facts in that respect. Subjective observation could be done consciously, but always unconscious subjective assumptions and predispositions come into such observation. Therefore, subjectivity is mainly conscious but always attached to unconsciousness. This combination of conscious and unconscious subjectivity which appears in the forms of narrative, theory, and so on, cannot be objective on the conscious level, where objects are seen only by subjective eyes and do not stand on their own independent from our subjective eyes. Meanwhile, on the unconscious level, such subjective inquiry cannot reach the objective psyche, which stands on its own independent from our subjective eyes. The attempt to apply objectivity from the study of material objects to the study of psychological facts cannot be achieved in the first place, and therefore such objectivity is a delusion: in a way, it is a projection from our subjectivity.

Jung's particular contribution to qualitative psychology might be presented as his awareness of two kinds of objectivity and, accordingly, his understanding of two kinds of subjectivity. He makes an implicit distinction between (1) objectivity which cannot be detached from subjectivity by being the object of our subjective inquiry and (2) objectivity which is out of the reach of subjectivity by being independent of our subjective experience. The former could be regarded as passive objectivity, and the latter as autonomous, active objectivity. Likewise, he makes an implicit distinction between (1) subjectivity which seeks for the object to make a direct, or conscious inquiry and (2) subjectivity which indirectly or archetypally receives part of the objective psyche. The former could be regarded as active subjectivity, and the latter as passive subjectivity (of the autonomous, objective psyche).[10]

Reason and Rowan present new paradigm research as 'objectively subjective', in the sense that it is a synthesis of naïve inquiry, which is 'subjective', and orthodox, old paradigm research, which is 'objective' (1981, p. xiii). In their account, what orthodox psychology has produced as psychological knowledge (which has been thought to be 'objective') and what is now thought to be involved in the study of psychology (that is, the 'subjective' which was neglected in orthodox psychology) are synthesised and presented as what qualitative psychology does and produces as psychological knowledge ('objectively subjective' knowledge, in their words). However, Jung might disagree with the view of orthodox research as 'objective', for the reasons that I discussed above, and might instead call it 'projected objective', since this notion of objectivity is a projection of subjectivity, or of part of subjectivity, that attempts to escape from itself or exclude itself. Jung might also add another dimension to this synthesis, that is, the objective psyche or the objective worlds beyond the reach of any individual's subjective inquiries.

Therefore, Jung appears to acknowledge two kinds of objectivity in which our subjectivity is involved in different ways. Taking the objective psyche into consideration allows us to have a holistic picture of psychology and psychological research: on the one hand, no single individual's subjectively biased inquiries are enough to know all the objective facts involved in psychological development, but, on the other, acknowledging subjective inquiries and alternative perspectives could help us to get a closer picture of the objective world. This approach does not aim at being objective in the old paradigm sense or at synthesising subjectivity with this kind of objectivity as is suggested by Reason and Rowan in their account of the new paradigm, but aims at getting the closest possible picture of the active objective psyche via both passive and active subjective experiences. In that respect, Jung's approach is closer to Banister *et al.*'s view of qualitative psychology/methods:

> Qualitative research does not make claims to be 'objective', but it does offer a different way of working through the relationship between objectivity and subjectivity. Objectivity and subjectivity are always defined in relation to one another, and the mistake that positivists make is to assume that the relationship is like a conceptual zero-sum game in which a diminution of one, the erasure of subjectivity, will lead to an increase in the other, the production of a fully objective account ... When researchers, whether quantitative or qualitative, believe that they are being most objective by keeping a distance between themselves and their objects of study, they are actually themselves producing a *subjective* account, for a position of distance is still a position and it is all the more powerful if it refuses to acknowledge itself to be such.
>
> (Banister *et al.*, 1994, p. 13)

Nevertheless, Jung might not entirely agree that considering the 'position of the researcher' with reference to the whole process of psychological research makes the research closer to being objective. The difference is that, in the old paradigm, objectivity has been thought of as the exclusion of subjectivity and, in the new paradigm, is still thought of as the researcher's active performance of including his or her subjectivity as part of the research process. In Jung's account, however, such objectivity does not exist as a human capacity. Objectivity can be hypothetically postulated either as the passive recipient of active subjectivity or as the active source of passive subjectivity. In turn, subjectivity can be hypothetically postulated either as active inquiry into passive objectivity or as the passive representation of active objectivity. Nevertheless, when an attempt is made to transform passive subjectivity into active subjectivity, the passive experience of active objectivity (e.g., in the form of symbols) becomes active understanding of passive objectivity (e.g., in the form of concrete ideas and thoughts). Therefore, this does not lead us to a complete or 'correct' picture, as there are still gaps between passive and active subjectivity and, consequently, between active and passive objectivity, or vice versa. However, it does illuminate what is involved in the process of meaning-making.

The question as to whether the unconscious develops, which was discussed in Chapter 1, could be revisited in relation to active and passive subjectivity and objectivity. In order to discuss such a hypothetical question, I postulated three different ways in which the word 'development' could be understood (whether the unconscious develops, develops something else, or develops itself). This question could be further explored elsewhere in terms of the two kinds of subjectivity of the personal unconscious and the two kinds of objectivity of the collective unconscious.

Also, to postulate active and passive objectivity in relation to passive and active subjectivity might solve the problem related to Jung's concept of the self that we looked at earlier (in Chapter 6). The argument that Jung's concept of the self cannot be the totality of the psyche and the archetypal contents within the self at the same time was raised by Fordham (1963) and has been debated widely including by Colman (2006, pp. 157–8).

If we try to work out the above two definitions of the self on their own, they do not seem to make sense. However, when considering the self, whether as the totality of the psyche or as one of the archetypal contents, this particular problem might cease to exist if we include explicitly in the picture the participation of an individual's psyche in the objective psyche. Then we would have the equation: the self as the totality of the psyche (including an individual's psyche participating in the objective psyche) = the self as an archetype in relation to an individual's psyche (both of which belong to the objective psyche). The view of the self as the totality of the psyche (which is to be worked towards in the course of individuation) could be seen as the universal phenomenon of every individual's psyche working towards psychological wholeness, the processes involving both the collective unconscious and consciousness (in the objective psyche) – therefore involving both the archetypes and one's conscious and unconscious psyche. This might be practically equivalent to viewing the self as one of the archetypal contents in relation to one's conscious and unconscious psyche. In this view, the self means the ongoing process or continuing relationship between the archetypes and one's psyche. Therefore, viewing the self independently and not in relation to both one's conscious and unconscious psyche could be seen as the reason why the two definitions of the self appear problematic. But if we see the self as an archetype in relation to an individual's psyche, this continuous relationship seems to be compatible with the view of the self as the process towards the totality of the psyche.

The relationships between active objectivity and passive subjectivity and between passive objectivity and active subjectivity seem to be helpful in explaining the above solution to Fordham's challenge to Jung's concept of the self. In terms of active and passive objectivity and passive and active subjectivity, the concept of the self as the totality of the psyche could be understood as follows. If we accept that the totality of the psyche is something only to be worked towards but not accomplished, then this implies that the self is an ongoing process – the process in which the relationship between the objective psyche and each individual's psyche could becomes closer, as the gap between the unknown and one's understanding becomes narrower, through the relationships between active and passive objectivity and passive and active subjectivity. When considering the concept of the self as an archetype in relation to an individual's psyche, the relationships between active and passive objectivity and subjectivity could be understood in the following way. The ego of one's psyche could make an enquiry into the archetypes (active subjectivity seeking for passive objectivity), but this is not the only psychological process. The unconscious or subconscious psychological processes outside of the ego-function could be stimulated or even transformed by the archetypes (passive subjectivity being triggered by active objectivity). In concrete terms, for instance, the self as an archetype manifests as symbolic images in one's psyche (active objectivity being perceived by passive subjectivity), and one tries to understand the meaning of the symbolic images (active subjectivity trying to grasp passive objectivity). Thus, Jung's concept of the self requires consideration of not only subjectivity but also objectivity – each both active and passive in relation to the other.

Recent discourses emerging from qualitative research demonstrate their openness to alternative discursive options. Qualitative research aims to live with 'the gap between objects and representations' (Banister *et al.*, 1994, p. 4) by accepting such factors as interpretative stance, diversity, and subjectivity, which quantitative research has been attempting to control. However, there still seems to be a considerable degree of reluctance to seriously examine what is thought to be 'irrational' or what Jung might regard as 'paradoxical' in psychological research in general as well as perhaps in other academic disciplines. Even qualitative researchers' foci on language and the process of meaning making can be blocked, when they are to express irrationality using language. The implications of Jung's concepts of symbols, archetypal images and the objective psyche and his implicit postulation of two kinds of objectivity and subjectivity keep alive a challenge within this area of psychology, which tends to be avoided if not totally dismissed.

Thus, Jung's perspective provides scope for the sense of self and relationships informed by the autonomy of the psyche, which not only is static or fixed or standardised or determined but also allows for irrationality and paradoxicality as part of the whole dynamics. The development of the self and relationships with others for Jung could be explained by both *intersubjectivity* and *intrasubjectivity*: i.e., *intersubjective* relationships with others and *intra-subjective* relationships with personal and symbolic images of the self and others. Approaches to this issue from a Jungian standpoint require a consideration of Jung's notion of the objective psyche, which includes what we see as biological and cultural, that is to say, instinctual and symbolic elements of psychological life. The idea of the objective psyche highlights Jung's distinctiveness, and this way of supporting objectivity does not seem to be found in qualitative psychology where universal truth is questioned and diversity is cerebrated.

Could Fordham be introduced to developmental psychology as a qualitative psychologist?

Let us next consider how Fordham might be introduced to contemporary developmental psychology. Would it be possible to present him as a qualitative psychologist, in the same way as we have attempted to render Jung's perspective into the language of contemporary debates? In this section I intend to identify some issues for debate and make suggestions for future research. Before one could look at Fordham's potential contribution to this area, there are some issues that need to be addressed.

Problems with introducing Fordham as a qualitative psychologist to developmental psychology

When we attempt to introduce Fordham as a qualitative psychologist to contemporary developmental psychology, some problems arise:

1   The notion, still dominant within analytical psychology, that Fordham is 'developmental' and 'scientific', in the senses understood by conventional psychology, distracts our attempt to render his perspective into the language of contemporary developmental psychology where qualitative psychology has now been welcomed.
2   Fordham himself seems to present what he means by 'developmental' and 'scientific' in more than one way, and since he fails to clarify these differences in relation to Jung's position, the coherence of his qualitative stance remains doubtful.
3   Fordham's self-reflexive analyses tend to lead us to his interests in his own professional and political position within analytical psychology, which clouds his contribution to the study of psychological development, and, accordingly, the ground for this contribution appears ambiguous.

First, within analytical psychology, Fordham's work seems to have been looked at predominantly in terms of the old paradigm of developmental psychology, which is characterised by empirical and often reductive approaches to the early periods of life. But a narrative about Fordham as 'developmental' in the context of contemporary developmental psychology has not yet been clearly distinguished from the widely accepted images of Fordham as 'developmental' within analytical psychology. Attempts have been made to connect depth psychology with modern psychology and, more specifically, with modern infant research (e.g., Frosh, 1989; Jacoby, 1996, 1999; Stern, 1985). These kinds of approaches seem to have been favourably received as a means of justifying the value of depth psychology. Since then, more connections have been established with the emerging new discourses in developmental psychology (e.g., Knox, 2003). However, though various attempts have been made by contemporary Jungians to fit Fordham into recent discourses, the emphasis still seems to be on his status related to the 'new' discourses and 'scientific' aspects of recent developmental psychology without critical evaluation of either what goes on in contemporary developmental psychology itself or the compatibility between Jung and contemporary developmental psychologists.

The second issue to be addressed is Fordham's own use of the words 'developmental' and 'scientific'. As we discussed in Chapter 6, Fordham shows ambivalence towards Samuels' classification of the SAP as the 'Developmental School': he does not see himself as 'developmental' in any way that implies his work departs from Jung's, but he sees 'developmental' in the same way as Jung is. Similarly, Fordham uses the word 'scientific' to support both his own work (Fordham, 1993b, p. 94) and Jung's work (Fordham, 1995, pp. 92–7) in two different ways. The word 'scientific' seems to have had a particular fascination for Fordham. He is evidently aware of two kinds of philosophical understanding of science. On the one hand, Fordham presents his own work as 'scientific' in a way that distinguishes it from Jung's, and on the other hand, he presents his work as in agreement with what Jung considers as 'scientific'. When distinguishing his 'science' from Jung's, Fordham's understanding seems close to what might now be called the old paradigm of science, and when seeing both Jung and himself as 'scientific', his understanding seems close to what might be referred to as the new paradigm. A question then arises as to how Fordham conceives objectivity in psychological research and the objective psyche postulated by Jung. For Jung expresses his doubt as to whether Fordham correctly understood what he meant by the objective psyche (Jung, 1973, p. 497). Whether or not Fordham understood Jung's notion of the objective psyche correctly could open up a crucial debate. I shall not discuss this issue here but would suggest that a thorough and systematic consideration of Jung's and Fordham's understandings of science and objectivity might prove illuminating.

The third issue to be considered is Fordham's subjective position in relation to his work on psychological development. Fordham seems to make an effort to accept both the earlier and the recent understandings of science and development, and even switches his positions, so that he can sustain his professional and political status and identity within analytical psychology. He shows his eagerness to present his own work as original and yet 'Jungian'. Thinking in terms of the reflexivity of qualitative research, Fordham's relationship with Jung in both personal and professional contexts appears to be a vital factor in the meaning-making processes of his psychology. Fordham several times compares Jung with his own father (1993b, pp. 67, 79, 111, 119), possibly because both men were very important to him but less accessible than he would have wished. He also expresses both his satisfaction at Jung's approval of his work (1993b, p. 132) and his dissatisfaction at Jung not referring to him when saying that individuation is a lifetime process (ibid., p. 138). It might be partly because of Fordham's ambivalent attempt to integrate Jung's work with his own, an attempt bound up with issues of power relationships and social identity within a professional circle, that we seem to lose sight of Fordham's own interests and motivation. To explore Fordham's position as a researcher in relation to his own psychology (apart from his political and personal position in relation to Jung) could be a project for future research.

Thus, Fordham does seem to have the voice of a qualitative psychologist, when we observe his engagement with the process of meaning-making and the way he confronts in his work his own subjectivity as a researcher and a human being. But he also seems to switch his voice and his self-representation in different contexts, sometimes being critical of the old paradigm of psychology and other times aligning himself with it. This makes it more difficult to have a consistent picture of Fordham's approach in his research. Whether Fordham would be willing to be presented as a qualitative psychologist, the reasons for his objections to conventional psychology, and what his distinctiveness is as a researcher are all questions for future discussion.

Conclusion

This chapter has examined how Jung's psychology, viewed as the work of a qualitative psychologist, could contribute to issues related to such topics as emotion, personality, and sense of self and relationships, which have been discussed in mainstream developmental psychology. Instead of covering an extensive range of issues debated in the field of developmental psychology, the chapter has focused on the ways in which Jung's psychology could be presented as that of a qualitative psychologist and linked with some of the topics involved. It has addressed Jung's qualitative stance in terms of his engagement with language and meaning, diversity, and subjectivity. In doing so, we have identified Jung's foci on symbols (rather than language) and their meaning, universality as well as diversity, and objectivity as well as subjectivity.

A possible way of presenting Jung as a qualitative psychologist is to see his approach as more hermeneutic than scientific in the sense of the old paradigm and to identify this approach with the strengths of qualitative psychology. For example, even though Jung was more deeply involved in symbols than language, his constant attempts to express the significance of symbols by using language could still be seen as comparable with the approaches of qualitative psychologists. More problematically, Jung's perspective on diversity seems to be in very close agreement with qualitative psychologists, but his perspective on universality casts doubt on the compatibility between them. Similarly, mainly due to his perspective on objectivity, Jung's perspective on subjectivity is potentially both a highly illuminating and a highly controversial aspect of his work from the point of view of presenting him as a qualitative psychologist.

Some aspects of Jung's approach which might limit the possibilities for viewing him as a qualitative psychologist seem to be rooted in his perspectives on: (1) subjectivity and objectivity; and (2) universality and diversity. First, his perspectives on two kinds of subjectivity and objectivity (passive and active) in his study of the human psyche in relation to the objective psyche, as discussed in this chapter, seem to differentiate his position from qualitative psychology, which does not share the same views on subjectivity and objectivity. Second, Jung's belief in the universality of the objective psyche and the diversity of its manifestations as well as of individual psyches makes his approach particularly distinctive. For although it supports the possibility of diverse interpretations, like qualitative psychology, it also supports the possibility of universal truths, unlike quantitative psychology.

Nevertheless, if qualitative psychology were to remain open to further discursive options, Jung's distinctiveness could still prove to be his strengths rather than his limitations in being considered as a qualitative psychologist. Whether in agreement or disagreement with qualitative psychology, Jung's distinctiveness seems to reside particularly in his idea of the objective psyche. This idea postulates two kinds of subjectivity and objectivity, which cannot be observed in any other psychological theories. The remaining controversy is whether to view this as Jung's original contribution to qualitative psychology and the field of psychology as a whole, or as something that limits the possibilities of presenting him as a qualitative psychologist. We have also briefly discussed the potentiality of and the impediments to introducing Fordham's work as a qualitative approach to development.

It has been noted that it would not be feasible for this book to speak about Jungian developmental psychology in the contexts of either analytical psychology or developmental psychology. However, we have established some of the many possible connections between Jung as a qualitative psychologist and contemporary developmental psychology in which the acknowledgement of qualitative research is increasing. At the same time, this attempt has also highlighted Jung's distinctiveness, whether this supports or limits the possibility of him being a qualitative psychologist. In order to speak about Fordham in the context of developmental psychology, further research would be necessary, and similarly in order to address analytical psychology as a whole in the same context, further discussion would be needed.

Chapter 9

Conclusion

Making connections between depth psychology and modern, scientific psychology has been one of the main ways of attempting to bolster the validity of depth psychology. Likewise, combining psychoanalysis with modern infant research has become a potent means of corroborating analyses of childhood and early infancy (i.e., both an adult's images of childhood and the actual mother–infant relationship). In contrast, the recent deconstruction of modern psychology and the further exploration of postmodern, post-scientific psychology have shed light on the hermeneutic value of depth psychology.

The questions we have been investigating are: in what way is Jung developmental?; in what way is Fordham developmental?; and in what way is analytical psychology developmental? – in the light of the shifts from the earlier to the more recent understanding of and approaches to development that are observed in contemporary developmental psychology. Moreover, questions have been asked concerning how Jung, Fordham, and analytical psychology could contribute to today's debates in contemporary developmental psychology and in a wider interdisciplinary context.

The book has illuminated various images and narratives of development in analytical psychology and compared and contrasted them with those in wider historical and disciplinary contexts: histories of children and childhood, psychology, developmental psychology, depth psychology, the 'Developmental School' of analytical psychology, and the children's rights movement. We have also examined the underpinning assumptions and implications of particular images of development. The focus of our discussion has been, first, on Jung's own images and narratives of development as these emerge from his texts (Part I), second, on Jung's and other analytical psychologists' perspectives on development in the context of developmental psychology (Part II), third, on Fordham's position within analytical psychology and the relation of his work to wider issues involving the history of children and childhood (Part III), and, finally, on the attempt to present Jung's work as a qualitative approach to psychological development and his potential contribution to contemporary developmental psychology (Part IV).

Our investigations into images and narratives of development have explicitly addressed the recent shifts both in the understanding of the notion of development and in psychological research on development. The book has explored ways in which analytical psychology differs from the earlier understanding of development and agrees with the more recent understanding of development. It has also explored ways in which analytical psychology resembles the earlier understanding of development and contradicts the recent understanding of development.

It has become apparent that the earlier, dominant notion of development, which is often associated with progress, has been present in analytical psychology to some extent, and some forms of it are related to the Developmental School of analytical psychology, which might have been expected to be more related to recent understandings of development. However, it has also become apparent that there are other images and narratives of development which challenge this dominant notion of development. These are mainly observed in Jung's texts. Exploration of Jung's understanding of psychological development has shown that he was different from other psychologists and psychoanalysts of his time in not presenting a clear-cut model of a child, or a stage-model of development, or a causal explanation for psychological development. Because of this, his ideas have affinity with recent challenges to the notion of development. Nevertheless, it has to be noted that postmodern psychologies challenge modern psychology for different reasons than Jung: the former challenge its alleged objectivity and universality, which often excludes human subjectivity and creates hierarchies, while the latter challenges its one-sidedness. Therefore, Jung, who believes not only in the subjectivity and diversity of individual psyches but also in the objectivity and universality of the objective world, cannot be seen as in total agreement with postmodern psychologies that favour subjectivity over objectivity and diversity over universality. It has also been shown that Fordham's approaches to development can create confusing images of his work. On the one hand, he joins with psychoanalysis in emphasising the importance of childhood and early infancy and in adopting the old paradigm understanding of 'scientific'. On the other, he remains aligned with Jung in not providing a causal account of development and in embracing the new paradigm understanding of 'scientific'.

We have observed the crucial role of language use in the whole process of psychological research. In particular, this study has advocated that analytical psychology should participate in contemporary discourses about psychological development by acquiring language which reflects today's concerns and issues about development, rather than by forcing its own language onto other disciplines. By this I do not refer only to the adoption of a new terminology but also to enhanced awareness of the active role of language in the generation of images and, reciprocally, the influence on language use of dominant images within particular contexts. Part I aimed to understand Jung's perspective on development in his own language. Part II introduced the discourses in developmental psychology and suggested qualitative psychology as a potential connector between contemporary developmental psychology and depth psychology in general and analytical psychology in particular. Part III attempted, on the one hand, to tease out the rhetoric of development observed within analytical psychology, and, on the other, to connect Fordham's perspective with discourses about images of children and childhood in general and children's rights in particular. Part IV, with the purpose of critically re-evaluating Jung's work, attempted to apply Jung's perspective to some of today's debates on developmental issues in more contemporary and generally accepted language, more specifically, as a form of qualitative psychology.

Through this attempt to introduce analytical psychology to contemporary developmental psychology, I have suggested that analytical psychology update its vocabulary especially in relation to social contexts. These contexts have recently attracted many psychologists' attention but have still not been fully considered in analytical psychology. Nevertheless, my attempt has also revealed its limitations: for some of the characteristics of the unconscious aspects of psychological development, such as autonomy, paradox, and irrationality, cannot quite be conveyed in the language of social contexts, i.e., in images and narratives, but tend to be pulled back into the language of symbolic and spiritual contexts, i.e., symbols and myths.

Bearing in mind the significance of Jungian approaches to symbols and myths, I tried to present them in the clearer form of images and narratives. However, as soon as I tried to explain symbols and myths, my arguments diminished in clarity and things became less definable so that I had to use some words as metaphors, e.g., the gap between objects and representations, the archetypes, and the unconscious. On the one hand, when we focus on clarity in the use of language, we seem to lose the sense of those characteristics which may be associated only with symbols and myths and may not belong to images and narratives, e.g., numinosity and autonomy, or perhaps what is categorised as 'irrational'. On the other hand, when we focus on what is symbolic and mythic, we lose clarity of meaning. Thus, our focus on images and narratives of development has made explicit both the lack of social consideration within analytical psychology and the lack of symbolic interpretation outside analytical psychology. Both ways of focusing represent challenges to particular epistemologies and could contribute to potential discourses aimed at integrating both aspects, the social and the symbolic. The book has identified the difficulties that Jung might have experienced in using language to make sense of what is paradoxical and might not be logically or rationally comprehensible.

Through exploring the images and narratives of development in analytical psychology, it is hoped that the book has achieved its aim of generating more discussions on psychological development not only within analytical psychology but also between analytical psychology and other kinds of discourses.

However, limitations in my material are that, mainly due to restrictions of space, it has not addressed a very extensive range of sources from developmental psychology and has not fully examined other works of analytical psychology than those of Jung and Fordham.

The book could have introduced more theories and research findings from the side of developmental psychology, but I refrained from going into the details of individual research evidence and remained at the level of addressing the controversial issues that more immediately called for discussion. Based on the present piece of research, however, a future project could involve more of the research within developmental psychology and could contribute to that field.

The book could also have explored further, for example, some of Hillman's work on emotion (1960) and his acorn theory (1996), Edinger's notion of the ego–self axis (1972), Neumann's notion of automorphism and centroversion (1954) and other researchers' work concerning the wider social contexts of psychological development. In the course of my research I noted that some of the elements in Jung's work which can be viewed as developmental in the context of contemporary developmental psychology are, unexpectedly, elaborated by Hillman. There is a correspondence between Hillman's way of thinking and methodology in his research on emotion and postmodern thinking and qualitative approaches to psychology. However, the implications of this work for development need to be discussed further. Again, Hillman's acorn theory, which seems at first sight to present a strong nativistic viewpoint with an admixture of interactionist viewpoints, could be more deeply investigated. Though effort might be required to re-interpret and translate his rhetoric of symbols and metaphors into today's wider discourses about development, nevertheless the ideas of 'growing down' and of 'neither nature nor nurture' in his acorn theory might find a place in contemporary debates. Edinger's notion of the ego–self axis could be useful for elaborating the relationship between subjectivity and objectivity, and perhaps also Jung's two kinds of subjectivity and objectivity which I proposed in Chapter 8 of this book. Neumann's concepts of automorphism and centroversion might be linked to today's debates on children's growing capacity for autonomy, though systematic research would need to be done both on his writings and on relevant sources by other authors in this area. Yet again, consideration of social contexts might be a crucial factor in future research. Contemporary work on analytical psychology concerning the significance of social contexts in psychological development could help it to join in wider social discourses about development.

In conclusion, the book has examined the distinctiveness and limitations of analytical psychological perspectives on development in relation to both conventional and contemporary developmental psychology and, more generally, in relation to images of children and childhood. It has identified the tendency of analytical psychology to express its perspectives in language understood only within its own circle and not to be alert to other discourses about psychological development. It has suggested that some of the images and narratives in analytical psychology might be connected with discourses in qualitative psychology as an alternative way of promoting communication. This has opened up for discussion the possibility of analytical psychology's active participation in today's debates on issues of development. The findings of this study suggest that Jung's approach could be presented, to a certain extent, by using the discourses employed in qualitative psychology and could be explored further in terms of his distinctiveness, which might lead to either expanding the framework of qualitative psychology or challenging and going beyond it. The book has demonstrated that analytical psychology does not present a single definition of psychological development, partly because of the co-existence within it of diverse images and narratives and partly because of its consideration of symbols through the method of amplification which fosters such diversity. Nevertheless, this could be a strength, for it means that analytical psychology can remain open to alternative interpretations and other perspectives.

If we are to move towards a Jungian developmental psychology, it will be necessary to understand today's debates, explore the ways (uses of language) in which analytical psychology makes sense of its perspectives, and re-examine the implications of analytical psychology for development. My suggestions for future research are to reinterpret the texts of analytical psychology, keep up with the shifts occurring in other disciplines, and actively participate in interdisciplinary debates from the psychological point of view. I hope that the present work has given at least a preliminary sense of the potential value of each of these tasks.

Notes

Introduction

1 For a comparison between analytical psychological and social constructionist approaches to child images, see Main (2008).
2 For the topic of narratives in the clinical context, see Papadopoulos and Byng-Hall (1997).

1 Psychological development

1 Jung's first use of the term 'archetype' appears in 'Instinct and the Unconscious' (1919) (Adler, 1973, p. xxii). For Jung's definition of the archetypes and recent critical discussion, see, e.g., Jung (1934/54); Hogenson (2004).
2 Jung first uses the term the 'self' in *Psychological Types*, 1921. For Jung's definition of the self and recent critical discussion, see, e.g., Jung (1940); Colman (2006).
3 For the distinction between 'archetype as such' and 'archetypal images', see Hillman (1983); Jacobi (1959); Samuels (1985).
4 See Segal (2007).
5 Jung writes that the *collective psyche* 'can be subdivided into the *collective mind* and the *collective soul*' (1916/1966, para. 456). He explains that the *collective mind* is 'collective thinking', the *collective soul* is 'collective feeling', and the *collective psyche* is the 'collective psychological functions as a whole' (ibid., para. 456, n. 7).
6 Regarding the idea of 'cosmic identity', Boholm refers to Montgomery (1973).
7 According to Boholm, this includes the 'animal and plant world, the stars and planets, physical entities such as minerals, metals and chemical substances, as well as man himself, his body and soul' (1992, p. 116).
8 For the definition of the word 'progression', see Chapter 2.

2 Regression

1 Jung refers to Freud's use of 'regression' in *The Interpretations of Dreams*, vol. II, p. 543. However, it is not clear which German word Jung refers to. Jackson reports that Freud's use of the German word 'Regression' first appeared in his published writings in Ch. VII of *The Interpretation of Dreams*. The word 'Rückbildung', which Freud used in 1891 to refer to Jackson's notion of dissolution, was translated as 'retrogression' and 'regression'. The word 'rückläufig', which Freud used in 1895, was translated as 'retrogressive'. (Jackson, 1969, p. 744, n.1).
2 On the differences among Freud's three kinds of regression (topographical, temporal, and formal), see Laplanche and Pontalis ([1973] 1988), pp. 386–8.

3 Jung cites (with modification) Abraham (1913: pp. 36 and 72).
4 Jung writes that 'the myth is nothing but a projection from the unconscious and not a conscious invention at all' (1928b, para. 71). For this reason, we come across the same myth-motifs, which actually represent typical psychic phenomena (ibid.).
5 What Jung means by constellation is explained here as the 'influence of the complex on thinking and behaviour' (1904–7, para. 733).
6 Freud published 'Formulations on the Two Principles of Mental Functioning' in 1911, in the same year as Jung's publication of 'Two Kinds of Thinking'. Freud presents the pleasure principle and the reality principle in this paper; the former governs the primary mental process, and the latter dominates the secondary mental process as the regulating principles of both unconscious and conscious mental processes. Freud associates Eugen Bleuler's term 'autistic' (Freud, 1911, p. 220, n. 4) with 'repression', which pushes internal unpleasurable stimuli into the external world. In contrast, Jung's notion of two kinds of thinking asserts the nonpathological nature of primitive thought, using the term 'archaic' rather than 'autistic' to indicate the universality of archaic thinking (ibid.). Jung is concerned with ontogenesis and phylogenesis in seeing both children and primitives in parallel with earlier evolutionary states (Jung, 1911–12/52, paras 26, 32). While Jung explains child thinking and the mythological thinking of ancients in a parallel way, he also sees the human body and psychology in a parallel way. Nevertheless, his use of these parallels should be examined cautiously. While Freud regards the early state of the mental as 'repressed' in the case of neurosis, Jung describes the characteristic of archaic thinking as non-pathological.
7 Nevertheless, Jung is cautious about this analogy: while progression and regression of libido are 'dynamic forms of a specifically determined transformation of energy', extraversion and introversion are 'the forms taken both by progression and by regression' (1928b, para. 77). In other words, progression can be either extraverted, adapting to objects and environmental conditions, or introverted, adapting to the conditions of the ego or the 'subjective factor'. Likewise, regression can be either extraverted, flying into extravagant experience of the outside world, or introverted, retreating from the outside world.
8 Piaget writes that 'adaptation presupposes an equilibrium between assimilation and adaptation', making a link between organic regulations and cognitive processes (1971, p. 173). He explains:

> Assimilation and accommodation are not two separate functions but the two functional poles, set in opposition to each other, of any adaptation . . . there can be no assimilation of anything into the organism or its functioning without a corresponding accommodation and without such assimilation's becoming part of an adaptation context.
>
> (ibid.)

He considers that the basic functions of adaptation and assimilation are observable 'at every hierarchical level, from the genome and epigenotype up to the cognitive mechanisms of the higher orders' (ibid.).
9 Fordham (1985b, pp. 50–63) postulates the dynamic activity of deintegration and reintegration from the beginning of life as the action of the self. He explains:

> Deintegration and reintegration describe a fluctuating state of learning in which the infant opens itself to new experiences and then withdraws in order to reintegrate and consolidate those experiences. During a deintegrative activity, the infant maintains continuity with the main body of the self (or its

centre), while venturing into the external world to accumulate experience in motor action and sensory stimulation.

(Fordham, cited in Astor, 1995, p. 229)

10 Klein's theory of the paranoid-schizoid position and depressive position postulates a continuous process throughout life, and in this model chronological time factors seem irrelevant to this continuous process of development. For Klein, the past and the present are one in one's unconscious phantasy, and therefore regression plays no role (Mitchell, 1986, p. 28).

11 Mahler conceives of separation and individuation as 'two complementary developments' (Mahler *et al.*, 1975, p. 4) with regard to the development of a major organisation of intrapsychic and behavioural life. She presents this process as the psychological birth of the individual, describing it as 'the establishment of a sense of separateness from, and relation to, a world of reality, particularly with regard to the experiences of *one's own body* and to the principal representative of the world as the infant experiences it, the *primary love object*' (ibid., p. 3). Unlike Piaget and Fordham, however, Mahler defines the separation-individuation process as the original infantile process, which refers to the period from around 4 to 5 months to 30 or 36 months of age, though it reverberates and remains always active throughout the life cycle (ibid., pp. 3–5, 292).

12 He also states that the 'retreat to the infantile level does not mean only regression and stagnation, but also the possibility of discovering a new life plan. Regression is thus in very truth the basic condition for the act of creation' (1913, para. 406).

13 Jung uses the words 'presexual stage' for the period from birth up to the time of the first clear manifestations of sexuality and describes the period between the first and the fourth year of life as analogous to the 'chrysalis stage in butterflies', in which the elements from the nutritional and sexual phases are mixed (1911–12/1952, para. 206). He later presents three phase of life: the *presexual stage* (the first year of life), *prepubertal stage* (the later years of childhood up to puberty), and *maturity* (the adult period from puberty on) (1913, paras 263–70). He further maintains that 'the caterpillar stage' possesses an alimentary libido but no sexual libido (ibid., para. 269). Here the limit of the presexual stage is considered to occur between the third and fifth year (subject to individual variation), during which the first signs of sexual interests and activities emerge (ibid., para. 266). An analogy is borrowed from the development of the caterpillar–chrysalis–butterfly, but a stage model is not retained in Jung's later theorisation.

14 Hierarchical mental models are later discussed in relation to repression. See Chapter 4.

3 Symbolic child psychology

1 In addition to observing his own child, in his consultations Jung dealt with some cases about children which were brought by adults, e.g., their parents or doctors. It was common practice in his time that children's cases were talked about by adults, rather than children themselves being taken to analytic sessions.

2 For further discussion of metaphor and literal and metaphorical approaches to developmental psychology, see Samuels (1989, pp. 27–8, 46–7).

3 On Jung and Lévy-Bruhl, see e.g., Segal (2007).

4 Likewise, when Jung speaks about parents, he refers to symbolic parents and not just to actual parents. He writes:

behind every individual father there stands the primordial image of the Father, and behind the fleeting personal mother the magical figure of the

Magna Mater. These archetypes of the collective psyche, . . . are the domin-
ants that rule the preconscious soul of the child and, when projected upon
the human parents, lend them a fascination which often assumes monstrous
properties.

(1927/1931a, para. 97)

5 The editors of *the Collective Works of C. G. Jung* write: the term 'parental imago'
was 'taken up by psychoanalysis, but in analytical psychology it has been largely
replaced by "primordial image of the parent" or "parental archetype" ' (Jung,
1928c, para. 293, n. 5).
6 Jung refers to a similar diagram which illustrates the marriage of the King and
Queen in an alchemical text (Jung, 1946).
7 For the comparison between Jungian and social constructionist perspectives on
child images, see Main (2008).

4 'Recapitulation' and 'development' in analytical psychology

1 E.g., human development, personal development, personality development, psychic development, psychological development, spiritual development, collective
development, conscious development, abnormal development, embryonic development, ontogenetic/phylogenetic development, and many other kinds. See *General
Index, Collected Works of C. G. Jung*, vol. 20.
2 Gould defines ontogeny as 'The life history of an individual, both embryonic and
post-natal' (1977, p. 483) and phylogeny as 'The evolutionary history of a lineage,
conventionally (though not ideally) depicted as a sequence of successive adult
stages' (ibid., p. 484). Hence, Gould regards recapitulation as 'The repetition
of ancestral adult stages in embryonic or juvenile stages of descendants' (ibid.,
p. 485).
3 Gould notes that the present meaning of evolution as 'organic change in phylogeny' was introduced by Spencer in the mid-nineteenth century. He also writes
that the term 'evolution' was used differently as a synonym for preformationism
in the eighteenth- and early nineteenth-century debate over epigenesis versus
preformation (Gould, 1977, p. 481).
4 Locke, who believed that the mind at birth was a *tabula rasa* and that ideas are
not inborn but acquired by means of experience, and Gassendi were the
seventeenth-century thinkers from whom the 'sensationalism' tradition stemmed
(Morss, 1990, p. 5).
5 Rousseau's writings are regarded as an important source, with which such idealist
philosophers as Schopenhauer, Hegel, and Fichte are associated (Morss, 1990, p. 6).
6 James Mill in the UK and Herbart in Germany maintained that 'mental contents
are derived from sensations' (Morss, 1990, p. 6).
7 For Hall's encounters with Nature Philosophy, Wundt's laboratory of experimental psychology, Darwinian biology, see Morss (1990).
8 'Wandlungen und Symbole der Libido. Beiträge zur Entwicklungsgeschichte des
Denkens', part. I. *Jb. Psychoanal. psychotath.* Forsch, III: 1, pp. 120–227.
9 Combined with 'Wandlungen und Symbole der Libido. Beiträge zur Entwicklungsgeschichte des Denkens', part II. *Jb. Psychoanal. psychotath.* Forsch, IV: 1,
pp. 162–464. Later revised and published with title change: *Symbole der Wandlung.
Analyse des Vorspiels zu einer Schizophrenie* (*Symbols of Transformation*, 1952).
10 In the same year as his completion of *Wandlungen und Symbole der Libido* in
1912, Jung also visited the USA for nine lectures at Fordham University in
New York (Hayman, 1999, pp. 156–8). Against Freud, Jung proposed his division
of individual development into three periods at these lectures: a presexual phase

(till about the age of 3), Oedipal (the period at which boys develop the Oedipus complex), and Elektral (the period at which girls develop the Elektra complex). However, this model does not focus on actual infantile experience, but on the symbolisation of the unconscious constellation, in which psychic energy activates (ibid.). Jung does not further foster this view of individual development.

11 'A Phobia in a Five-Year-Old Boy'.

12 Jung's third lecture, entitled 'Experiences Concerning the Psychic Life of the Child' (later changed to 'Psychic Conflicts in a Child' [1910]) (Rosenzweig, 1992, p. 151) on the observation of the 4-year-old girl Anna, was deliberately made on the same day as Freud's lecture on the 4-year-old boy Hans. Both were in the form of the father's observations reported to the lecturer (ibid., p. 138). Anna's case was actually that of Jung's own daughter, and Jung's reference to the girl's extreme mistrust of the father would have been written when the scandalous relationship of Jung to Sabina Spielrein had climaxed and threatened Jung (ibid., pp. 147, 148). See further detail in ibid., Chapter 8.

13 Hall's child studies made parallels with the mind of primitive people in terms of fears, anger, sympathy and pity, social impulses, suggestion and imitation, fun, wit, and humour, rhythm and dancing, dreams, folklore, curiosity and interest, spontaneous drawings, attempts at artistic creations, fetishes, collections, the beginnings of property ownership, punishments, concepts of and attitude toward childhood in different nations, races, and stages of development, attitude toward authority, the earliest expressions of the religious instinct, the idea of number, the growth of language in young children, and so on (Hall *et al.*, 1921).

14 Freud noted the comparison of madness and dreaming in the philosophers Kant and Schopenhauer as well as in psychologist Wilhelm Wundt (Morss, 1990, p. 24).

15 Jung's use of these parallels persists through his work: children (infantile thinking), dreams (dream-thinking), and primitives (earlier evolutionary stage) in terms of mythological thinking (1911–12/1952); children, dreams, and dementia praecox in terms of mythological references (1913); childhood and prehistory of the race and of mankind in terms of possession of animal instincts (1927/1931b); childish fear (fairy tales) and primitive psychology ('night religion' of 'primitives') in terms of myth (1927/1931b); dreams, primitive levels of development, mental disturbances, the unconscious in terms of earlier stages of evolution (1930/1950); and childhood and a state of the past in terms of the pre-rational, pre-scientific world, i.e., the 'world of the men before us' (1943).

16 Jung writes that the collective psyche is the 'collective psychological functions as a whole', which consists of 'collective thinking', i.e., the collective mind, and 'collective feeling', i.e., the collective soul (1916/1966, para. 456, n. 7).

17 Jung makes parallels between embryonic mutation and racial history (1911–12/1952); body and mind (1913); the universal similarity of human brains and universal possibility of a uniform mental functioning (1916/1966); and anatomical and psychic structures (1930/1950).

18 Zschokke believed that there is a fixed evolutionary hierarchy of 'higher' and 'lower' functions based on his morphological view of the human body (Portman, 1976).

19 Hughlings Jackson originally presented this view in the late nineteenth century (Morss, 1990, pp. 24–5). On Meynert, see Sulloway (1979).

20 Hall's approach to education in the USA, which was seen as being recapitulatory, was not original to him but was a doctrine influential in Germany as well as elsewhere in Europe, and is already seen in Rousseau in the eighteenth century. Rousseau invented the modern notion of childhood as a distinct period of human life with particular needs for stimulation and education (Burman, 1994, p. 53). Likewise, Gould quotes Herbert Spencer who wrote in 1861 that 'Education

should be a repetition of civilization in little' (Spencer, 1861, p. 76, quoted in Gould, 1977, p. 148).

21 Greene illustrates feminist writers, who have shown us the histories of patriarchal society and women's development. For further discussion on women's development, see, e.g., Gilligan (1982).

22 Samuels classifies three different schools of analytical psychology: Classical, Developmental, and Archetypal (1985, pp. 1–22). He has since modified this classification into four different schools: fundamentalist, classical, developmental, and psychoanalytic (1998, pp. 21ff).

23 Jung wrote the foreword to the book.

24 Giegerich also challenges Fordham's scientific, empirical approach to development. See Samuels (1985, Chapter 5).

25 Circularity in Hillman's account is that 'every element in personality is seen as always present and as always having been so, and that development is construed as development of something into itself, into the nature that was always there' (Samuels, 1985, p. 141; see also Hillman, 1975).

26 With regard to the argument about dichotomy (1994), Samuels proposes to unite and integrate both diachronic-causal and synchronous-acausal models of development, giving both equal weight (1989). See Samuels (1994, p. 12, 1989, Chapter 2).

27 For the application of systemic theories to Jungian perspectives, see Papadopoulos (1996a); and for that of ecological thinking, see Papadopoulos (1998).

5 Methodological issues in developmental psychology and analytical psychology

1 This was written before the time when the word was changed from 'subjects' to 'participants' in the BPS 'Code of Conduct, Ethical Principles, & Guidelines'.

2 Pearson (1995, p. 761) refers to Hammersley (1992, Chapter 9).

3 Krantz (1995, p. 91) refers to Reichardt and Cook (1979, p. 10).

4 Rabinowitz and Weseen (2001, p. 23) refer to Morawski (1986, pp. 47–66).

5 In certain discourses such as the children's rights discourse, when it is connected with the notion of 'well-being' of an individual, particularly of a child, narrative truth could be seen as a powerful and convincing factor which explicates the child's psychological well-being. In this framework, the acts of denying or rejecting such narrative truth expressed in children's own voices could even be seen as politically inappropriate. – We will return to some of the issues related to children's rights in Chapter 7.

6 It officially ceased at the Society of Analytical Psychology AGM November 2006 (Slater, the Librarian at the SAP, personal communication, 2007).

7 Nevertheless, Covington also questions the popularity – and frequently the requirement – of infant observation among various trainings, since the six lessons she mentions can also be learned in the course of work with adult patients (1991, p. 73).

8 Fulani (2000, p. 156) quotes Vygotsky (1978, p. 65).

9 I have discussed elsewhere analytical psychological perspective on universality and diversity in comparison with social constructionist views (Main, 2008).

6 Jung, Fordham, and the 'Developmental School'

1 Samuels argues that the Schools should be spelled in title cases, starting with capitals, e.g., the Developmental School (Samuels, personal communication, 2001). He does so in his first classification in his own book, though he changes the

names into lower case in his new classification, following the style of the book edited by Casement (see Samuels, 1998).

2 Kirsch basically agrees with Samuels' quadripartite division, presenting four types as 'ultra-classical, classical, developmental, and "merging" with psychoanalysis' (2000, pp. 53–4).

3 For further details, see Kirsch (1998, 2000); Casement (1995); Fordham (1979, 1993b); Lambert (1976); Shamdasani (1996); Prince (1963).

4 The SAP does not possess any documents that constitute an official history of the SAP as such (Stobart, SAP, personal communication, 2001).

5 I have discussed Fordham's work in 'Fordham's Contribution to Jungian Child Therapy: Individuation in Childhood', unpublished Masters dissertation, University of Kent at Canterbury, 1998.

6 Fordham mainly accepted Klein's practice but not all her theories. For instance, he did not believe in Klein's concept of the death drive (Astor, personal communication, 1998), but he found similarities between Klein's notion of unconscious phantasies and Jung's concept of archetypes.

7 I have discussed elsewhere Fordham's disagreement with Jung's notion of the self and of the child's psyche. See Miyagi (1998).

7 The children's rights movement and Fordham's work with children

1 The comparisons between Jung's and the social constructionist perspectives on adults' images of children and childhood are discussed elsewhere (Main, 2008).

2 See further details in Van Bueren (1995, Chapter I); Veerman (1992a, Chapter X).

3 See Veerman (1992a, Chapter VI).

4 Having read history and then education at Oxford, Jebb became a primary school teacher for children of poor families in a church school in Marlborough. Giving up teaching for reasons of health, she moved to Cambridge to live with her mother, and there received information about the horrific fate of children during the war from influential Red Cross officials with whom she had made contact during her visit to Macedonia before the war. With her sister, Jebb published the facts about civilian victims of the war in the *Cambridge Magazine*, and after the war, also with some friends, founded the *Fight the Famine Council*. The members of this council held meetings to influence public opinion in favour of lifting the food blockade. See further Van Bueren (1995, Chapter 1).

5 See Veerman (1992a, Chapter IV).

6 Freeman refers to P. B. Mayer, 'The Exploitation of the American Growing Class', in Gottlieb, *Children's Liberation* (1973, p. 51).

7 According to Urban, the reasons for the cessation of the Child Analytic Training (CAT) as stated in the CAT annual report of 2005 point to the consequences of child psychotherapy training having links with NHS training posts. The consequences included difficulties in meeting a growing number of NHS-related requirements with only a few child analysts in the SAP as well as the difficulty for trainees to sustain their private training, which is costly, without having training posts, which are far fewer than the number of trainees.

8 Lopatka refers to Braibant, 1990 (Lopatka, 1992, p. 48).

9 Cunningham points out the problem in the translation of the French '*sentiment*', used by Ariès, by the English 'idea', which fails to convey the meaning of the original word, i.e. 'the sense of a feeling about childhood as well as a concept of it' (1995, p. 30). He argues that, by using this particular word, Ariès attempted to make a clear 'distinction between a "*sentiment*" about childhood and the way adults treated children' (ibid.).

10 In the ancient world, 'there was a relative neglect of young children' (Cunningham. 1995, p. 25), who were discussed primarily in terms of 'their deficiencies, the adult qualities which they lack' (ibid., pp. 25–6). Childhood was seen 'as part of a process towards producing a good citizen' and not as important for itself; children were predominantly seen in terms of the services they could provide and not as individual human beings; and they were seen as being close to the divine world because they were thought of, together with women and slaves, as unimportant, and also because their life was thought of as uncertain, having possibilities of death before reaching adulthood. Children were therefore marginal to society. He asks whether children were held in low esteem, and whether slaves and servants were in the same position as children (ibid., p. 23). Moreover, it is hard to determine whether the words signifying child, which are found in Greek (*pais*) and Latin (*infans, puer*), from which some of the English words signifying the child originate, relate to age or status. For 'in the ancient world a slave or a servant, of whatever age, could be *pais* or *puer*' (ibid., p. 23). See further Cunningham (1995, pp. 19–27); Shahar (1990, Chapter 1).
11 See further ibid., Chapter 2.
12 On *patria potestas*, the power of the father or force of paternal authority in Roman law, see Cunningham (1995, pp. 24ff); Shahar (1990, p. 13).
13 'Childhood was most commonly divided into three stages': *infantia, pueritia*, and *adolescentia* (1990, p. 22). See further Shahar (1990, Chapter 2).

8 Jung as a qualitative psychologist

1 On the erotic transference between Jung and his cousin during the seances, see Goodheart (1984).
2 The design of the study varied in terms of the variables controlled. The participants were asked to say what is immediately called to mind when a stimulus word is called out. (The numbers and categories of the stimulus words used and the participants involved varied.) See further Jung, *CW2*.
3 The word 'correlation' is not used in the original texts.
4 Qualitative psychology works with problems which conventional psychology finds intolerable and therefore attempts to control. What Woolgar (1988) calls the 'methodological horrors' are such problems as (a) 'indexicality (where explanation is tied to particular occasions and uses, and changes correspondingly)'; (b) 'inconcludability (where the meaning of an account is inexhaustible and will continually change as more is added)'; and (c) 'reflexivity (where the process of interpretation structures the phenomenon under consideration and this correspondingly changes the ways we view it)' (Burman, 2001, p. 265). For further discussion, see Woolgar (1988).
5 Twenty-four families participated, consisting altogether of 100 individuals. See further details in Jung (1910b).
6 For further discussion on the concept of the self, which has been one of the most controversial topics within analytical psychology, see, for example, Colman (2006).
7 Similarly, Knox (2003) draws a parallel between developmental cognitive science and psychoanalytic/psychodynamic work in terms of internal objects. See Chapter 4 of this book.
8 For further discussions on the concept of the 'other' in the context of analytical psychology, see, e.g., Papadopoulos (1984, 2002).
9 The editors of *C. G. Jung Letters* draw our attention to the origin of the term (Jung, 1973, p. 497). See 'Basic Postulates of Analytical Psychology' in *CW8*, para.

666. In many places Jung seems to use such terms as objective psyche, objective world, autonomous psyche, the collective unconscious as though equivalent. But more cautious and systematic study is required to distinguish between these terms.

10 For Jung's discussion on active/passive fantasies, see Jung (1921, paras 711–14). For his explanation of active/passive extraversion, see ibid., para. 710, and that for active/passive introversion, see ibid., para. 769.

Bibliography

Abraham, K. (1913) *Dreams and Myths*, trans. W. A. White. (Nervous and Mental Disease Monograph Series, 15), New York.

Adams, M. V. (1996) *The Multicultural Imagination: 'Race,' Color, and the Unconscious*, London: Routledge.

Adler, G. (ed.) (1973) *C. G. Jung Letters I: 1906–1950*, London: Routledge and Kegan Paul.

Andersen, T. (1997) 'Researching client–therapist relationships: a collaborative study for informing therapy', *Journal of Systemic Therapies*, vol. 16, no. 2, pp. 125–33.

Anderson, H. (2000) 'Reflections on and the appeals and challenges of postmodern psychologies, societal practice, and political life', in L. Holzman and J. Morss (eds), *Postmodern Psychologies, Societal Practice, and Political Life*, London: Routledge.

Ariès, P. (1962) *Centuries of Childhood: A Social History of Family Life*, trans. R. Baldick, New York: Vintage Books; London: Jonathan Cape Ltd.

Astor, J. (1995) *Michael Fordham: Innovations in Analytical Psychology*, London: Routledge.

—— (1996) 'A tribute to Michael Fordham', *Journal of Child Psychotherapy*, vol. 22, no. 1, pp. 5–25.

—— (2007) 'Analytical psychology and Michael Fordham', in A. Casement (ed.), *Who Owns Jung?*, London: Karnac.

Balint, M. ([1968] 1995) *The Basic Fault: Therapeutic Aspects of Regression*, London: Routledge.

Banister, P., Burman, E., Parker, I., Taylor, M. and Tindall, C. (1994) *Qualitative Methods in Psychology: A Research Guide*, Buckingham and Philadelphia: Open University Press.

Barnes, P. (ed.) (1995) *Persona, Social and Emotional Development of Children*, Milton Keynes: Open University Press; Oxford: Blackwell.

Baynes, H. G. ([1940] 1969) *Mythology of the Soul: A Research into the Unconscious from Schizophrenic Dreams and Drawings*, London: Rider & Company.

Berger, P. and Luckmann, T. ([1966] 1971) *The Social Construction of Reality*, Harmondsworth: Penguin.

Billig, M. (1999) *Freudian Repression: Conversation Creating the Unconscious*, Cambridge: Cambridge University Press.

Bliwise, N. G. (1999) 'Securing attachment theory's potential', *Feminism and Psychology*, vol. 9, no. 1, pp. 43–52.

Boholm, Å. (1992) 'How to make a stone give birth to itself: reproduction and auto-reproduction in medieval and renaissance alchemy', in G. Aijmer (ed.), *Coming into Existence: Birth and Metaphors of Birth*, Göteborg, Sweden: IASSA.

Bowlby, J. (1944) 'Forty-four juvenile thieves: their characters and home life', *International Journal of Psychoanalysis*, 25, pp. 1–57, 207–28.

—— (1969) *Attachment and Loss: Attachment*, New York: Basic Books.

Braibant, G. (1990) *Les Droits de l'Homme: Universalité et Renouveau, 1789–1989*. Works published under the direction of G. Braibant and G. Marc, Paris: Edition l'Harmattan.

Brems, C. (1991) 'Self-psychology and feminism: an integration and expansion', *The American Journal of Psychoanalysis*, vol. 51, no. 2, pp. 145–60.

Bruner, J. (1986) *Actual Minds: Possible Worlds*, Cambridge, MA: Harvard University Press.

Burman, E. (1994) *Deconstructing Developmental Psychology*, London: Routledge.

—— (1997) 'Minding the gap: positivism, psychology, and the politics of qualitative methods', *Journal of Social Issues*, vol. 53, no. 4, pp. 785–801.

—— (2000) 'Method, measurement, and madness', in L. Holzman and J. Morss (eds), *Postmodern Psychologies, Societal Practice, and Political Life*, London: Routledge.

—— (2001) 'Minding the gap: positivism, psychology, and the politics of qualitative methods', in D. L. Tolman and M. Brydon-Miller (eds), *From Subjects to Subjectivities: A Handbook of Interpretive and Participatory Methods*, New York: New York University Press.

Butterworth, P. and Bryant, P. (eds) (1990) *Causes of Development: Interdisciplinary Perspectives*, New York: Harvester Wheatsheaf.

Cambray, J. (2006) 'Towards the feeling of emergence', *Journal of Analytical Psychology*, vol. 51, no. 1, pp. 1–20.

Carey, S. (1990) 'On some relations between the description and the explanation of developmental change', in G. Butterworth and P. Bryant (eds), *Causes of Development: Interdisciplinary Perspectives*, New York: Harvester Wheatsheaf.

Casement, A. (1995) 'A brief history of Jungian splits in the United Kingdom', *Journal of Analytical Psychology*, vol. 40, no. 3, pp. 327–42.

—— (ed.) (1998) *Post-Jungians Today: Key Papers in Contemporary Analytical Psychology*, London: Routledge.

Chamberlain, A. F. (1900) *The Child: A Study in the Evolution of Man*, London: Walter Scott.

Colman, W. (2000) 'Models of the self', in E. Christopher and H. M. Solomon (eds), *Jungian Thought in the Modern World*, London: Free Association.

—— (2006) 'The self', in R. K. Papadopoulos (ed.), *The Handbook of Jungian Psychology: Theory, Practice and Applications*, Hove and New York: Routledge.

Cooper, T. and Kaye, H. (2002) 'Language and meaning', in T. Cooper and R. Ilona (eds), *Challenging Psychological Issues*, Milton Keynes: Open University.

Covington, C. (1991) 'Infant observation reviewed', *Journal of Analytical Psychology*, vol. 36, no. 1, pp. 63–76.

Cowie, H. (1995) 'Child care and attachment', in Peter Barnes (ed.) *Personal, Social and Emotional Development of Children*, Oxford: Blackwell.

Cunningham, H. (1995) *Children and Childhood in Western Society since 1500*, London and New York: Longman.

Dalal, F. (1988) 'Jung: a racist', *British Journal of Psychotherapy*, vol. 4, no. 3, pp. 263–79.

Das Gupta, P. (1994) 'Images of childhood and theories of development' in J. Oates (ed.), *The Foundation of Child Development*, Milton Keynes: Open University; Oxford: Blackwell.

Davidson, D. (1986) 'The child analytic training, 1960–1985: the first quarter', *Journal of Analytical Psychology*, vol. 31, no. 1, pp. 213–22.

Davin, A. (1999) 'What is a child?', in A. Fletcher and S. Hussey (eds), *Childhood in Question: Children, Parents and the State*, Manchester: Manchester University Press.

de Mause, Lloyd (ed.) (1974) *The History of Childhood*, New York: The Psychohistory Press.

Edinger, E. (1972) *Ego and Archetype*, New York: Penguin.

Ford, R. M. (2004) 'Thinking and cognitive development in young children' in T. Maynard and N. Thomas (eds), *An Introduction to Early Childhood Studies*, London: Sage.

Fordham, F. (1969) 'Some views on individuation', in M. Fordham (ed.), *Analytical Psychology: A Modern Science*, The Library of Analytical Psychology, vol. 1, London: William Heinemann Medical Books.

Fordham, M. (1949) 'A discussion on archetypes and internal objects: I. on the reality of archetypes', *Journal of Medical Psychology*, vol. 22, no. 1, pp. 3–7.

—— (1957) *New Developments in Analytical Psychology*, London: Routledge and Kegan Paul.

—— (1960) 'Counter-transference', *Journal of Medical Psychology*, vol. 33, no. 1, pp. 1–8.

—— (1963) 'The empirical foundation in Jung's works', in *Analytical Psychology: A Modern Science*, The Library of Analytical Psychology, vol. 1, London: William Heinemann Medical Books.

—— (1965) 'The importance of analysing childhood for assimilation of the shadow', in *Analytical Psychology: A Modern Science*, The Library of Analytical Psychology, vol. 1, London: William Heinemann Medical Books.

—— (1968) 'Individuation in childhood', in J. B. Wheelwright (ed.), *The Reality of the Psyche*, New York: Putnam.

—— (1971) 'Maturation of ego and self in infancy', in *Analytical Psychology: A Modern Science*, The Library of Analytical Psychology, vol. 1, London: William Heinemann Medical Books.

—— (1976) *The Self and Autism*, The Library of Analytical Psychology, vol. 3, London: William Heinemann Medical Books.

—— (1979) 'Analytical psychology in England', *Journal of Analytical Psychology*, vol. 24, no. 4, pp. 279–97.

—— (1981) 'Neumann and childhood', *Journal of Analytical Psychology*, vol. 26, no. 2, pp. 99–122.

—— (1985a) 'Abandonment in infancy', *Chiron*, vol. 2, no. 1, pp. 1–21.

—— (1985b) *Explorations into the Self*, Library of Analytical Psychology, vol. 7, London: Academic Press.

—— (1988) 'The emergence of child analysis', in M. Sidoli and M. Davis (eds), *Jungian Child Psychotherapy: Individuation in Childhood*, London: Karnac.

—— (1993a) 'The Jung–Klein Hybrid', *Free Associations*, vol. 3, pt 4, no. 28, pp. 631–41.

—— (1993b) *The Making of an Analyst: A Memoir*, London: Free Association Books.

—— ([1988] 1994) *Children as Individuals*, London: Free Association Books.

—— (1995) *Freud, Jung, Klein – the Fenceless Field: Essays on Psychoanalysis and Analytical Psychology*, London and New York: Routledge.

Fottrell, D. (1999) 'Children's rights', in A. Hegarty and S. Leonard (eds), *Human Rights – An Agenda for the 21st Century*, London: Cavendish Publishing.

Freeman, M. (1992a) 'Introduction: rights, ideology and children', in M. Freeman and P. Veerman (eds), *The Ideologies of Children's Rights*, International Studies in Human Rights, vol. 23, Dordrecht: Martinus Nijhoff Publishers.

—— (1992b) 'The limits of children's rights', in M. Freeman and P. Veerman (eds), *The Ideologies of Children's Rights*, International Studies in Human Rights, vol. 23, Dordrecht: Martinus Nijhoff Publishers.

Freud, S. (1900) *The Interpretation of Dreams, Standard Edition of the Complete Psychological Works of Sigmund Freud*, trans., ed. J. Strachey, in collaboration with A. Freud, assisted by A. Strachey and A. Tyson, 24 vols. (1953–74), vols 4 and 5, London: Hogarth.

—— (1909) 'A phobia in a five-year-old boy', in *Standard Edition of the Complete Psychological Works of Sigmund Freud*, trans., ed. J. Strachey, in collaboration with A. Freud, assisted by A. Strachey and A. Tyson, 24 vols. (1953–74), vol. 10, London: Hogarth.

—— (1911) 'Formulations on the two principles of mental functioning', in *Standard Edition of the Complete Psychological Works of Sigmund Freud*, trans., ed. J. Strachey, in collaboration with A. Freud, assisted by A. Strachey and A. Tyson, 24 vols. (1953–74), vol. 12, London: Hogarth.

Frosh, S. (1989) *Psychoanalysis and Psychology: Minding the Gap*, New York: New York University Press.

Fulani, L. (2000) 'Race, identity, and epistemology', in L. Holzman and J. Morss (eds), *Postmodern Psychologies, Societal Practice, and Political Life*, London: Routledge.

Giegerich, W. (1975) 'Ontogeny = phylogeny? a fundamental critique of Erich Neumann's analytical psychology', *Spring*, vol. 75, pp. 110–29.

Gilligan, C. (1982) *In a Different Voice: Psychological Theory and Women's Development*, Cambridge, MA: Harvard University Press.

Goldfarb, W. (1947) 'Variations of adolescent adjustment of institutionally reared children', *American Journal of Orthopsychiatry*, vol. 17, pp. 449–57.

Goodheart, W. (1984) 'C. G. Jung's first "patient": on the seminal emergence of Jung's thought', *Journal of Analytical Psychology*, vol. 29, no. 1, pp. 1–34.

Gottlieb, D. (ed.) (1973) *Children's Liberation*, Englewood Cliffs, NJ: Prentice Hall.

Gould, S. J. (1977) *Ontogeny and Phylogeny*, Cambridge, MA: Belknap Press of Harvard University Press.

Greene, S. (1997) 'Child development: old themes and new directions', in L. Fuller *et al.* (eds), *A Century of Psychology: Progress, Paradigms and Prospects for the New Millennium*, London: Routledge.

Halasz, G. (1996) 'The rights of the child in psychotherapy', *American Journal of Psychotherapy*, vol. 50, no. 3, pp. 285–97.

Hall, G. S. *et al.* (eds) (1921) *Aspects of Child Life and Education.* New York: MCMXX, D. Appleton.

Hammersley, M. (1992) *What's Wrong with Ethnography? Methodological Explorations*, London: Routledge.

Hauke, C. ([1994] 1996) 'The child: development, archetype, and analytic practice', *San Francisco Jung Institute Library Journal*, vol. 15, no. 1, pp. 17–38.

—— (2000) *Jung and the Postmodern: The Interpretation of Realities*, London: Routledge.

Hayman, R. (1999) *A Life of Jung*, London: Bloomsbury.

Hillman, J. (1960) *Emotion: A Comprehensive Phenomenology of Theories and Their Meanings for Therapy*, London: Routledge and Kegan Paul.

—— (1967) 'Senex and puer: an aspect of the historical and psychological present', *Eranos-Jahrbuch*, vol. 36, *Polarität des Lebens*, Zürich: Phein-Verlag.

—— (1975) 'Abandoning the Child', in J. Hillman (ed.), *Loose Ends: Primary Papers in Analytical Psychology*, New York: Spring Publications.

—— (1983) *Archetypal Psychology: A Brief Account*, Texas: Spring Publications.

—— (1996) *The Soul's Code: In Search of Character and Calling*, New York: Random House.

Hinde, R. (1990) 'Causes of social development from the perspective of an integrated developmental science', in G. Butterworth and P. Bryant (eds), *Causes of Development: Interdisciplinary Perspectives*, New York: Harvester Wheatsheaf.

Hinde, R. A. and Stevenson-Hinde, J. (eds) (1988) *Relationships within Families: Mutual Influences*, Oxford: Clarendon.

Hogenson, G. B. (2004) 'Archetypes: emergence and the psyche's deep structure', in J. Cambray and L. Carter (eds), *Analytical Psychology: Contemporary Perspectives in Jungian Analysis*, Hove and New York: Brunner-Routledge.

Holzman, L. (2000) 'Performance, criticism, and postmodern psychology', in L. Holzman and J. Morss (eds), *Postmodern Psychologies, Societal Practice, and Political Life*, London: Routledge.

Holzman, L. and Morss, J. (eds) (2000) *Postmodern Psychologies, Societal Practice, and Political Life*, London: Routledge.

Hopcke, R. (1989) *Jung, Jungians and Homosexuality*, Boston: Shambhala.

Jackson, S. W. (1969) 'The history of Freud's concepts of regression', *Journal of the American Psychoanalytic Association*, vol. 17, no. 3, pp. 743–84.

Jacobi, J. (1959) *Complex/Archetype/Symbol in the Psychology of C. G. Jung*, New York: Princeton University Press.

—— (1965) *The Way of Individuation*, trans. R. F. C. Hull, London: Hodder & Stoughton.

Jacoby, M. (1996) ' "Reductive" analysis in the light of modern infant research', *Journal of Analytical Psychology*, vol. 41, no. 3, pp. 387–98.

—— (1999) *Jungian Psychotherapy and Contemporary Infant Research: Basic Patterns of Emotional Exchange*, translated from the German, in collaboration with the author, by R. Weathers, London: Routledge.

Jones, R. A. (2007) *Jung, Psychology, Postmodernity*, London: Routledge.

Jung, C. G. (1902) 'On the psychology and pathology of so-called occult phenomena', in *The Collected Works of C. G. Jung*, 20 vols. (1953–1979) ed. H. Read, M. Fordham, and G. Adler, trans. R. F. C. Hull, London: Routledge and Kegan Paul, [hereafter *CW*], vol. 1.

—— (1904–7, 1910) 'Studies in word association', in *CW* 2.

—— (1906a) 'The psychological diagnosis of evidence', in *CW* 2.

—— (1906b) 'Psychoanalysis and association experiments', in *CW* 2.

—— (1906c) 'The psychopathological significance of the association experiment', in *CW* 2.

—— (1910a) 'The association method', in *CW* 2.

—— (1910b) 'The family constellation', in *CW* 2.

—— (1910/1946) 'Psychic conflicts in a child', in *CW* 17.

—— (1911–12/1952) *Symbols of Transformation, CW* 5.

—— (1913) 'The theory of psychoanalysis', in *CW* 4.

—— ([1911] 1913) 'On the doctrine of complexes', in *CW* 2.

—— (1916) 'Psychoanalysis and neurosis', in *CW* 4.

—— ([1916]/1957) 'The transcendent function', in *CW* 8.

—— (1916/1966) 'The structure of the unconscious', in *CW* 7.

—— (1917/1926/1943) 'On the psychology of the unconscious', in *CW* 7.

—— (1919) 'Instinct and the unconscious', in *CW* 8.

—— (1921) *Psychological Types, CW* 6.

—— (1923) 'Psychological types' in 'Appendix, four papers on psychological typology', in *CW* 6.

—— (1925) 'Marriage as a psychological relationship', in *CW* 17.

—— (1926/1946) 'Analytical psychology and education: three lectures', in *CW* 17.

—— (1927) 'Woman in Europe', in *CW* 10.

—— (1927/1931a) 'Introduction to Wickes's "Analyses der Kinderseele" ', in *CW* 17.

—— (1927/1931b) 'Mind and earth', in *CW* 10.

—— (1928a) 'Child development and education', in *CW* 17.

—— (1928b) 'On psychic energy', in *CW* 8.

—— (1928c) 'The relations between the ego and the unconscious', in *CW* 7.

—— (1928d) 'The significance of the unconscious in individual education', in *CW* 17.

—— (1928/1931) 'Analytical psychology and *Weltanschauung*', in *CW* 8.

—— (1929a) 'Commentary on "The Secret of the Golden Flower" ', in *CW* 13.

—— (1929b) 'Problems of modern psychotherapy', in *CW* 16.

—— (1929c) 'Freud and Jung: contrasts', in *CW* 4.

—— (1930b) 'Some aspects of modern psychotherapy', in *CW* 16.

—— (1930–31) 'The stages of life', in *CW* 8.

—— (1930/1950) 'Psychology and literature', in *CW* 15.

—— (1933/1934) 'The meaning of psychology for modern man', in *CW* 10.

—— (1934a) 'The development of personality', in *CW* 17.

—— (1934b) 'The soul and death', in *CW* 8.

—— (1934c) 'The state of psychotherapy today', in *CW* 10.

—— (1934/1954) 'Archetypes of the collective unconscious', in *CW* 9 (i).

—— (1935a) 'Principles of practical psychotherapy', in *CW* 16.

—— (1935b) 'The Tavistock lectures', in *CW* 18.

—— (1936) 'The concept of the collective unconscious', in *CW* 9 (i).

—— (1938/1954) 'Psychological aspects of the mother archetype', in *CW* 9 (i).

—— (1940) 'The psychology of the child archetype', in *CW* 9 (i).

—— (1942/1948) 'A psychological approach to the dogma of the Trinity', in *CW* 11.

—— (1943) 'The gifted child', in *CW* 17.

—— (1943/1948) 'The spirit Mercurius', in *CW* 13.

—— (1944a) 'Epilogue', in *CW* 12.

—— (1944b) 'Introduction to the religious and psychological problems of alchemy', in *CW* 12.

—— (1945) 'Psychotherapy today', in *CW* 16.

—— (1946) 'Psychology of the transference', in *CW* 16.

—— (1947/1954) 'On the nature of the psyche', in *CW* 8.

—— (1950) 'Concerning mandala symbolism', in *CW* 9 (i).

—— (1952) 'Answer to job', in *CW* 11.

—— (1956) *Gegenwart und Zukunft* ('The Undiscovered Self', *CW* 10).

—— (1957) 'The undiscovered self (present and future)', in *CW* 10.

—— ([1963] 1995) *Memories, Dreams, Reflections*, ed. A. Jaffé, trans. R. and C. Winston, reprinted, London: Fontana Press.

—— (1973) *C. G. Jung: Letters I: 1906–1950*, ed. G. Adler in collaboration with A. Jaffé, trans. R. F. C. Hull, London: Routledge and Kegan Paul.

Karmiloff-Smith, A. (1996) 'The connectionist infant: would Piaget turn in his grave?', in A. Slater and D. Muir (eds), *The Blackwell Reader in Developmental Psychology*, Oxford: Blackwell.

King, M. (1985) 'Are rights relevant?', *Educational and Child Psychology*, vol. 2, no. 2, pp. 49–57.

Kirsch, T. B. (1998) 'Approaching the millennium: origins of analytical psychology in Great Britain', afternoon talk at Society of Analytical Psychology, London.

—— (2000) *The Jungians: A Comparative and Historical Perspective*, London: Routledge.

Krantz, D. L. (1995) 'Sustaining vs. resolving the quantitative-qualitative debate', *Evaluation and Program Planning*, vol. 18, no. 1, pp. 89–96.

Kris, E. (1952) *Psychoanalytic Explorations in Art*, Oxford: International Universities Press.

Knox, J. (2003) *Archetypes, Attachment, Analysis: Jungian Psychology and the Emergent Mind*, Hove and New York: Brunner-Routledge.

—— (2004) 'Developmental aspects of analytical psychology: new perspectives from cognitive neuroscience and attachment theory', in J. Cambray and L. Carter (eds), *Analytical Psychology: Contemporary Perspectives in Jungian Analysis*, Hove and New York: Brunner-Routledge.

Lambert, K. (1976) 'Michael Fordham', *Journal of Analytical Psychology*, vol. 21, no. 1, pp. 88–91.

—— (1981) *Analysis, Repair and Individuation*, The Library of Analytical Psychology, London: Karnac.

Laplanche, J. and Pontalis, J. B. ([1973] 1988) *The Language of Psychoanalysis*, trans. D. Nicholson-Smith, London: Karnac.

Lopatka, A. (1992) 'The rights of the child are universal: the perspective of the UN Convention on the Rights of the Child', in M. Freeman and P. Veerman (eds), *The Ideologies of Children's Rights*, International Studies in Human Rights, vol. 23, Dordrecht: Martinus Nijhoff Publishers.

McGowan, D. (1994) *What Is Wrong with Jung?*, New York: Prometheus Books.

McNamee, S. (2000) 'Dichotomies, discourses, and transformative practices', in L. Holzman and J. Morss (eds), *Postmodern Psychologies, Societal Practice, and Political Life*, London: Routledge.

Marcus, W. (2007) *Feeling, Being, and the Sense of Self: A New Perspective on Identity, Affect and Narcissistic Disorders*, London: Karnac.

Mareschal, D., Johnson, M. H. and Grayson, A. (2004) 'Brain and cognitive development', in J. Oates and A. Grayson (eds), *Cognitive and Language Development in Children*, Milton Keynes: Open University Press; Oxford: Blackwell.

Mahler, M. S., Pine, F. and Bergman, A. (1975) *The Psychological Birth of the Human Infant: Symbiosis and Individuation*, New York: Basic Books.

Maidenbaum, A. and Martin, S. (eds) (1991) *Lingering Shadows: Jungians, Freudians and Anti-Semitism*, Boston: Shambhala.

Main, S. (2008) 'Re-imagining the child: challenging social constructionist views of childhood', in L. Huskinson (ed.), *Dreaming the Myth Onwards: Revisioning Jungian Theory and Thought*, London: Routledge.

Marlan, S. (2006) 'Alchemy', in R. K. Papadopoulos (ed.), *The Handbook of Jungian Psychology: Theory, Practice and Application*, London: Routledge.

Miell, D. (1995) 'Developing a sense of self', in P. Barnes (ed.), *Personal, Social and Emotional Development of Children*, Oxford: Blackwell.

Mitchell, J. (ed.) (1986) *The Selected Melanie Klein*, London: Penguin.

Miyagi [Main], S. (1998) 'Fordham's contribution to Jungian child therapy: individuation in childhood', unpublished MA dissertation, University of Kent at Canterbury.

Montgomery, J. W. (1973) *Cross and Crucible: Johann Valentin Andreae (1586–1654), Phoenix of the Theologians*, 2 vols, The Hague: Martinus Nijhoff.

Morawski, J. G. (1986) 'Contextual discipline: the unmaking and remaking of sociality', in R. L. Rosnow and M. Georgoudi (eds), *Contextualism and Understanding in Behavioral Science: Implications for Research and Theory*, New York: Praeger.

Morss, J. R. (1990) *The Biologising of Childhood: Developmental Psychology and the Darwinian Myth*, Hove: Lawrence Erlbaum Associates.

—— (1996) *Growing Critical: Alternatives to Developmental Psychology*, London: Routledge.

Muir, D. (1999) 'Theories and methods in developmental psychology', in A. Slater and D. Muir (eds), *The Blackwell Reader in Developmental Psychology*, Oxford: Blackwell.

Neumann, E. (1954) *The Origins and History of Consciousness*, Bollingen Series, vol. 42. New York: Pantheon Books.

Newman, F. and Holzman, L. (1997) *The End of Knowing: A New Developmental Way of Learning*, London: Routledge.

Oates, J. and Grayson, A. (2004) *Cognitive and Language Development in Children*, Milton Keynes: Open University Press; Oxford: Blackwell.

Ognjenovic, V. (2000) 'Life is where we are', in L. Holzman and J. Morss (eds), *Postmodern Psychologies, Societal Practice, and Political Life*, London: Routledge.

Papadopoulos, R. K. (1984) 'Jung and the concept of the Other', in R. K. Papadopoulos and G. S. Saayman (eds), *Jung in Modern Perspective*, London: Wildwood House.

—— (1996a) 'Archetypal family therapy: developing a Jungian approach to working with families', in L. Dodson and T. Gibson (eds), *Psyche and Family*, Wilmette: Chiron.

—— (1996b) 'The tyranny of change', paper based on a presentation at the Champernowne Trust's Cumberland Lodge Conference, July 1996.

—— (1997) 'Is teaching Jung within the university possible?: A response to David Tacey', *Journal of Analytical Psychology*, vol. 42, no. 2, pp. 297–301.

—— (1998a) 'Destructiveness, atrocities and healing: epistemological and clinical reflections', *Journal of Analytical Psychology*, vol. 43, no. 4, pp. 455–77.

—— (1998b) 'Jungian perspectives in new contexts', in A. Casement (ed.), *Post-Jungians Today: Key Papers in Contemporary Analytical Psychology*, London: Routledge.

—— (2002) 'The other other: when the exotic other subjugates the familiar other', *Journal of Analytical Psychology*, vol. 47, no. 2, pp. 163–88.

—— (2006) 'Jung's epistemology and methodology', in R. K. Papadopoulos (ed.), *The Handbook of Jungian Psychology: Theory, Practice and Applications*, London: Routledge.

Papadopoulos, R. K. and Byng-Hall, J. (eds) (1997) *Multiple Voices: Narratives in Systemic Family Psychotherapy*, London: Duckworth.

Pearson, G. (1995) 'The quantitative-qualitative dispute: an unhelpful divide, but one to be lived with', *Addiction*, vol. 90, no. 6, pp. 759–61.

Perret-Clermont, A., Carugati, F. and Oates, J. (2004) 'A socio-cognitive perspective on learning and cognitive development', in *Cognitive and Language Development in Children*, Milton Keynes: Open University Press; Oxford: Blackwell.

Pestalozzi, J. H. (1927) *Ideen (Pestalozzis Werk)*, ed. by Martin Hürliman, II, Zurich.

Piaget, J. (1971) *Biology and Knowledge: An Essay on the Relations between Organic Regulations and Cognitive Processes*, Edinburgh: Edinburgh University Press.

Pollock, L. A. (1983) *Forgotten Children: Parent-Child Relations from 1500 to 1900*, Cambridge: Cambridge University Press.

Portman, A. (1976) 'Jung's biology professor: some recollections', *Spring*, pp. 148–54.

Prince, G. S. (1963) 'Jung's psychology in Britain', in *Contact with Jung: Essays on the Influence of His Work and Personality*, London: Tavistock Publications.

Rabinowitz, V. C. and Weseen, S. (2001) 'Power, politics, and the qualitative/quantitative debate in psychology', in D. L. Tolman and B. M. Mary (eds), *From Subjects to Subjectivities: A Handbook of Interpretive and Participatory Methods: Qualitative Studies in Psychology*, New York: New York University Press.

Reason, P. (ed.) (1988) *Human Inquiry in Action: Developments in New Paradigm Research*, London: Sage.

Reason, P. and Rowen, J. (eds) (1981) *Human Inquiry: A Sourcebook of New Paradigm Research*, Chichester: Wiley.

Reichardt, C. and Cook, T. (1979) 'Beyond qualitative versus quantitative methods', in T. Cook and C. Reichardt (eds), *Qualitative and Quantitative Methods in Evaluation Research*, London: Sage.

Richardson, K. (2000) *Developmental Psychology: How Nature and Nurture Interact*, London: Macmillan.

Rose, S. (1997) *Lifelines: Biology, Freedom, Determinism*, London: Penguin Books.

Rosenzweig, S. (1992) *Freud, Jung, and Hall the King-Maker: The Historic Expedition to America (1909), with G. Stanley Hall as Host and William James as Guest*, Seattle: Hogrefe & Huber.

Rycroft, C. (1988) 'Comments to Farhad Dalal "Jung: a racist" ', *British Journal of Psychotherapy*, vol. 4, no. 3, p. 281.

Samuels, A. (1985) *Jung and the Post-Jungians*, London: Routledge.

—— (1988) 'Comments to Farhad Dalal "Jung: a racist" ', *British Journal of Psychotherapy*, vol. 4, no. 3, p. 280.

—— (1989) *The Plural Psyche: Personality, Morality and the Father*, London: Routledge.

—— (1993) 'Jung, anti-Semitism and the Nazis', Chapter 12, in *The Political Psyche*, London: Routledge.

—— (1994) 'The hidden reactionary politics of object relations psychoanalysis: my different journey to similar conclusions to those of Dr. Nathan Adler', *NCSPP Newsletter*, Northern California Society for Psychoanalytic Psychology, A Regional Affiliate of the Division of Psychoanalysis (39), American Psychological Association.

—— (1998) 'Will the post-Jungians survive?', in A. Casement (ed.), *Post-Jungians Today: Key Papers in Contemporary Analytical Pscyhology*, London: Routledge.

—— (2001) *Politics on the Couch: Citizenship and the Internal Life*, London: Routledge.

Samuels, A., Shorter, B. and Plaut, F. ([1986] 1991) *A Critical Dictionary of Jungian Analysis*, London: Routledge.

Schlossman, S. L. (1973) 'G. Stanley Hall and the Boys' Club: conservative applications of recapitulation theory', *Journal of the History of the Behavioral Sciences*, vol. 9, no. 2, pp. 140–7.

Seagull, E. A. W. (1978) 'The child's rights as a medical patient', *Journal of Clinical Child Psychology*, vol. 7, no. 3, pp. 202–4.

Sears, E. (1986) *The Ages of Man: Medieval Interpretations of the Life Cycle*, Princeton, NJ: Princeton University Press.

Segal, R. A. (2007) 'Jung and Lévy-Bruhl', *Journal of Analytical Psychology*, vol. 52, no. 5, pp. 635–58.

Shahar, S. (1990) *Childhood in the Middle Ages*, London and New York: Routledge.

Shamdasani, S. (1996) 'Introduction', in M. Fordham, *Analyst-Patient Interaction: Collected Papers on Technique*, London: Routledge.

Shotter, J. (2000) 'From within our lives together: Wittgenstein, Bakhtin, Voloshinov and the shift to a participatory stance in understanding understanding', in L. Holzman and J. Morss (eds), *Postmodern Psychologies, Societal Practice, and Political Life*, London: Routledge.

Sidoli, M. and Davies, M. (1988) *Jungian Child Psychotherapy: Individuation in Childhood*, London: Karnac.

Siegelman, E. Y. (1994) 'Reframing "reductive" analysis', *Journal of Analytical Psychology*, vol. 39, no. 4, pp. 479–96.

Spencer, H. (1861) *Education: Intellectual, Moral and Physical*, London: G. Manwaring.

Stern, D. N. (1985) *The Interpersonal World of the Infant: A View from Psychoanalysis and Developmental Psychology*, New York: Basic Books.

Stevens, A. (1982) *Archetype: A Natural History of the Self*, London: Routledge.

Stevens, A. and Price, J. (1996) *Evolutionary Psychiatry: A New Beginning*, London: Routledge.

Sulloway, F. (1979) *Freud: Biologist of the Mind: Beyond the Psychoanalytic Legend*, New York: Basic Books.

Tajfel, H. (1972) 'Experiments in a vacuum', in J. Israel and H. Tajfel (eds), *The Context of Social Psychology: A Critical Assessment*, London: Academic Press.

—— (ed.) (1978) *Differentiation between Social Groups: Studies in the Social Psychology of Intergroup Relations*, London: Academic Press.

Tajfel, H. and Turner, J. (1986) 'The social identity theory of intergroup behaviour', in S. Worchel and W. Austin (eds), *Psychology of Intergroup Relations*, Chicago: Nelson-Hall.

Thomas, K. (2002) 'The individual differences approach to personality', in D. Miell, A. Phoenix and K. Thomas (eds), *Mapping Psychology I*, Milton Keynes: Open University Press.

Thorndike, L. (1927) *A History of Magic and Experimental Science*. New York and London: Columbia University Press.

Urban, E. (1992) 'The primary self and related concepts in Jung, Klein, and Issacs', *Journal of Analytical Psychology*, vol. 37, no. 4, pp. 411–32.

—— (1994) 'Infant studies and Fordham's model of development', paper presented at 8th Jung Studies Day, The University of Kent.

—— (1998) 'States of identity: a perspective drawing upon Fordham's model and infant studies', *Journal of Analytical Psychology*, vol. 43, no. 3, pp. 261–75.

Urwin, C. (1986) 'Developmental psychology and psychoanalysis: splitting the difference', in M. Richards and P. Light (eds), *Children of Social Worlds*, Oxford: Blackwell.

Van Bueren, G. (1995) *The International Law on the Rights of the Child*, International Studies in Human Rights, vol. 35, Dordrecht: Martinus Nijhoff Publishers.

Veerman, P. E. (1992a) *The Rights of Children and Changing Images of Childhood*, International Studies in Human Rights, vol. 18, Dordrecht: Martinus Nijhoff Publishers.

—— (1992b) 'Towards a more integrated basis for the children's rights movement: the aims and outcome of the first International Interdisciplinary Study-Group on Ideologies of Children's Rights', in M. Freeman and P. Veerman (eds), *The Ideologies of Children's Rights*, International Studies in Human Rights, vol. 23, Dordrecht: Martinus Nijhoff Publishers.

von Franz, M.-L. (1990) *Individuation in Fairy Tales*, Boston: Shambhala.

Vygotsky, L. S. (1978) *Mind in Society*, Cambridge, MA: Harvard University Press.

Wehr, D. (1988) *Jung and Feminism: Liberating Archetypes*, London: Routledge.

Wetzler, S. (1985) 'The historical truth of psychoanalytic reconstructions (1)', *International Review of Psychoanalysis*, vol. 12, pp. 187–97.

Winnicott, D. W. (1954) 'Withdrawal of regression', in *Through Paediatrics to Psychoanalysis: Collected Papers*, London: Karnac.

—— (1959–64) 'Classification: is there a psycho-analytic contribution to psychiatric classification?', in *The Maturational Processes and the Facilitating Environment*, London: Karnac.

—— (1964) *The Child, the Family and the Outside World*, Harmondsworth: Penguin Books.

Wood, C., Littleton, K. and Oates, J. (2002) 'Lifespan development', in T. Cooper and I. Roth (eds), *Challenging Psychological Issues*, Milton Keynes: Open University Press.

Woolgar, S. (1988) *Science: The Very Idea*, London: Tavistock.

Zinkin, L. (1991) 'The Klein connection in the London School: the search for origins', *Journal of Analytical Psychology*, vol. 36, no. 1, pp. 37–61.

Index

Adams, M.V. 65–6
adaptation
    adjustment and 157–8
    neurosis as 34, 35
    outer and inner 35–6, 37, 38, 51
adults
    'child in the adult' 45, 49, 55, 56
    children's rights perspectives 124–7
    see also child archetype; parent–child
        relationship
alchemy 23–6
analyst–analysand relationship 97–8
analytical psychology
    'Archetypal School' 74–5, 75–6,
        103–4, 111
    'Classical School'('Zurich School') 74,
        75–6, 103–4, 105, 111
    postmodern perspectives 98–100
    see also developmental psychology;
        Developmental School; Jung,
        C.G.
Andersen, T. 98
Anderson, H. 98
archaic/subjective and directed/logical
        thinking 31–2, 34–5, 163
'Archetypal School' 74–5, 75–6, 103–4,
        111
archetypes 11–12, 13–14, 18–19, 40, 162
    Developmental School 106–7, 108, 109
    Object Relations School 106–7
    senex–puer 46, 52–3, 54, 140
    see also child archetype
Ariès, P. 139
Association of Jungian Analysts (AJA)
        105, 106, 111, 116
association tests 33, 153–6
Astor, J. 110, 116, 118, 127–8
attachment theory 91

autonomous psyche 158, 162, 185
autonomy
    of the psyche 97, 158, 167
    of the child 47, 73, 77, 125, 138, 145,
        175

Banister, P. et al. 83, 85, 86, 87, 97–8, 153,
        160, 165, 167
Baynes, G. 93
Baynes, H.G. Peter 105, 107, 129–30
biology 56–7
    foundations of psychological types
        157–8
    homeodynamics 19
    nature and culture 21–8, 41, 158
    recapitulation theory 68–9, 72
        dynamic interaction/self-
            organisation 72–3, 77
        evolution 62–3, 68, 73
        life-span perspective 71
    see also science
birth and rebirth 14, 42
Bliwise, N.G. 91
Boholm, Å. 25
Bowlby, J. 89–90, 91, 161
Brems, C. 135
Burman, E. 3, 5, 44, 72, 77, 78, 82, 84, 86,
        87, 91
Butterworth, P. and Bryant, P. 72

Carey, S. 72
Casement, A. 74, 105–6, 110
change 16–17
    and stability 18–19, 37–8
Child Analytical Training (SAP) 94, 107,
        124, 134
child archetype 45–7
    and actual child 47–50, 113–14

child archetype – *Contd.*
  and 'archetype in childhood' 50–2
  'development' critique 77–8
  Developmental School 111–12
  and medieval views of children 141–2
  significance in second half of life 52–5
child–parent relationship *see* parent–
    child relationship
child psychology 46–58, 67, 78, 115,
    179
'child-savers' 125, 126, 132–3
children's rights movement 118–46
Christian beliefs 139–42
'Classical School'('Zurich School') 74,
    75–6, 103–4, 105, 111
collective psyche 42, 48–9, 65–70, 177,
    180–1
collective unconscious
  global parallelism 65–8
  and personal unconscious 19–20, 34,
      37–8, 156
  psycho-physical parallelism 68–9, 70
  see also archetypes; child archetype
Colman, W. 13, 18, 166
complexes 33, 154–5, 156
  incest 33–4, 41
conscious and unconscious, relationship
      between 31–2, 36–7, 41–2, 66–70,
      157
Convention on the Rights of the Child
    124
Covington, C. 94–5
culture
  nature and 21–8, 41, 157–8
  and notion of progress 69
Cunningham, H. 125, 127, 128, 132,
    139–41

Dalal, F. 65–6
Darwinism (evolution) 62–3, 68, 73
Davin, A. 137
Declaration of the Rights of the Child
    123–4
depth psychological approaches to early
    infancy 89–91
development
  concepts of 70–3
  Jung's understanding of psychological
      11–29
  and progress 28, 64–78
  and recapitulation 61–80
  and regression 35–8

developmental psychology
  and analytical psychology 172–3,
      174–6
    perspectives on the child and
        childhood 142–4
    practice and methodology 92–100
  and depth psychological approaches to
      infancy 89–91
  methodological shift 7, 81–2, 90, 100
  see also qualitative approach
Developmental School 2–3, 74, 75–6, 92,
    169
  Child Analytical Training (SAP) 94,
      107, 124, 134
  'developmental' aspects 109–12
  distinctive aspects of 106–9
  elements and rhetoric 112–17
  emergence of 103–6
  individuation process 107–9, 119–21,
      126, 133, 136–7
  see also Fordham, M.
dialectical relationship, unconscious and
      conscious 36–7, 41–2
dialogically-structured activity 85
dichotomies
  gene/environment 71
  legal 126
  postmodern critique 82–3
  quantitative/qualitative 86
  vs dynamic systems theory 72–3, 77
diversity 151, 152, 153
  psychological types 156–60
  universality and 135–7
dreams 31
dynamic systems/self-organisation
      theory 72–3, 77

education 69
emotion
  language and meaning 153–6
  see also private and public lives of
      children; subjectivity
evolution (Darwinism) 62–3, 68, 73

fantasies, regression 31–5, 36
feminist perspectives 135
Fordham, F. 120–1
Fordham, M. 1, 2–3
  and children's rights movement
      121–39
  individuality of the child 107–9,
      119–21, 126, 132, 133, 136–7

personal analysis 107, 128–30, 133
as qualitative psychologist 168–70
see also Developmental School
Franz, M.-L. von 46
Freeman, M. 122, 124, 125–6, 131,
132–3, 143
Freud, S. 3–4, 31, 32–5, 64–5, 66, 68–9,
141, 163–4
Frosh, S. 96, 98
Fulani, L. 83

Giegerich, W. 74–5, 76, 78
global parallelism 65–8
Greene, S. 44–5, 61, 71–2, 76

Haekel, E. 63, 68
Hall, G.S. et al. 64–5, 66, 69
Hauke, C. 27, 76, 119
Henderson, J. 129
hierarchical models see stage/hierarchical
models
Hillman, J. 46, 52–3, 54, 75
history
concepts of childhood 121–3, 139–42
and notion of progress 69–70
Holtzman, L. 83, 84
and Morss, J. 84
homeodynamics 19

incest complex 33–4, 41
independence of children 120–1
individual–society relationship 26–8
'individualism' 27
individuality of the child 107–9, 119–21,
126, 132, 133, 136–7
children's rights perspective 121–5,
131–3, 137–9, 143–4
primary self 108–9, 118–19, 120,
126–7, 131–2
individuation process 11–15, 23–4, 27,
161
see also Developmental School
infant observation see observed infant
infantile memories (regressive fantasies)
32–5
infantile sexuality 33, 34, 141
inter and intrasubjectivity 160, 161,
167–8

Jacobi, J. 14, 163–4
Jacoby, M. 3, 92, 93
Jebb, E. 123–5, 132

Jung, C.G. 1
children's rights perspective 139–44
psychological development theories
11–29
as qualitative psychologist 150–68
symbolic child psychology 44–58
see also archetypes; autonomous
psyche, child archetype; collective,
psyche, individuation process;
nature and culture; objective
psyche, recapitulation; regression;
symbols, unconscious

'kiddy-libbers' 125, 126
King, M. 125, 134–5, 137–8
Kirsh, H. 93, 105, 107, 110, 116
Klein, M. 106–7
Knox, J. 3, 76
Krantz, D.L. 86, 88

Lamarckism 63
language 151–2, 173–4
association tests 33, 153–6
and methodology: quantitative/
qualitative debate 85–9
Lapatka, A. 136, 138
Lévy-Bruhl, L. 18, 49, 121
libido/psychic energy
regression of 35–8
symbols 39
'London School' see Developmental
School

McNamee, S. 82–3, 84
medieval concepts of childhood 139–42
memory
infantile (regressive fantasies) 32–5
reconstruction of childhood in
analysis 92–3
methodological issues 81–100, 155–6
see also qualitative approach
midlife 53–4
Morss, J. 16, 62, 64, 66, 68, 78, 82
mother–child relationship 40–1, 89–90,
91, 140–1
myths 56, 74–5, 76, 115, 174
themes in Fordham's analysis 129–30
see also archetypes; child archetype;
primitives

nature and culture 21–8, 41, 157–8
needs, children's rights perspective 131–3

Neumann, E. 73–5, 76, 78
neurosis 11, 32–5, 36, 39, 64–5
non-progressive development 70–1

Object Relations School 106–7
objective and subjective psyche 163–7
objectivity in research 96–7, 98, 99,
    163
observed infant 94–5
    vs clinical infant 90–1
ontogeny–phylogeny relationship *see*
    recapitulation theory
outgrowing, psychological development
    as 15–16

Papadopoulos, R. 18, 105, 111, 112, 113,
    115, 116
parent–child relationship
    children's rights perspective 143–4
    Development School/Fordham's
        perspective 108, 120–1, 127–8,
        131, 132
    individuation 120–1, 132
    mothers 40–1, 89–90, 91, 140–1
    symbolic interpretation 40–1, 47–8,
        49–52, 54–5, 56
parental imago 50–2, 54–5, 55
parental pathology 48, 49, 108
participation mystique 18, 20, 49
Pearson, G. 86, 87, 88
personality
    and psychological types 156–60
    of children 121
Pestalozzi, J.H. 27–8
philosophical influences 63–4
Pollock, L.A. 139
postmodern perspectives
    on analytical psychology 98–100
    on developmental psychology 82–5
pre-sexual stage 39–40
primary self 108–9, 118–19, 120, 126–7,
    131–2
primitives
    and child comparison 32, 67–8, 77
    and collective psyche, global
        parallelism 65–8
private and public lives of children
    127–31, 132–3
professionals, children's rights 128,
    133–5
progress 28, 64–78
    see also development

psychology, methodological shift in
    82–91
public and private lives of children
    127–31, 132–3

qualitative approach
    developmental psychology
        Fordham 168–70
        Jung 150–68
    and quantitative approach 85–9, 98,
        153, 154
    research methods and analytical
        practice 96–8

Rabinowitz, V. and Weseen, S. 88–9
racist accusations 65–8
Reason, P. and Rowan, J. 81, 164, 165
rebirth 41, 54
    birth and 14, 42
recapitulation theory
    definition and significance in
        psychology 62–4
    and notion of progress 64–70, 72, 73–7
reconstructed child in analysis 92–4
regression
    connecting 'child archetype' and
        'archetype in childhood' 51
    fantasies 31–5, 36
    of libido/psychic energy 35–8
    symbolic interpretations of 38–42
relativity of children's rights and
    individuality 137–9
researcher–researched relationship 97–8,
    160, 162–3
Richardson, K. 72–3, 77
Rose, S. 19, 56–7, 115

Samuels, A. 66, 74, 75–6, 99, 103–4, 105,
    109, 113–14, 119
science
    Developmental School 90, 115–16,
        118, 132, 169
    see also biology
self 11–12, 13, 23–4, 107–9
    child as symbol of 16
    and 'identity' 158–9
    loss of 27
    primary 108–9, 118–19, 120, 126–7,
        131–2
    see also child archetype; subjectivity
self-organisation/dynamic systems
    theory 72–3, 77

senex–puer archetype 46, 52–3, 54, 140
'sensationalism' 63–4
sexuality
    aetiology of neurosis 33–4, 39, 64–5
    infantile 33, 34, 141
Shahar, S. 140, 141–2
Siegelman, E. 93–4
social constructionism 71, 76, 137–9,
        144
    and historical concepts of childhood
        121–3, 139–42
Society of Analytical Psychology (SAP)
        see Developmental School
society–individual relationship 26–8
spirituality
    development of 35
    and physicality, culture and nature as
        21–3, 24–6, 41
stability, change and 18–19, 37–8
stage/hierarchical models 61, 141
    and recapitulation theory 64, 65,
        68–70, 74–6
Stern, D. 3, 90–1, 92, 94
Stevens, A. 73–4
subjectivity
    archaic and logical/directed thinking
        31–2, 34–5, 163
    of children 120
    dimension of research 90–1
    inter and intrasubjectivity 160, 161,
        167–8
    and objective psyche 163–7
    researcher–researched relationship
        97–8, 160, 162–3
    sense of self and relationships 160–8
symbolic child psychology 44–58

symbolic interpretations of regression
        38–42
symbols, concept of 38–9

transcendent function of development
        41–2
transference 106
    and countertransference 107, 129
    delusional 128–9

unconscious 16–21
    child–parent relationship 50–2, 54–5,
        56, 108
    and conscious, relationship between
        31–2, 36–7, 41–2, 66–70, 157
    personal and collective 160
    see also archetypes; child archetype;
        collective unconscious
universality and diversity 135–7
Urban, E. 109, 118–19, 134, 145
Urwin, C. 89–90

Van Bueren, G. 122, 123
Veerman, P. 121–2, 123, 124, 125, 131,
        132, 133, 136, 137, 142
'Vienna School' 105
Vygotsky, L. 71, 84, 95

Winnicott, D. 35, 120–1
'wise old man' 12
    senex–puer archetype 46, 52–3, 54, 140
word association tests 33, 153–6

Zinkin, L. 94
'Zurich School' (Classical School) 74,
        75–6, 103–4, 105, 111